Providing Health Care Benefits in Retirement

Pension Research Council Publications

A complete listing of PRC publications appears in the back of this volume.

Providing Health Care Benefits in Retirement

Ralph H. Blanchard Memorial Endowment Series
Volume V

Edited by
Judith F. Mazo
Anna M. Rappaport
Sylvester J. Schieber

Published by
Pension Research Council
The Wharton School of the University of Pennsylvania

and
University of Pennsylvania Press
Philadelphia

The chapters in this volume are based on papers presented at the Pension Research Council Conference, "Providing Health Care Benefits in Retirement," held at the University of Pennsylvania on May 6 and 7, 1993.

Library of Congress Cataloging-in-Publication Data

Providing health care benefits in retirement / edited by Judith F. Mazo, Anna M. Rappaport, Sylvester J. Schieber.
    p.   cm.
    Includes bibliographical references and index.
    ISBN 0-8122-3270-4
    1. Insurance, Health–United States–Finance–Congresses. 2. Retirees–Medical care–United States–Finance–Congresses. 3. Medicare–Finance–Congresses. I. Mazo, Judith F. II. Rappaport, Anna M. III. Schieber, Sylvester J. HD7102.U4P784 1994
    331.25'5–dc20   94-13655
                                                        CIP

Printed in the United States of America

Alicia H. Munnell, *Assistant Secretary,* Office of Economic Policy, U.S. Department of the Treasury, Washington, DC

Robert J. Myers, *International Consultant on Social Security,* Silver Spring, MD

George J. Pantos, Esq., *Partner,* Vedder, Price, Kaufman, Kammholz & Day, Washington, DC

Richard Prosten, *Director,* Coordinated Bargaining and Research, Industrial Union Department, AFL-CIO, Washington, DC

Anna M. Rappaport, FSA, *Managing Director,* William M. Mercer Companies Inc., Chicago, IL

Jerry S. Rosenbloom, *Frederick H. Ecker Professor,* Department of Insurance and Risk Management, The Wharton School, University of Pennsylvania, Philadelphia, PA

Sylvester J. Schieber, *Vice President and Director,* Research and Information Center, The Wyatt Company, Washington, DC

Ray Schmitt, *Specialist in Social Legislation,* Congressional Research Service, Washington, DC

Richard B. Stanger, *National Director,* Employee Benefits Services, Price Waterhouse, Washington, DC

Marc M. Twinney, FSA, *Director,* Pension Department, Ford Motor Company, Dearborn, MI

Jack L. VanDerhei, *Associate Professor of Risk and Insurance,* Temple University, Philadelphia, PA

Paul H. Wenz, FSA, *Second Vice President and Actuary,* The Principal Financial Group, Des Moines, IA

Howard Young, FSA, *Adjunct Professor of Mathematics,* University of Michigan, Ann Arbor, MI

The Pension Research Council

The Pension Research Council of the Wharton School of the University of Pennsylvania is an organization committed to generating debate on key policy issues that affect pensions and other employee benefits. The Council sponsors interdisciplinary research on the entire range of private and social retirement security and related benefit plans in the United States and around the world and seeks to broaden public understanding of these complex arrangements through basic research into their social, economic, legal, actuarial, and financial foundations. Members of the Advisory Board of Council, appointed by the Dean of the Wharton School, are leaders in the employee benefits field, and though they recognize the essential role of social security and other public sector income maintenance programs, they share a strong desire to strengthen private sector approaches to economic security.

The Leonard Davis Institute of Health Economics

The Leonard Davis Institute of Health Economics is the University of Pennsylvania's primary center for research, policy analysis, and education in health care. It is a cooperative venture among Penn's schools of Medicine, Business (Wharton), Nursing, and Dental Medicine and has linkages with other schools, including Arts and Sciences, Education, Social Work, Communications, and Law. The Leonard Davis Institute and its over 100 senior fellows work to improve the health of the public through multidisciplinary studies on the medical, economic, and social issues that influence how health care is organized, financed, managed, and delivered in the United States and worldwide. It is composed of the Center for Research, the Center for Health Policy, and the Center for Advanced Management Education. It also supports and works collaboratively with several of Penn's graduate and postdoctoral programs.

Contents

Preface

This is a book about health care insurance for retirees in the United States. In the past, many employers automatically extended to workers who retired before age 65 the same health insurance package provided to active employees. At and after age 65, older retirees would turn to Medicare coverage for large components of their medical care needs.

Unfortunately, health insurance coverage patterns have changed in the last decade, leaving many older (as well as younger) Americans susceptible to economic insecurity occasioned by inadequate health insurance coverage. One objective of this volume is to evaluate several explanations for recent trends in retiree health insurance patterns. These explanations are often complex, as illustrated by contributors to this volume who come from private sector management and labor, and who are economists, physicians, and policymakers.

As the health care reform debate continues, a second objective of this book is to underscore the need to focus on retirees' special health issues. Policy discussions frequently have overlooked both the costs of offering retiree health insurance coverage and the benefits of providing health care to the elderly. As many contributors to this volume note, the elderly are caught between the pincers of reform proposals: prospective benefits legislation that certainly will affect employer willingness to continue support for expensive retiree health benefits, and Medicare changes that also may curtail benefits obtainable from the government. The fact that these reforms often are targeted at the types of medical care most often consumed by older people makes this group deserving of special attention.

The last and, perhaps, most important goal of this book is to offer new perspectives and evaluative tools that readers then may use to examine these as well as other health reform concerns. To this end, the contributors have supplied an unusually rich combination of facts and philosophical insights, derived from ethicists and academicians as well as from medical and benefits practitioners. These discussions should inform the public by supplying a much needed perspective on health care insurance for retirees.

This volume owes its existence to the vision and hard work of Judith Mazo, Anna Rappaport, and Sylvester Schieber, who conceived of the May 1993 conference at which earlier versions of these papers and discussions were presented. On behalf of the Pension Research Council of the Wharton School of the University of Pennsylvania, I wish to thank the editors and all contributors. The Pension Research Council also acknowledges the groups that supported the excellent research that led to this volume, including the Institutional Members of the Pension Research Council, the Office of the Dean of the Wharton School which designated this event as a Wharton Impact Conference, and the Leonard Davis Institute of Health Economics.

Olivia S. Mitchell
Executive Director
Pension Research Council

Chapter 1
Overview

Anna M. Rappaport and Sylvester J. Schieber

During the national political campaigns in 1992, deep concerns emerged about many aspects of the health delivery and financing systems in the United States. President Clinton was elected, at least in part, because he promised to reform the health care system in this country. As the debate has unfolded, however, very little of the public discussion has centered on the special plight of retirees and how health care reforms might affect them.

The elderly are much less able than younger people to adjust to evolving health insurance patterns. In addition, dissatisfaction from providers and consumers alike about the costs of the current health care delivery system has introduced the prospect of limitations (or "caps") on resources devoted to health care. As the largest consumers of health care, the elderly will be profoundly affected by any such restrictions.

The purpose of this book is to first identify and then explore the challenges faced by private and public sector policymakers in providing retiree health care insurance in the current economic environment and under probable national health care reform. The chapters and commentaries were first presented as papers and discussions at a Wharton School Impact Conference in May, 1993, that was hosted by the Pension Research Council at the University of Pennsylvania, with additional sponsorship from the Leonard Davis Institute of Health Economics (University of Pennsylvania). Participants in the symposium represented the diverse constituencies involved in direct provision, funding, and evaluation of health care delivery to older Americans. The group included policymaking and academic economists, actuaries, statisticians, physicians, employee-benefit-plan sponsors, represenatives of labor, attorneys, and health care policy specialists. The combination of practical, research, and policy expertise brought together a rich diversity of perspectives and resulted in this book, which addresses the ongoing debate over health care funding and delivery issues, particularly as these things apply to retiree health care needs.

Several common themes emerge in the chapters and commentaries that follow and are highlighted here to provide readers with an overview of salient issues related to the funding and delivery of retiree health services.

The Challenges

Judith Mazo, Senior Vice President of The Segal Company, takes up the general question of how to provide health benefits to elderly Americans in Chapter Two, where a distinction is made between two diverse groups of retirees: those early retirees who are not yet Medicare eligible, and those retirees over age 65 or disabled who are Medicare eligible.

Before Medicare, most retirees who received Social Security benefits did not have health insurance coverage and could not afford to purchase health care coverage directly. Today, most Social Security beneficiaries aged 65 and older, as well as many disabled persons, enjoy coverage from Medicare, a program that cost American taxpayers $82 billion in 1992 (for Medicare Part A). Despite this massive growth in health care protection, the elderly's out-of-pocket health care spending as a share of their income is as high today as it was before Medicare was introduced,[1] and the federal Medicare program faces a difficult economic future. Recently, payroll taxes financing Medicare Part A grew at a rate of 6.9 percent, whereas expenditures rose at an annual rate of 11.1 percent.[2] This scenario leads Dr. Mark Pauly, Chairman and Professor of Health Care Systems, The Wharton School, and Director of the Center for Research at the Leonard Davis Institute, to remark that "the fundamental conclusion is that Medicare has to change" (see Chapter Six).

In addition to Medicare, some retirees are eligible for health benefits provided through their former employers' health benefit programs. These benefits often are provided to people who retire before age 65, typically with a reduction in benefits and coverage once the Medicare eligibility age is attained. Employers who provide health insurance protection for retirees have found that recent private health insurance coverage premiums rose far more rapidly than the other costs of doing business. This cost pressure was exacerbated in 1990 when a new financial accounting standard (FAS 106) required employers to recognize the financial obligations incurred by promising such benefits.

Problems with the current employer-sponsored group retiree health benefit system may be summarized as follows:

- When employers offer early retiree health care coverage, the costs often are high and variable. Early retirees cost about two-and-one-half times as much to insure on average as younger active workers. Companies face substantial uncertainty regarding future company-sponsored plan costs, as well as costs of related government programs (e.g., Medicare). In addition, frequently changing rules and legal uncertainties regarding national reform make it difficult to manage the benefits.

- Employer-provided health insurance coverage often is costly to retirees; benefit caps and cost-sharing make coverage unaffordable for some people.
- Because employers usually reserve the right to alter and amend benefit offerings, active and retired workers sense some insecurity with regard to benefits. Also, employer plans are typically not prefunded, nor is there plan termination insurance. Long-term care generally is not covered, and many plans do not cover prescription drugs.
- Many companies offer no retiree coverage, and early retirees' income often is inadequate to cover the full cost of health coverage, particularly before Medicare eligibility sets in.

As a consequence of these uncertainties, firms that provide health benefits to current workers not only expend more in current operating costs but also reduce their reported financial values because they need to forecast future retiree health care cost liabilities. The net result has been that many employers have curtailed the health benefits offered to retirees. As Mazo concludes in Chapter Two, "overall, the outlook is for less employer-paid retiree health coverage."

Reviewing the Current Situation

Anna Rappaport, Managing Director of William M. Mercer, Inc., and Carol Malone, also from William M. Mercer, Inc., examine aspects of the retiree health insurance market in Chapter Four of this book. They focus on plan coverage, benefit levels (including cost sharing), and the types of services provided. Their chapter notes that retiree health insurance coverage depends on the employer's size and other characteristics. Coverage levels are relatively high for large employers in established industries such as heavy manufacturing and financial services and are also high in unionized industries and in the public sector. In contrast, there is virtually no coverage for retirees given by employers who have fewer than 100 employees or by companies that have been in operation for only a few years. A serious concern is that privately provided benefits may be cut even more in the future in response to the cost concerns just discussed.

Two specialists comment on Chapter Four. William Custer, Director of Research at the Employee Benefit Research Institute, observes that a degree of subjectivity is required when evaluating the adequacy of employer-provided health benefits, but he concludes that current benefits are "clearly inadequate" because only about one third of current retirees receive them. He predicts that health care reform packages will allow retirees to join community-rated risk pools, in which case employers may offer reduced retiree health benefits in exchange for meeting retiree income needs through cash-income retirement plans. This is likely because current retiree health insurance plans cannot be prefunded on a tax-preferred basis. This approach clearly places the responsibility of purchasing private retiree health insurance on the individual.

In contrast, Paul Grant, Associate Professor of Human Resources and Industrial Relations at Loyola University, expresses concern over asking individuals to pay for their own care, because health insurance markets are thin for early retirees. In part, this is because the lack of good data on this population and also because greater needs for new types of coverage such as long-term care are thwarted by changing social patterns, making the benefits less available.

The trade-off between retiree health insurance and cash benefits is taken up by Deborah Chollet, Associate Director at the Alpha Center in Washington, D.C. In Chapter Three, she asks whether the high and rapidly growing cost of retiree health benefits is putting pressure on other benefits, particularly pensions, while recognizing that pension savings have a tax-preferred status in contrast to the less tax-favored retiree health insurance coverage. Chollet's analysis suggests that reductions in retiree health benefits are more likely than reductions in pension benefits, and she concludes that retiree health obligations will not jeopardize pension benefits in the near future. She also contends that the future of employer-sponsored retiree health plans is highly uncertain, in light of the financial disclosure requirements recently imposed on retiree health care plans and the dire straights in which Medicare finds itself.

Diana Murray, Senior Manager of Group Insurance Plans for the Sara Lee Corporation, offers the corporate perspective on Chollet's chapter, concluding that many firms "do not want to have to tell employees when, where, and how to buy care." If retiree health insurance benefits do decline, then this might have a serious and perhaps unpredictable effect on older workers' willingness and ability to retire, warns Olivia Mitchell, Executive Director of the Pension Research Council and International Foundation of Employee Benefit Plans and Professor of Insurance and Risk Management at The Wharton School. In her commentary to Chollet's chapter, Mitchell notes that reluctant retirees will present human resource specialists with yet a new and potentially unexpected spillover effect in the health insurance problem. This point is shared by Rappaport and Malone in Chapter Four, where they state that both employers and employees tend to be dissatisfied in situations in which early retirement must be delayed.

Looking Forward

One theme that runs through the chapters and their related commentaries is the view expressed by Joseph Antos, Director of the Office of Research and Demonstrations in the Health Care Financing Administration. In his commentary to Chapter Five, Antos states that the nation is "nearing a practical limit to health care expenditures." Somewhat optimistically, Mark Pauly suggests in Chapter Six that policymakers may have another six years to resolve the Medicare funding problem. Antos counters that governmental budgets are straining now under the burden of medical plans at federal and state levels alike. The Medicare trust fund deficit over the next 25 years is projected to be $1.4 trillion in present value terms (Board of Trustees, 1993). In addition, employer-provided retiree health benefits always have been limited, and now even those employers who traditionally offered benefits are driven to curtail their commitments. At some point, the problems simply become too pressing to postpone.

What should be the proper role for employers in this retiree health care puzzle? G. Lawrence Atkins, Director of Health Legislative Affairs in the law firm of Winthrop, Stimson, Putnam & Roberts, suggests in Chapter Five that many companies that currently provide these benefits in fact stumbled into offering them, having thought of them in the past as merely an extension of active-worker benefits. Supporting his point is the evidence that these benefits were relatively inexpensive, at least at the outset. Now that retirees are more numerous, and because the benefit cannot be prefunded in a tax-favored vehicle, the benefit payments have become a burden on current workers and shareholders alike. Atkins notes that the extent of the burden depends on the employer's current and retired workforce, as well as on the extent of benefits promised. No matter what else applies, as Atkins points out, redistribution of these obligations will be controversial. Still, he feels that employee obligations for retiree health benefits should be limited to coverage for early retirement benefits, because this allows companies to induce early retirement if necessary. Atkins also argues that employer responsibility for health benefits for retirees aged 65 and over should be phased out, and, over time, more responsibility for the benefit should be shifted to elderly consumers of health services.

In his commentary, Donald Snyder, Assistant Director of the U.S. General Accounting Office's Human Resources Division, critiques Atkins' stance by arguing that Medicare benefits are inadequate and insecure. Although Atkins believes that the beneficiaries themselves should be required to undertake a larger share of the overall burden of financing their own benefits, Snyder does not agree. Others take a different tack. For instance, Mark Pauly suggests that the thrust of Medicare should be redirected, moving away from its current emphasis on inpatient care and "caps" on coverage toward a catastrophic coverage program that does not distinguish between different categories of medical expense. It should be noted that even if Medicare promises were revamped, retirees will probably remain insecure about the value of the health care promise. Funding cuts in both Medicare and Medicaid have been experienced in recent years, and many costs have been shifted to private payers over time.

The financing issues in health benefit reform are taken up by Sylvester Schieber, Vice President of The Wyatt Company and Director of its Research and Information Center. His Chapter Eight suggests that governments and employers have reached their "practical limit" of what they can pay for health care, to borrow Antos' terminology. Several reform options are discussed, and Schieber concludes that there are no "magic bullets." In particular, current proposals to simplify health care delivery and to reform malpractice insurance will not fix major problems in the current system, nor will they generate needed revenues to fund expanded insurance coverage. Schieber concludes that the underlying incentives that face health service providers today must be changed.

One popular policy approach to changing health care system incentives involves "managed competition." This option is reviewed favorably by William Greer, Markey Clinical Scholar at the University of Pennsylvania School of Medicine, and Alan Hillman, Associate Professor of Medicine and Health Care Systems and Director of the Leonard Davis Institute's Center for Health Policy. In Chapter Seven, they state that moving the elderly into a basic benefit package anticipated under health system reform would provide better care and more comprehensive benefits than now available under Medicare. They also caution that creating a cost-conscious system will alter the philosophy of medical delivery decisions drastically. Their warning is that the elderly will be at particular risk of reduced care because they consume most of the public health care budget. Greer and Hillman suggest that any health care reform proposal will need to consider the elderly's special health care needs. Their point illustrates the two sides of this coin: moving retirees into purchasing cooperatives could drive up the cost of coverage to everyone if premiums are not age linked, whereas coverage could become expensive for the elderly if premiums are linked to age.

A commentary on the Greer and Hillman chapter is offered by John Rother, Director of Legislation and Public Policy Division for the American Association of Retired Persons. He concurs that Medicare must be overhauled but does not believe that rationing is required. Instead, Rother supports the extension of managed competition techniques to the Medicare program, "coupled with vigilant external review of the quality of care provided and rigorous enforcement." A labor union perspective is explored by Peggy Connerton, Chief Economist and Director of Public Policy at the Service Employees International Union, AFL-CIO, and by Peter Nixon, a policy analyst with the same organization. In their commentary to Chapter Seven, they express skepticism about managed competition proposals, particularly as they refer to retirees. The authors note that when the Medicare program moved toward a Health Maintenance Organization (HMO) mode, hospital utilization rates fell but overall costs did not, suggesting that competition and budget-capping may not reduce medical expenditures as much as expected. Also, retirees do have substantially different needs and find it more difficult to obtain private insurance, compared to the younger population.

Some policymakers already advocate the extension of a drug benefit and long-term care to the elderly under Medicare, as Pauly notes. If the national health insurance reform bill that emerges does offer benefits to the entire non-Medicare population, and if they receive significantly more generous benefits than those granted to the Medicare population, then it is likely that the elderly also will seek this extended coverage. Undoubtedly, questions will be raised about the cost of including the elderly under a comprehensive national benefit package and the consequences of doing so.

At issue here are the practical limits that society is willing to place on health care expenditures and the philosophical premise that every American has a "right" to a wide range of health care services. In Chapter Eight, Schieber concludes that the "hope that all Americans are willing to pay for every possible health service or product that the current system might devise and make that service or product available to anyone who might want it is not viable in the current economic situation."

A unique perspective on this theme is offered by John Burns, Vice President for Health Management at Honeywell and a medical doctor as well. In his commentary to Schieber's chapter, Burns indicates that the United States has failed to address "the issue of the necessity and appropriateness of care," and that until unnecessary and unwanted care is eliminated, the "conflict between cultural values and limited resources is a perception, not a reality." In contrast is the assessment of David Asch, Assistant Professor of Medicine, the University of Pennsylvania. In his view, the conflict between individual needs and social goals cannot be resolved. Accepting that practical limits to health care budgets exist at the "global level" ultimately means saying "No" at the micro level, and Asch concludes that "we need to say "No" a bit more often in the provision of medical care. We need to say it to our physicians, and our physicians need to say it to their patients. If we learn, finally, how to say "No," then the elderly are going to hear that word more often than other segments of the population."

Conclusion

An underlying tension marks the chapters and many of the commentaries found here. On the one hand, many authors are deeply concerned about the elderly population's particular risk of health problems and its precarious position as health reform proposals unfold. On the other hand, all participants recognize the vulnerability of the economic and political institutions that must meet the needs of taxpayers, both the young and the elderly. Inevitably, these issues must be confronted in the political arena. The collection of papers and commentaries in this volume highlights many of the special health insurance problems that face the elderly and offers some solutions that the reform process might consider.

References

Board of Trustees, Federal Hospital Insurance Trust Fund. *1993 Annual Report of the Board of Trustees of the Federal Hospital Insurance Trust Fund.* Washington, DC: USGPO, 1993.
National Health Policy Forum. Medicare Beneficiary Burdens, Part I: Out-of-Pocket Health Care Costs. Issue Brief, No. 462. Washington DC: George Washington University, March, 1987; p. 3.

Chapter 2
Introduction to Retiree Health Benefits

Judith F. Mazo

This discussion offers a brief overview of employer-provided retiree health benefits, describing what they look like, who is likely to receive them (and why), and the immediate and long-term issues that they pose for employers, employees and the economy. It also aims to set the stage for those who are not employee benefits professionals, to give a common context for the substantive matters that will be explored in the chapters and commentaries that follow. This overview speaks in generalities, to give a sense of what is "typical." In fact many, and perhaps most, real-life situations depart from the norm to greater or lesser degrees.

Retiree Health Coverage: A Roadmap

Retiree health plans often are continuations of the health coverage that the employer provides for similarly situated active workers, but just as often there are distinctions in the retiree coverage that reflect the special needs of that population. In particular, all employer-provided retiree health coverage is designed around Medicare or its absence.

The 800-pound gorilla in the retiree health coverage field is the federal Medicare program. Virtually all Americans aged 65 and older are entitled to hospitalization insurance under Medicare Part A, paid for by the Medicare Trust Fund. They also are eligible for major medical insurance under Medicare Part B, which is funded in part by premiums paid by enrollees and, therefore, is voluntary.[1] If a retiree has Medicare and other coverage that overlaps it, Medicare is the primary payor, that is, it pays an eligible claim first and the other coverage pays any remaining balance. So, retiree health plans most commonly distinguish between coverage for retirees who are Medicare eligible and those who are not.

Medicare-Covered Retirees

Employer plans for Medicare-covered retirees recognize substantial savings from the fact that Medicare pays its share of a claim first, leaving only deductibles and copays to be picked up by the employer's plan.[2] In addition, employer plans cover items for over-65 retirees that Medicare excludes, such as prescription drugs. Some plans even cover retirees for items that are not part of the employer's general health benefit plans for active employees.

Some retiree health plans reimburse the Medicare Part B premiums for the retiree and, if the plan has dependent coverage, for the retiree's spouse. This is not only a valuable benefit for the retiree, but it also makes it easier for the employer's plan to coordinate with Medicare's primary coverage. In some instances, reimbursement of the Part B premiums *is* the employer-sponsored plan's coverage for retirees.

Early Retirees

Because it is so much more expensive than coverage for retirees who also have Medicare, employer-provided coverage for early retirees has been somewhat less common (except in connection with early retirement windows, as discussed later). Where it is offered, it usually is a simple continuation of the active-employee coverage (perhaps without noncore coverages, such as vision and dental) rather than a specially tailored retiree benefit package.

Financing

Many employers pay at least some part of the cost of the retiree coverage that they offer, at least for the retired employee. Some plans require contributions from retirees that are higher than what active employees have to pay. Implicitly if not expressly, this recognizes that active employees also are "paying" the employer's share, which is offset directly or indirectly against their wages. Even where the employee and retiree contributions are set at the same levels, retiree payments are effectively higher because they are after tax, whereas almost all companies now enable their employees to pay their share of the cost of health coverage on a pre-tax basis.

It is not unusual for an employer to offer retiree health coverage on a retiree-pay-all basis. The plan offered to retirees is ordinarily the employer's active-employee health plan. The ability to buy it at cost (i.e, at age-neutral, large-group rates) could be a substantial benefit for retirees. The employer plan thus becomes another option for retirees who are shopping for Medigap coverage.

Eligibility

Retiree health coverage is typically made available only to people who retire from active employment, with the company sponsoring the health plan. This means that covered retirees must qualify and apply for a pension from that company (i.e., they must have a minimum of five years of service) and that the plan sponsor essentially must be their last employer. Some companies offer retiree coverage to people who move to jobs elsewhere before returning to claim their pensions, but this is not common outside the multiemployer plan arena.

Extent of Retiree Coverage

The federal government, all state governments, and most local governments provide health coverage for early retirees and for those persons who retire after 65. This reflects the traditional pattern of public employers offering richer benefits than much of the private sector in return for lower cash compensation. It also is probably an artifact from the time when many public sector employees were not eligible for Medicare because they were not covered by Social Security.

Private employers' health coverage for retirees is much more narrow. In March 1990, the General Accounting Office (GAO) reported that companies employing 40 percent of the private sector workforce offered retiree health coverage, and that about 5 million retirees (2 million below age 65) were covered at that point by employer-sponsored health plans. Predictably, retiree health coverage was most likely to be found in larger companies: 43 percent of those with 500 or more employees had retiree health coverage, compared with 2 percent of companies with fewer than 25 employees. Retiree health coverage was more common in the manufacturing, transportation, and utilities sectors than in such service industries as construction and retail.

Although multiemployer health plans, set up under the Taft-Hartley Act to cover collectively bargained employees working for a number of employers that bargain with the particular union that cosponsors the fund, cover a much smaller percentage of the private sector work force, a companion GAO report issued in July 1990 reported that about two thirds of those plans offered retiree coverage. According to that report, about 6 percent of current retirees with employer-provided health coverage were in multiemployer plans.

Early Retirees

Despite the costs and the lack of Medicare coverage to cushion them, early retirement incentives, sweetened with promises of continued health insurance, became an important instrument in the widespread corporate restructurings of the 1980s, continuing into the 1990s.

Some employers that pared back their workforces had labor agreements that bound them to extend the retiree-health safety net to the affected workers. Other companies might have been free, technically, to fire people without making any health care arrangements for them, and many did so. But many other employers chose to avoid the political and legal confrontations that that approach would trigger by attempting to ease people out with the offer of generous lifetime health coverage.

Funding

Employers generally have not prefunded retiree medical coverage. Unlike pensions, employer health plans have no meaningful reserves to cover the costs for retirees if the employer no longer is able or willing to do so. In part, this is because employers have, until recently, viewed retiree health coverage as a current benefit, like the active-employee coverage to which it was appended. This perspective has been shared and reinforced by Congress, which has not set vesting or funding standards for retiree health coverage, and which, in 1984, eliminated the opportunity for tax-favored prefunding for retiree health benefits.[3]

Legal Status

At present, employer-provided health benefit plans are subject to substantial regulation, but only on essentially peripheral aspects of their operations. Private sector plans are covered by the federal Employee Retirement Income Security Act (ERISA), which sets reporting, disclosure, and fiduciary standards but whose main significance in the health plan area may come from the fact that it prevents the states from regulating the plans (ERISA pre-emption). In complex, ambiguous, and often overlooked terms, section 105(h) of the U.S. Internal Revenue Code (IRC) bars self-funded plans from discriminating in favor of certain highly paid employees. Section 125 of the IRC sets ground rules for health plans funded with pre-tax employee contributions and, as noted, sections 419, 419A, and 512 govern the tax treatment of funding for health plans.

Other pertinent federal laws include Title VII of the 1964 Civil Rights Act, which prohibits discrimination in employment, benefits, and compensation based on race, gender, religion, and national origin; the Age Discrimination in Employment Act; the provisions of the Social Security Act that prescribe rules for health plans' coordination with Medicare (MSP, or Medicare Secondary Payor rules); and the Americans with Disabilities Act. On a different note, section 1114 of the Bankruptcy Code was intended to provide special protection for retiree health coverage when an employer goes into Chapter XI proceedings.

The Consolidated Omnibus Budget Reconciliation Act of 1985 (COBRA), which actually was passed in the Spring of 1986, requires employer plans to give employees and their families the right to continue health coverage that they otherwise would lose when the employee terminates service (a concept that includes retirement), by paying for it themselves. Health coverage continuation under COBRA on this basis can last for up to 18 months, but it is terminable when the individual becomes covered under Medicare. COBRA coverage thus can be viewed as a type of (and prototype for) mandatory, employer-provided health coverage for early retirees. COBRA applies to the private sector and to federal, state, and local governments.

In the middle and late 1980s, employers were alarmed, and employee/retiree advocates were encouraged, by a flurry of federal court decisions that prevented employers from cutting back retiree health coverage. For a while it looked as if ERISA might be read to imply something akin to vesting in the right to retiree health coverage, or even in the right to a particular design of retiree health coverage (i.e., first dollar), if employees had not been warned explicitly, while working or at the point of retirement, that the employer had reserved the right to alter, cut back, or eliminate coverage. In the majority of later cases, the courts have tended to find that the employer has no ongoing obligation if the written plan document and summary plan description include reservation-of-rights language, at least in the absence of express commitments to the contrary in bargaining agreements or elsewhere. Nevertheless, many employers have been reluctant to alter the terms of health coverage for people who already have retired, other than passing through generally applicable plan design changes.

The Cost Spiral

Retiree Coverage Costs in General

Although employer-provided retiree health coverage predated Medicare, which was passed in 1965, its general expansion was spurred by the introduction of the federal program, which focused employees' and society's attention on the health care needs of the over-65 population, and at the same time, made it much less expensive for employers to offer to help meet those needs. As health care costs generally have exploded, however, so has the cost of even the supplementary coverage that employer plans provide for over-65 retirees. For example, the $3 monthly enrollee premium set in 1965 for Medicare Part B coverage climbed to $36.60 in

1993; in 1993, a Medicare-covered hospital patient must pay a $676 for the first-day hospital deductible under Part A, compared to the $40 deductible that applied initially. From a relatively inexpensive add-on to ease employees' transition to retirement, retiree medical coverage has become a major corporate cost item.

And, apart from the direct cost of covering Medicare-eligible retirees, the health care cost crisis has precipitated cutbacks in health coverage for active workers that make it difficult economically and from a personnel-policy perspective to continue to devote available compensation funds to relatively rich retiree coverage.

Demographic Factors

The cost of retiree health coverage is not only driven by the general pace of health care cost inflation. The happy fact is that people who retire are now living longer than they used to, so that "lifetime coverage" entails benefits for a significantly larger total amount of health care, as later chapters discuss. The unhappy implications of this are that older people use a disproportionate share of health care services as their bodies wear out. As life spans increase, many older people seem to stay fairly healthy in their initial retirement years, becoming frailer as their ages climb past 80 and 85. Illnesses and conditions that used to end people's lives fairly quickly, such as infections, certain kinds of cancer, and heart disease, can now be conquered through expensive health care procedures (e.g., heart transplants, chemotherapy and the like) and are replaced by drawn-out, chronic diseases such as Alzheimer's disease, congestive heart failure, and emphysema. Both elements push up health care costs.

FAS 106

These assorted social and political concerns and pressures have been brought to a head by the unlikely agency of the Financial Accounting Standards Board (FASB). Completing a project launched in the early 1980s to rationalize the accounting treatment for post-employment benefits, in 1990 FASB adopted Financial Accounting Statement 106 (FAS 106), to govern employer accounting for post-retirement health benefits.[4]

FAS 106 went into effect for most public companies in 1993. It requires employers that provide retiree health coverage to recognize an obligation to pay for that coverage on their balance sheets, and, in the future, to accrue it as an expense over the careers of the employees who (the employer expects) will be entitled to it. In effect, FAS 106 requires employers to treat retiree health coverage much like pension obligations, for accounting purposes. A company must set a present value on their expected future outlays for the coverage, which, net of assets set aside to meet those costs, is treated as a company liability.

Aside from the fact that this was revolutionary because health care costs had always been taken into account on a year-by-year, pay-as-you-go basis, the impact has been dramatically different from that of the similar pension accounting requirement (FAS 87) because, unlike pension plans, health plans have virtually no assets to offset corporate America's retiree health obligations. Moreover, given current trends in health care costs, companies that began calculating their FAS 106 exposure found that the total cost of an open-ended promise to pay health care expenses on the traditional health plan model was staggering.

Corporate Response

FAS 106 has precipitated a massive effort at corporate consciousness raising on the cost of retiree health coverage. Whether or not FAS 106 measures it correctly and has the right answer for the expense accrual, there now is no doubt that, even though fewer than half of American workers are in plans that offer them retiree health coverage, employers' exposure for this cost is enormous.

Most employers are looking for ways to reduce that unfunded liability. Funding might be one way, but as noted, there are tax impediments that make it uneconomic, and, in any event, it would be an expensive and drawn-out process. The other way is to reduce the liability by redesigning (read "reducing") the health coverage that companies promise to retirees.

Companies are taking various routes to this end. Most, but far from all, are preserving the current health coverage design for workers who already have retired and are putting changes into place prospectively. Some of the revised approaches being considered or adopted include:

- Terminating of retiree health coverage, sometimes softening the impact by substituting enhanced retirement savings in the form of an Employee Stock Ownership Plan;
- Setting a maximum per-person dollar amount that the company will pay in the future for health insurance premiums or premium equivalents;
- Introducing or increasing retiree contributions and setting a ceiling on the share of future coverage costs that the company will absorb;
- Introducing defined-dollar health coverage "accounts" that increase with the employees' years of service, in lieu of defined benefit type health coverage. The amount in each person's account defines the

maximum that the company will spend for that person's retiree health coverage.

- Linking the extent of company-paid coverage at retirement to the length of the retiree's service.

Overall, the outlook is for less employer-paid retiree health coverage just as the demographic trends converge to create a greater need for it. The chances for a successful national health care reform depend on a creative response to this challenge.

In the chapters and commentaries that follow, the themes touched on here are explored in some depth. This book does not try to come up with definitive solutions for all the problems. Rather, the hope is that the insights and observations presented here will shed some useful light on the issues that now confront those charged with shaping public policy.

Notes

1. Technically, Part A coverage is voluntary as well, in that an individual must enroll to have claims honored. Enrollment is automatic for those who have applied for Social Security benefits.

2. Medicare is secondary when its coverage duplicates that provided by an employer plan for an active employee or the spouse of an active employee.

3. Under IRC sections 419, 419A, and 512, companies can take a current deduction for amounts contributed to reserves for retiree medical benefits but only to the extent that they do not anticipate inflation in medical costs, and earnings on funds held in those reserves are taxable, except for collectively bargained and employee-pay-all arrangements.

4. FAS 106 actually covers all post-retirement benefits other than pensions, but the costs for other benefits, such as life insurance, are so minor in comparison with health coverage that they typically are overlooked in general discussions to focus on the impact of FAS 106 in connection with retiree health care accounting. FASB standards define "generally accepted accounting principles," with which auditors must comply to produce an unqualified opinion on a company's financial statements.

Chapter 3
Is Retiree Health Insurance Crowding Out Retiree Cash Benefits?

Deborah J. Chollet

Employer payments for health insurance in the United States have surpassed payments for any other employee benefit. In 1990, employers paid an estimated $174.2 billion in contributions for health insurance, equal to 5.3 percent of total compensation.[1] Employer payments to health insurance now represent nearly one third of aggregate employer payments for all benefits combined, including voluntary benefits and social insurance (U.S. Department of Commerce 1992). Obviously, since not all firms offer health insurance to current workers or to retirees, these relative measures understate the burden assumed by firms that do offer them.

Most employer payments for health insurance benefits finance coverage for active workers. However, employer promises to continue benefits after retirement, often made as an inducement for workers to take early retirement, have changed the balance of cost for many employers during the last decade. Some older manufacturing companies, with a long history of collectively bargained contracts, now count more retirees and retiree dependents in their health plans than active workers and their dependents. In 1988, 7.8 million retirees aged 55 or older received health insurance as a retiree benefit in their own name. These people represented 42 percent of all retirees aged 55 or older who were not currently employed (Zedlewski 1993).[2]

As of December 15, 1992, most private employers that are obligated to pay health insurance benefits for current or future retirees must report the present value of that obligation as a liability against corporate assets and income. The present value of corporate liabilities for retiree health

The views expressed in this paper are solely those of the author. The author wishes to acknowledge the generous advice and assistance of Jack L. VanDerhei of Temple University and Daniel J. Beller of the U.S. Department of Labor in tabulating the Form 5500 data.

insurance, estimated by the U.S. General Accounting Office (GAO), approached $300 billion in 1989—as much as one half of aggregate spending for health care in the United States and approximately twice the level of all employer payments for current health insurance benefits in that year.[3]

This chapter is an overview of issues and evidence related to the burden of funding retiree health insurance liabilities and is organized as follows: first, the nature of employer obligations to recognize the present value of unfunded liabilities on their balance sheets, as well as evidence about employer responses to date are reviewed. Second, employer options for funding liability for retiree health benefits are summarized. Drawing on simple economic theory to suggest the likely distribution of burden, the incidence of increases in the cost of retiree health benefits related to funding future obligations is then discussed. Finally, the current relationship between health insurance benefits and pension benefits is described, together with inferential evidence about how that relationship may change for future retirees.

Employer Responses to the Recognition of Retiree Health Liabilities

Financial Accounting Standard (FAS) 106 requires corporations to "book" the actuarial present value of retiree health insurance benefits attributable to the accrual period, net of plan assets, as of December 15, 1992. Compliance with FAS 106 requires firms to amortize accumulated obligations for retiree health insurance benefits for active workers and retirees alike, and to fund future benefits as workers earn them, rather than as they are received.

Issued in 1990, FAS 106 had been anticipated for a decade before the statement's actual effective date for compliance.[4] A series of preliminary conclusions issued by the Financial Accounting Standards Board (FASB) that accrual accounting was appropriate for post-retirement benefits other than pensions had resulted in FASB taking two steps in 1984: establishing a major project to explore issues related to the recognition and measurement of liability, and issuing an interim statement (FAS 81) in November 1984 that required disclosure of the current cost of these benefits to the extent possible.[5] It is noteworthy that in the years immediately following FAS 81, many firms were unable to identify and, thus, to report the current cost of health insurance benefits for retirees.[6]

In addition to clear signals from FASB that accrual accounting standards for retiree health insurance liabilities were virtually inevitable, employers also received strong signals from both the courts and Congress that corporate retiree obligations were taken seriously. Litigation that tested employer rights to modify or terminate retiree health insurance benefits increased markedly during the 1980s.[7] Persistent increases in the cost of health benefits as well as the acceleration of merger and acquisition activity led many corporations to seek ways to cut the cost of current and prospective benefits. Retirees, in turn, sued for reinstatement of benefits that had been modified or terminated. These cases ultimately confirmed the contractual nature of employer promises related to retiree health insurance and served to alert employers to the importance of language used in plan documents and personnel interviews to describe the nature and durability of retiree health insurance benefits.

In 1985 and again in 1988, Congress passed legislation affecting the rights of retirees to continued coverage in employer-sponsored health insurance plans. In 1985 (and as subsequently amended), the Consolidated Omnibus Budget Reconciliation Act (COBRA) required employers to offer retiring and other terminating workers and their dependents the opportunity to continue health insurance benefits for a period of 18 to 36 months following termination of employment.[8] A special bankruptcy provision enacted in 1986, moreover, requires that in the event of Chapter XI bankruptcy reorganization, retirees be offered indefinite continuation of coverage—that is, until the retiree dies or regains group coverage as a consequence of re-employment or marriage.

Although COBRA allows employers to charge as much as 102 percent of average plan cost for such continuation, employer experience suggests that adverse selection is a substantial problem (Charles D. Spencer and Associates 1992). As a result, employers' obligation to offer continued coverage to retirees at approximately average plan cost represents in effect an obligation to offer a contribution for continued coverage. In 1988, approximately 244,000 retirees reported having coverage from a past employer that would continue for not longer than 18 months; such coverage is presumed to represent COBRA continuation (Zedlewski 1993).

In 1988, the Retiree Benefits Bankruptcy Act again addressed the matter of retiree health insurance benefit continuation in cases of sponsor bankruptcy. That legislation prohibits companies filing for Chapter XI bankruptcy from modifying or terminating retiree health benefits unless they are able to prove in court that they must do so to avoid liquidation. Although various proposals to improve tax incentives for the funding of future liabilities have been discussed at length, none of these has been considered seriously in light of the significant potential for federal revenue loss.

These consistent signals from FASB, the courts, and Congress over the last decade or more have given employers both reason and opportunity to reconsider the nature of their retiree health benefits that they promise to current workers. Preliminary evidence from the U.S. Department of

Labor (DOL) suggests that employers have in fact modified their obligations to current workers in ways that would reduce the current cost of retiree health benefits, as well as liability for future cost.

In 1991, 42 percent of workers in private firms with 100 employees or more had health insurance plans that would continue coverage after early retirement; 40 percent had plans that continued coverage after normal retirement (see Table 3.1). These counts represent a decline in reported coverage from two years earlier and contrast with an expansion of retiree coverage promises to workers in large firms between 1981 and 1986. Clark et al. (1992) report that the decline in coverage promised to both early and normal retirees between 1988 and 1989 was most dramatic among firms in wholesale trade.

TABLE 3.1   Percent of Employees in Larger Establishments with Health Insurance Benefits that Continue After Retirement [a,b]

Year	Retirement before Age 65	Retirement at Age 65 or Older
1981	61	55
1985	64	59
1986	82	68
1988[c]	45	37
1989[c]	40	35
1991[c]	42	40

[a] *Source:* Tabulations of survey data from the United States Department of Labor, Bureau of Labor Statistics, various years.
[b] Data include only benefits to which the employer will contribute and that continue for one month or more after retirement.
[c] Data are based on a sample of firms with 100 or more employees; prior years' data are based on a sample of firms with 250 employees or more.

Funding Employer Liability for Retiree Health Benefits

For many firms, the obligation to fund accrued liability for the health benefits promised to current and future retirees represents a substantial increase in current spending for those benefits—by one estimate, five to ten times annual pay-as-you-go costs (Cotter 1993). The burden of funding these benefits on an accrual basis is further magnified by restrictions on recognized funding that are imposed by FASB, as well as restrictions on allowable funding imposed by the federal tax code.

FAS 106 recognizes funding as an offset to liability for retiree health benefits only if the funds are held exclusively for that purpose. Funds held in a trust that is usable for funding welfare benefits other than retiree health insurance (for example, a 501(c)(9) trust) would not qualify as an offset to liability under FAS 106; the trust must be designated specifically and exclusively for the purpose of funding retiree health benefits.

Employers may make tax-preferred contributions to fund current and future retiree health benefits under various sections of the federal tax code. Of those summarized here, the most generally useful funding options available to employers are 501(c)(9) plans and 401(h) plans.

501(c)(9) Plans

Also called Voluntary Employee Benefit Associations (or VEBAs), these plans can be used to hold and invest assets against retiree health obligations. However, the federal tax code tightly limits both the amount of the contribution (by disallowing contributions against future inflation, regardless of how reasonable the assumptions used) and the effective rate of return on assets held in a VEBA for the particular purpose of funding retiree health insurance benefits. Earnings against such assets are subject to tax as unrelated business income. Note that these provisions affect only single-employer plans; 501(c)(9) trusts established under collective bargaining agreements are subject to neither the zero-inflation restriction nor the tax on earnings.

401(h) Plans

Federal law also allows the use of 401(h) medical accounts for the purpose of funding retiree health benefits but restricts contributions to such plans to 25 percent of the employer's contribution to the pension plan. That is, while employer contributions to a 401(h) trust are tax deductible and earnings in the trust accumulate tax free, use of the 401(h) plan requires that the employer be able to make a pension contribution within the plan's full funding limit. A revision of the "incidental" rule governing 401(h) plans has been discussed, allowing 401(h) contributions against the accrual of employer pension liabilities regardless of the pension plan's funding status. As with other proposals that might ease funding of retiree health liabilities, however, these discussions have foundered on the issue of potential federal revenue loss.

Employers with money purchase pension plans may also use 401(h) plans for the purpose of funding retiree health liabilities. In this case, the pension plan in effect never reaches a full funding limit, so that a tax-qualified contribution to the 401(h) trust is always allowable. Even in this case, however, the 25-percent limit on such contributions may bear no relationship to the employer's actual accrued liability for retiree health benefits.

Transferring Excess Pension Assets to a 401(h) Plan

The Omnibus Budget Reconciliation Act of 1990 created Internal Revenue Code (IRC) Section 420. Section 420 addresses the effective prohibition on employers from using 401(h) plans if their pension plan has reached the full funding limit. Section 420 allows for a limited transfer of excess pension assets into 401(h) plans to fund current-period retiree health benefits. Section 420 does not allow this transfer to fund liability for *future* benefits; therefore, it helps to amortize neither past-accrued liability nor current-period accrual of liability for future benefits.

The use of Section 420 transfers is also restricted in other ways:

- All current pension plan participants must be fully vested in all accrued benefits at the time of the transfer.[9]
- Employers that make a Section 420 transfer cannot reduce per-retiree health care spending for five years following the transfer. This means that employers whose cost experience improves may actually need to enhance retiree health benefits to maintain cost.
- Employers can transfer only those amounts that exceed 125 percent of the amount needed to cover current pension liabilities.
- Transfers to the 401(h) trust can be made only once per year through 1995.
- Transferred funds not used to pay health benefits must be transferred back to the pension plan account and are subject to the excise tax on asset reversions.
- No transfer can be made to pay benefits for key employees.

These restrictions are such that few employers are likely to use Section 420 transfers. Indeed, one employer has done so only with the expectation of terminating its retiree health benefit altogether in 1997 (Mintz 1993). Millholland (1992) notes that Section 420 transfers are useful primarily to employers with substantially overfunded pension plans and immediate cash-flow needs. However, the transfer reduces the employer's current tax deduction for medical benefits and hastens the time when the employer must begin making tax-deductible contributions to the pension plan.

Designated Qualified Retirement Plans

Employers may also use conventional qualified profit-sharing or stock bonus plans to fund retiree health liability. As with 501(c)(9) and 401(h) plans, assets held in these plans offset the employer's FAS 106 liability if the plans are designated exclusively for the purpose of funding retiree health benefits. This degree of segregation may be prohibited under the rules governing qualified retirement plans (Hutchison 1991), although professional opinion on this point appears to be divided.

The use of a designated qualified plan allows the employer to make tax-deductible contributions within the current-law limits governing contributions to such plans for the purpose of retirement saving, and earnings accumulate tax free. Retirees may use plan distributions to pay their share of the cost of health benefits at the time of receipt. Although both contributions and earnings to the plan are tax deferred, distributions are taxable income to retirees. Millholland (1992) suggests that the qualified plan itself may purchase a health insurance plan, which then may provide tax-exempt medical benefits to retirees.[10]

Corporate-Owned Life Insurance (COLI)

Although COLIs may not be counted toward an employer's FAS 106 liability, they may help employers manage cash-flow needs associated with retiree health benefits. Employers may purchase a COLI on part or all of their active work force; as deaths occur, the company collects the life insurance distributions tax free. The company may also borrow against the cash value of the policy to create cash flow to meet all or part of its current costs for retiree health benefits. Interest on loans under $50,000 is tax deductible.

Employers also may combine a COLI with a 501(c)(9) plan (or VEBA) to provide additional tax benefits. Such plans, called *trust-owned life insurance (TOLI)*, allow employers to deduct the life insurance premium and to accumulate earnings as inside-buildup (and, therefore, not subject to tax as unrelated business income). Unlike a COLI, the cash value of a TOLI does count against the employer's FAS 106 liability.

Both COLIs and TOLIs carry some potential disadvantages. Both require that the employer transfer risk to an insurance company, including the risk of asset performance. Employers also may have to comply with some states' insurable interest laws and may need employee consent to structure retiree health plan funding in this way. Finally, in the near term, neither COLIs nor TOLIs may have sufficient asset value to fund accrued retiree health liability for current retirees or for workers near retirement.

Despite the variety of funding options available to employers, none necessarily offers employers the ability to fund accrued retiree health benefit obligations with the same tax advantages that apply to funding pension obligations. Depending on the firm's particular circumstances, there may be no option that would allow full funding of the true present value of liability for retiree health benefits with fully deductible contributions and exemption of plan earnings. Arrangements that are most like conventional defined-contribution pension plans in their tax implications may be unable to provide the tax-exempt benefit after retirement that is normally associated with an employer-sponsored health plan. Although TOLIs may come closest to replicating the tax advantages allowed employer pension funding, their usefulness depends critically on the demographics of the covered work force. The difficulty of configuring adequate funding against employer liabilities for retiree health benefits under current law may prove to be among the most important factors in an ongoing decline of these benefits.

The potential difficulty of designing an adequate, tax-preferred funding arrangement for employer contributions, however, does not mean that employers would not sponsor group coverage for retirees without a contribution. Various conventional defined-contribution pension plans may be used to accumulate employee contributions to finance future participation in a group retiree health plan. Such arrangements help offset employer reductions in plan benefits or in their obligation to contribute to benefits and may enable employers to redesign their liability as a defined contribution.

Various surveys indicate that many employers have in fact redesigned their retiree health plans in ways that increase retiree costs to participate in the plan and limit employer liability either absolutely or relative to total plan cost. Plan reports tabulated by Clark et al. (1992) suggest that retiree contributions for coverage became much more common even between 1988 and 1989. In 1989, fewer than one half of workers (45 to 47 percent) with a health benefit that would continue after retirement either before or after age 65 would have the benefit wholly paid by their employer, although this proportion varies widely among industry groups

TABLE 3.2   Workers with Wholly Employer-Paid Retiree Health Benefits as a Percent of All Workers with Retiree Health Benefits: Establishments with 100 Workers or More, 1989 [a]

Industry group	Retirees Under Age 65	Retirees Aged 65 or Older
Mining	28	30
Construction	58	67
Manufacturing	46	44
Transportation, communications, and utilities	73	75
Wholesale trade	75	70
Retail trade	10	10
Finance, insurance, and real estate	32	37
Services	29	40

[a] *Source:* Clark RL, Headen Jr. AE, Shumaker L. *Retiree Health Insurance Benefits and the Retirement Decision.* Final Report, HHS Grant No. 90-ASPE-231A (June 1992), Table III-6. Washington, DC: Department of Health and Human Services, 1992.

(see Table 3.2). A survey conducted by Hewitt Associates (1990) indicated that more than one third of the nearly 300 surveyed employers with retiree health benefits had made changes in either 1988 or 1989 that increased retiree contributions for single or family coverage or raised the deductibles or coinsurance provisions of the plan. Of these, approximately one third had provided offsetting increases in other benefits such as pensions.[11]

The Incidence of Increases in the Cost of Retiree Health Benefits

Some simple economics of employer responses to the increased current cost of health benefits are described in this section. The expected increase in employer cost, both now and over the foreseeable future, comes from a number of sources.

Before 1993, most employers that sponsored retiree health benefits neither recognized nor funded any accrual of liability.[12] By forcing balance-sheet recognition of the present value of employer promises to provide retiree health benefits, FAS 106 has forced plan sponsors to increase current spending for health benefits greatly, to avoid significant loss of financial net value. This cost can be taken as a one-time "hit" to the corporate balance sheet; however, FAS 106 allows employers to amortize past accruals over as many as 20 years.[13]

The cost of health benefits, both for retirees and current workers, has exceeded growth in any other sector of the economy and probably will continue to do so for some time. As a result, the relative cost of health benefits compared to wages, other benefits, capital, and corporate gross income will continue to grow for many if not most employers. Thus, even if plan sponsors were to continue pay-as-you-go financing of retiree health benefits, the relative cost of these benefits would continue to rise.

Employers' limited ability to fund against retiree health obligations in a tax-effective way magnifies the cost of retiree health liabilities relative to other retirement benefits that the employer might offer. If employers are more willing to fund pension benefits than health benefits, the effect of increasing retiree health costs on retiree cash benefits—the central question of this Chapter—may be less than if funding options for both were equally tax-advantaged.

The discussion that follows distinguishes between the cost of funding accrued retiree health benefits and the cost of funding current benefit accruals. Although this distinction is conventional in a discussion of pension liability, where standards for vesting and accruals are established in law, with respect to retiree health insurance benefits the distinction is relatively novel.

Funding benefits pay-as-you-go, most employers have eschewed the notion of pre-retirement vesting for retiree health benefits. Typically, employers have in effect cliff-vested workers at the point they became eligible to receive pension benefits.[14] However, FAS 106 is premised on FASB's determination that terminal accrual of liability (that is, accrual at retirement) is inappropriate (FASB 1990). Instead, FAS 106 requires employers to recognize benefit accruals using a benefits/years of service approach that attributes the expected benefit obligation to each year of service in the attribution period.[15] Thus, FAS 106 requires employers to fund liabilities for current workers during their working years, even if the employer retains terminal vesting for the benefit. It is this provision of FAS 106 that makes the question of incidence especially interesting.

Anticipating new accounting rules and seeking to control the cost of funding for short-service workers, some employers have established explicit, graduated benefits schedules for retiree health benefits. In general, such schedules provide for greater employer payment for coverage after retirement (in either dollar terms or as a percentage of plan cost) for workers with longer service, and less or no payment after retirement for short-service workers (for example, workers with fewer than ten years of service at retirement). Such graduated schedules for retiree health benefits may become more common as employers begin to adjust to the new accounting rules.

Funding Past Accruals

In the simplest scenario, the cost of funding past-accrued liability (either for retiree benefits that already are in pay status or for benefits that are fully obligated to current workers) has no bearing on current production decisions. Even if the firm is able to alter its contractual obligation to pay these benefits, to the extent that the firm retains liability related to past service, funding that liability raises the firm's fixed cost: the cost of funding the liability cannot be altered by changing any short-term production decision. Thus, the firm suffers reduced profit but will make no adjustment in the level of production or the price of its product, unless reduced profit affects the firm's cost of obtaining capital.[16] An increase in the cost of capital may cause the firm to scale back production and employment, and, as a result, the product price may rise. Obviously, even firms with relatively little need for external capital can be forced out of business if their fixed costs for past accruals are sufficiently high, perhaps affecting market prices for labor, capital, and their product more widely.

In any case, the magnitude of the potential effect on product price depends on the structure and regulation of product markets. Reduced output could raise product prices in markets with relatively few competitors. Regulated monopolies, such as public utilities, may be especially successful in shifting the cost of funding past accruals forward to con-sumers, as rate increases are administratively determined and generally gauged to maintain a fixed margin of profit for the firm. In fact, firms in transportation, communications, and public utilities (TCU) may bear the greatest liability for health benefits related to current retirees;[17] together with firms in finance, insurance, and real estate, TCU firms are the most likely to offer retiree health benefits to current workers. In more com-petitive industries, where firms have limited ability to raise prices inde-pendently, plan sponsors and, in turn, shareholders would bear the cost of funding past accruals.

To the extent that employers fail to fund past accruals as they are rec-ognized, past research on pension funding suggests that the firm's share prices may adjust quite accurately to the magnitude of unfunded liability for benefits (Feldstein and Seligman 1981; Landesman 1986). It seems likely that most firms with very large accrued liability for retiree health benefits will avail themselves of the 20-year amortization period that FAS 106 allows for past accruals. As a result, the impact of past accruals on employers' financial statements is likely to be gradual and cumulative, whether funded or otherwise. Nevertheless, it is noteworthy that equity markets apparently have not been sensitive to retiree health liabilities since FAS 81 required disclosure.[18]

Finally, if the firm is able to alter its obligations to current retirees, how the employer handles health benefits for current retirees may affect the employer's credibility in negotiating compensation for current work-ers. That is, the funding of past accruals may affect the incidence of the cost of funding current accruals. The value to the employer of sending the "right" signal to current workers may be so significant that employers who would reduce substantially or terminate benefits for current retirees must do the same for current workers, even if the employer believes that a retiree health plan is critical in attracting and retaining good workers. This effect is discussed next.

Funding Current Accruals

The accrual of liability for retiree health benefits stretches the attribu-tion period for benefits over the worker's career.[19] As a result, the employer's recognition of liability becomes a current cost of labor and production decisions, rather than a fixed cost of retiring the worker. This adjustment in employers' (and perhaps employees') view of retiree health benefits may have implications for wages and other benefits, short-run and long-run production decisions, and employment.

Figure 3.1 offers a simple graphical exposition of the hypothetical trade-off between retiree health benefits and other forms of labor compensation. We assume that employers are interested only in total compensation, not necessarily the relative components of the compensation package. After Smith and Ehrenberg (1983), the firm's "isoprofit" curve—a curve along which any combination of benefits and cash compensation yields equals profits to the firm—is depicted as YY'. In effect, this is the firm's offer curve to workers in negotiating compensation.

In this case, we consider retiree health benefits separately from wages and all other benefits. For simplicity, one may assume that employer contributions to pensions and benefits other than retiree health are monotonically (and positively) related to wages. If employee productivity does not change systematically with the mix of retiree health benefits and other compensation, then the firm's isoprofit curve is a straight line. YY' can easily be nonlinear (convex or concave) if the presence of retiree health benefits enhances employee work effort by reducing turnover or, conversely, if retiree health benefits are structured so as to be independent

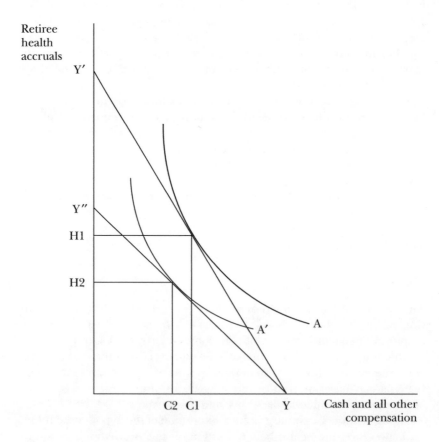

Figure 3.1   Retiree health benefits versus other forms of labor compensation.

of work effort and, therefore encourage absenteeism (Lazear 1990). However, the essential results of the analysis are the same for our purposes.

Adopting standard convexity assumptions, employee demand for retiree health benefits relative to wages and other benefits is depicted as indifference curve A. Employees with different preferences for retiree health benefits versus cash or other benefits will have indifference curves situated at different tangencies to the firm's offer curve. Each worker's utility is maximized at a tangency point; the differences among workers' preferences and their resulting tangency points define a range of compensation offers that the firm will make to employees (at a given target profit) and the resulting mix of wages and benefits in employee compensation. A uniform increase in the cost of funding retiree health benefits produces a downward swing of the firm's offer curve and a reduction in the worker's utility maximizing level of retiree health benefits relative to wages and other benefits. Whether wages and/or other benefits fall in equilibrium depends on employees' relative preferences for retiree health benefits and, therefore, the relative income and substitution effects of the new funding requirement.

The incidence of the cost of funding current accruals has to do with the willingness of employees to tolerate a reduction in wages and other benefits to sustain retiree health benefits. Worker tolerance for reduced wages and other benefits, in turn, depends on their relative preferences for retiree health benefits, their ability to find a preferred mix of compensation in alternative employment, and the degree to which they believe that their retiree health benefit is guaranteed.

Figure 3.2 depicts the market demand for and supply of labor for comparable workers. Required new funding for retiree health benefit accruals represents a downward shift in employer-sponsors' demand for labor by the full cost of funding. Guaranteeing the benefit to workers, in turn, shifts their supply curve outward by an amount equal to their valuation of the benefit. If the value of retiree health benefits to workers equals the cost of funding the benefit, then the supply of labor shifts outward to S', and the cost of funding is offset fully by a reduction in current compensation (to C3). Given time for market adjustment, plan sponsors would bear none of the cost of funding accruals.[20]

Workers who have little confidence that they ultimately will receive a health benefit in retirement will place a lower value on retiree health benefits than workers who are more confident of receiving the benefit, and they will be less tolerant of a reduction in current compensation to fund the benefits. The supply curve for these workers will shift outward less (to S''), and their current compensation in equilibrium will fall only to C2. The employer burden of funding retiree health benefits will be

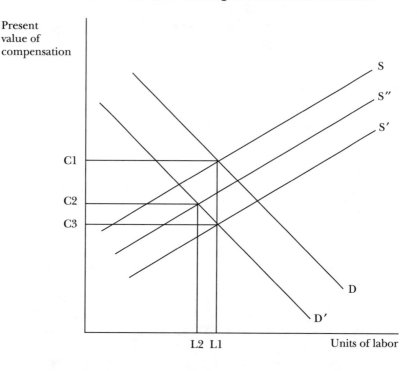

Figure 3.2   Market demand for and supply of labor in response to required new funding for retiree health benefit accruals.

greater (by the distance C2 - C3) than if these workers placed a higher probability on receiving the benefit.

It is this difference in the incidence of the cost of funding that may drive employers to adopt explicit (contractual) graduated benefit schedules, despite the absence of any requirement in law that employers establish vesting for retiree health benefits comparable to that required for pensions. By contractually guaranteeing partial benefits to workers, even if they terminate employment before retirement, the plan sponsor may be able to bargain much more effectively to fund accruals by reducing other forms of current compensation. Failure to convince workers of the current value of retiree benefits, conversely, places the burden of funding entirely on the plan sponsor, with little likelihood of obtaining any offset in other forms of compensation.

Furthermore, employers that retain the right to modify or terminate retiree benefits at will (and demonstrate that right with respect to benefits in payment to current retirees) may seriously diminish workers' confidence that they ultimately will receive the benefit, regardless of the agreement struck with current workers. As a result, these employers reduce the likelihood of obtaining wage concessions to offset the cost of funding current accruals.[21]

Although the relatively simple scenario described above captures the essence of the problem of incidence, the level of retiree health insurance benefits likely to emerge in the marketplace may be affected greatly by the idiosyncracies of the tax rules that govern funding of these benefits. For example, at present, the rules governing 501(c)(9) plans limit the level of tax-deductible contributions well below the full current value future benefits by disallowing any inflation assumption. Similarly, funding in a 401(h) plan is limited by the firm's pension funding status. Obviously, funding options that do not protect the plan sponsor from taxation of earnings on assets reduce the value to the employer of a dollar spent to fund retiree health benefits relative to a dollar spent on benefits that are relatively tax preferred, such as pensions or current insurance.

Although the second matter—taxation of earnings at all levels of funding—is important, analysis of its effect is qualitatively the same as that already presented. That is, the cost of funding retiree health benefits is simply higher, at every level of the benefit, than it would be were earnings in the plan tax deferred or tax exempt, and employers are correspondingly less willing to offer retiree health benefits at any level.

The presence of effective limits on tax-deductible contributions, however, may produce a qualitatively different result by producing a "kink" in the employer's compensation offer curve. Such a case is depicted in Figure 3.3.

YY'' in Figure 3.3 represents the firm's isoprofit curve, reflecting the current cost of funding retiree health benefit accruals with full deductibility of employer funding. A limit on deductible funding at H1 produces a new, kinked isoprofit curve, YY'''. In the limit, the equal-profit level of retiree health benefit funding becomes Y''', where

$$Y''' = Y''(1 - t)$$

and t is defined as the marginal tax rate on employer contributions above the deductible limit.

For workers with relatively strong preferences for retiree health benefits, such as that depicted by A' in Figure 3.3, the limit on tax-deductible employer funding of the benefit will have the effect of further reducing worker utility from compensation (relative to the no-limit case) and also fixing worker demand for retiree health benefits nearer (or at) H1. That is, although the equilibrium level of retiree health benefits (at a given level of profit) is likely to drop for all workers as employers begin to fund retiree benefits, it will drop most for workers who prefer relatively extensive retiree health benefits and, as a result, represent funding that ex-

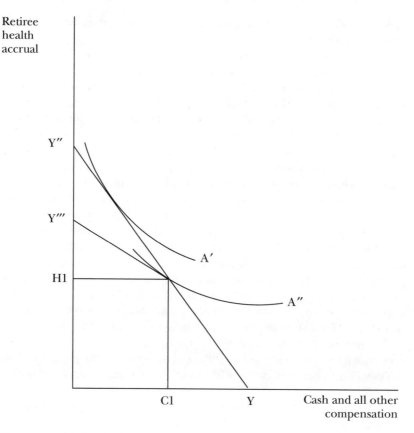

Figure 3.3 Effects of limits on tax-deductible contributions, or the so-called "kink" in the employer's compensation offer curve.

ceeds the tax-deductible limit. For such workers especially, employers may seek to improve employee satisfaction with total compensation (at the same level of profit) by redesigning the retiree health plan—for example, by using a conventional qualified plan to fund defined employer contributions as well as employee contributions to the benefit.

One reason why employees may have strong preferences for retiree health benefits relative to pension benefits, in particular, may relate to historically high rates of health care cost inflation. That is, if employees perceive that the discounted present value of retiree health benefits exceeds the discounted present value of equal employer contributions to a pension plan, they may prefer greater funding of retiree health benefits to maintenance of the pension benefit. By trading retiree health benefits for pension benefits, employees would, in effect, buy inflation protection with respect to a major expense item—health care. For workers anticipating retirement before Medicare eligibility, this may be especially attractive. This scenario might lead one to expect that pension coverage and benefits might deteriorate in favor of retiree health benefits.

Such preferences for retiree health benefits in lieu of pension benefits seem unlikely for several reasons. First, workers likely to value retiree benefits most also are likely to be near retirement. Such workers would have the most to lose from significant reductions in the pension formula in order to gain inflation protection for relatively few years. They may be more willing to delay retirement instead. Second, recent changes to Medicare (in particular, limiting physician balance billing) lessen the value of inflation protection after age 65. Finally, employers would seem unlikely to favor such a trade, accepting the open-ended liability of a retiree health benefit in lieu of the close-ended liability of a pension benefit.

Implications of Health Benefit Cost Increases for Retirement Benefits

The simple analysis already offered suggests that the impact of employer funding for retiree health benefits may be limited substantially by the relative tax disadvantages of funding these benefits. There are good reasons to expect employers to respond to FAS 106 by redesigning retiree health benefits to reduce or eliminate liability. Conversely, few scenarios would suggest that employers simply would commence funding an unaltered obligation unless otherwise constrained to do so. And, to the point of this chapter, there is little reason to believe that retiree health benefits would flourish at the expense of retirement cash benefits.

The intuition that employers would be reluctant to retain generous retiree health benefits is consistent with the recent erosion of retiree plans in general and the erosion of retiree plans that are fully employer-paid in particular. These patterns were described earlier in the section about employers' initial responses to the required recognition of accrued liability for retiree health benefits. Because the shortness of available time-series data supports (at best) only preliminary conclusions about trends toward scarcer and less generous retiree benefits, the issue clearly bears watching.

The funding of retiree health benefits, however, may affect pension benefits in other ways. Under IRC Section 420, employers may transfer excess pension assets for the purpose of funding current retiree health benefits. Because no available data describe the funding status of pension plans sponsored by firms that also provide retiree health benefits, the potential impact of Section 420 can be inferred only very generally from funding reports on all plans. Examination of Form 5500 reports on defined benefit pension plans, in particular, indicates that firms in industries that are the most likely to offer a concurrent retiree health benefit (in finance, insurance, and real estate) are also the most likely to have very high pension asset ratios.

A second way that retiree health benefit funding may affect pension plans is also an artifact of tax code restrictions on allowable retiree health plan funding. That is, employers who wish to use a 401(h) trust to fund retiree health benefits may contribute to the 401(h) plan only an amount that is not more than 25 percent of their contribution to the pension plan. As a result, consideration of retiree health obligations may force significant change in employers' pension funding strategies, encouraging greater contributions within the plan's full funding limit. These points are developed in greater detail in the following section.

Tabulation of the U.S. Department of Labor (DOL) employee benefit survey data indicates that about 40 percent of all establishments that sponsor a defined-benefit pension plan also sponsor retiree health benefits (see Table 3.3). Conversely, few firms (16 percent in 1989) offer a retiree health benefit, but no pension (Clark et al. 1992).

TABLE 3.3 Percent of Defined Benefit Pension Sponsors that Offer Retiree Health Benefits, by Age of Retiree Eligibility, 1989 [a]

	Retirees Under Age 65	Retirees Aged 65 or Older
Total, all establishments	44	40
Industry Group:		
Mining	56	43
Construction	24	36
Manufacturing	48	44
Transportation, communications, and utilities	58	46
Wholesale trade	29	22
Retail trade	42	29
Finance, insurance, and real estate	57	61
Service	21	17
Establishment Size:		
250 - 499	41	28
500 - 999	38	33
1000 - 2499	46	39
2500+	68	62

[a] *Source:* Calculations based on: Clark RL, Headen, Jr. AE, and Shumaker L. *Retiree Health Insurance Benefits and the Retirement Decision.* Final Report, HHS Grant No. 90-ASPE-231A (June 1992), Tables III-11 and III-12. Washington, DC: Department of Health and Human Services, 1992.

The contingent probability of a retiree health benefit, given the presence of a defined benefit plan, is highest in firms that have 2500 or more

TABLE 3.4   Distribution of Defined Benefit Pension Plans by Funding Status, 1990 [a]

	Number of Plans	Participants (in millions)	Plan Assets as a Percent of Current Liability				
			Less than 50%	50–99%	100–124%	125–149%	150% or more
			Percent of Plans				
Total, all plans	15,561	33.21	3.2	16.7	22.4	20.7	36.8
Industry Group:							
Agriculture, mining, and construction	1100	1.86	1.9	17.0	32.7	25.0	23.4
Manufacturing	7835	14.27	4.3	22.2	24.4	19.4	29.8
Transportation, communications, and utilities	811	4.45	2.7	14.3	15.5	21.9	45.5
Wholesale and retail trade	1203	3.27	2.7	12.6	23.4	20.7	40.6
Finance, insurance, and real estate	1405	3.32	1.6	5.3	12.6	22.1	58.4
Service	3165	6.01	2.2	10.4	19.8	21.6	45.9
Missing	42	0.03	11.9	19.0	19.0	16.7	33.3
Number of Employees:							
<100	233	0.04	3.4	16.7	24.5	19.3	36.1
100 - 499	3044	0.75	2.5	9.1	17.0	23.2	48.3
500 - 999	1321	0.75	3.2	11.0	17.9	20.5	47.5
1000 - 2499	1408	1.70	2.2	9.9	17.0	23.8	47.2
2500 or more	1992	12.52	2.0	8.7	18.5	22.3	48.5
Missing	7563	17.44	4.1	24.2	27.4	18.8	25.5

[a] *Source:* Form 5500 reports.

employees; in 1989, 68 percent of firms that offered a defined benefit pension plan also offered a health benefit to early retirees, and 62 percent offered a health benefit to retirees aged 65 or older. The contingent probability of retiree health benefits is the highest among firms in finance, insurance, and real estate (FIRE) and among TCU firms. In 1989, 57 percent of FIRE firms that sponsored a defined-benefit pension plan also provided health benefits for early retirees; 61 percent provided health benefits for retirees aged 65 or older. Among TCU firms, 58 percent of firms that sponsored a defined-benefit pension plan also provided health benefits for early retirees, but only 46 percent provided health benefits for retirees at age 65. This latter rate is not substantially different from that reported by firms in manufacturing or mining.

Tabulations of Form 5500 reports for defined benefit pension plans indicate that most plans are well funded. In 1990, nearly 58 percent of defined benefit pension plans reported asset ratios that exceeded 125 percent, and in that respect would qualify for use of Section 420 transfers (*see* Table 3.4). Among plans in FIRE—and most likely to have a concurrent retiree health benefit—82 percent reported funding ratios that exceeded 125 percent; 58 percent reported funding ratios that exceeded 150 percent. In no other industry group were pension plans so likely to be substantially overfunded. Pension plans sponsored by TCU firms also were likely to be substantially overfunded relative to the average among industries: two thirds reported a funding ratio in excess of 125 percent, and 45 percent reported a funding ratio in excess of 150 percent.

A multiple regression analysis of the determinants of pension funding

TABLE 3.5   Determinants of Pension Plan Asset Ratios in 1990: Multiple Regression Results [a]

Variable Name	Estimated Coefficient
Intercept	1.3954 [b]
Industry Variables (omitted=manufacturing):	
Agriculture	- 0.0510
Mining and construction	0.3770
Trade	0.0493
Transportation, communications, public utilities	0.1766 [b]
Finance, insurance, real estate	0.2516 [b]
Services	0.1735 [b]
Number of Employees	0.0113
1988 Asset ratio	0.0002
Equation F-value = 4.542; Adjusted r^2 = 68%	

[a] Dependent = 1990 Assets as a percent of current liability; n=4138.
[b] Significant at 0.99 (two-tailed).

status among plans that reported both in 1990 and in 1988 confirms the industry variation in pension funding status already described. These results are reported in Table 3.5. Furthermore, it demonstrates that pension funding status in 1990 did not vary significantly with firm size, suggesting that very large firms are not necessarily better positioned to use Section 420 to finance current retiree health benefits than are smaller firms. Nor was pension overfunding in 1990 significantly related to funding status two years earlier. This latter result, indicating apparent volatility of asset ratios over a relatively short period of time among firms that could be matched to an earlier report, was somewhat surprising. Employers that have experienced such volatility may be especially unwilling to use Section 420 transfers to fund current retiree benefits.

The accumulation of substantial excess assets in a defined contribution plan may offer a limited opportunity to use Section 420 transfers to fund current retiree benefits, but this opportunity is of no use to firms that have few retirees and a relatively large number of workers with past and current accruals. In contrast, 401(h) plans can be used to fund accruals as well as current benefits. Their use is limited, however, by the

TABLE 3.6   Average Contribution per Participant to Defined Benefit Pension Plans, 1990 [a]

	Total Number of Plans	Percent of Plans with a Contribution	Average Contribution per Participant [b]
Total, all plans [c]	15,561	63.4%	$1123
Industry Group:			
Mining and construction	993	80.4	1336
Manufacturing	7835	62.4	737
Transportation, commu- nications, and utilities	811	57.7	4447
Wholesale and retail trade	1203	59.6	995
Finance, insurance, and real estate	1405	50.4	1817
Service	3165	69.5	981
Missing	42	68.9	1273
Number of Employees:			
<100	233	52.7	2076
100 - 499	3044	59.2	1010
500 - 999	1321	61.1	929
1000 - 2499	1408	59.2	860
2500 or more	1992	54.8	832
Missing	7563	68.9	1273

[a] *Source:* Form 5500 reports.
[b] Includes only plans with nonzero contributions in 1990.
[c] Includes plans in agriculture not included in industry detail.

employer's current contribution to the pension plan. Consequently, current pension contributions are of as much interest as the plan's funding status as a gauge of employers' opportunity to fund retiree health liabilities with the same tax advantages as apply to pension funding.

In 1990, fewer than two thirds of defined benefit plans reported any current-year contribution to the plan (see Table 3.6). Pension plans in FIRE and TCU were less likely than the average plan to report a current-year contribution. Although the variance in current contributions (among plans with non-zero contributions) was substantial, the average contribution per participant was approximately $1100.

On average, these contributions were markedly lower than the levels that might provide an opportunity to fund retiree health benefits adequately. As reported in one survey, the median level of funding required to fund accrued retiree health liabilities for current retirees alone in compliance with FAS 106 was estimated to exceed $9000 per year in 1990—although again the variance among firms was substantial (ranging from $0 to more than $30000) (Hewitt Associates 1990).

Finally, a Tobit analysis of employer contribution levels in 1990 among plans that also reported in 1988 indicates that the plans' reported funding ratio in 1990 had no significant bearing on the level of pension contributions that year. The absence of a statistical relationship between funding status and current contributions appears to demonstrate the flexibility with which employers make pension contributions to achieve current-year financial and tax objectives. The coefficient estimates reported in Table 3.7, however, indicate that firms in industry groups and firm sizes most likely to have retiree health benefits (firms in FIRE and firms with more than 2500 employees) were also significantly less inclined to

TABLE 3.7   Determinants of Defined Benefit Pension Contributions in 1990: Tobit Results [a]

Variable Name	Estimated Coefficient
Intercept	187.3158 [b]
Industry Variables (omitted=manufacturing):	
Agriculture	107.2888
Mining and construction	39.8286
Transportation, communications, and utilities	41.3764
Trade	-145.7760 [c]
Finance, insurance, real estate	-271.1919 [b]
Services	81.5744
Number of Employees	-53.3406 [b]
1990 Asset ratio	0.0988
Normal scale parameter	1570.5663
Log likelihood = -39602.93	

[a] Dependent = Contributions per participant; noncensored n = 4266; left-censored n=3148.
[b] Significant at 0.99 (two-tailed).
[c] Significant at 0.95 (two-tailed).

make greater pension contributions in 1990. For such firms, use of a 401(h) trust to fund retiree health liabilities would appear to require a significant departure from past pension funding strategies.

Conclusion

The need for employers to fund their retiree health obligations is driving re-evaluation of these benefits by both employers and employees. Some employers, anticipating unsustainable cost for these benefits, have altered their retiree health plans significantly or terminated them altogether for current employees. Data sufficient to indicate the prevalence of this be-havior are unlikely to accumulate for some time. One recent survey indi-cated that only about one third of 306 employers with retiree health plans had completed their analysis of the initial impact of FAS 106 at the time of the survey (Hay Group 1993).

It seems unlikely that employers' need to fund retiree health benefit liabilities would significantly jeopardize pension benefits. Indeed, the analysis presented in this chapter suggests that significant reductions in retiree health benefits are much more likely than any reduction in pen-sion benefits. The relative tax disadvantage of funding retiree health benefits adequately may be among the most important factors in employ-ers' reluctance to adjust pension formulas in favor of greater funding for retiree health benefits. Furthermore, the analysis presented in this chap-ter indicates that pension funding ratios may be volatile, even in the short term. As a result, firms may be unwilling to use Section 420 transfers to pay retirees' current health benefits and, in turn, provide cash flow to fund past and current accruals.

Finally, although funding retiree health benefits through a 401(h) plan offers the greatest tax advantages, full funding limits on pension plans may not offer employers sufficient latitude to fund large retiree health obligations. Firms' pension contributions apparently are gauged to serve corporate financial and tax needs; at the margin, these considerations appear to outweigh consideration of the plan's current funding status. For many firms, use of a 401(h) plan to fund retiree health liabilities would seem to force a significant reconfiguration of their pension-fund-ing strategy.

In general, FAS 106 has come at a difficult time. Uncontrolled infla-tion in health care costs is driving national re-evaluation of our entire system of financing health care and paying health care providers. Medi-care Part A, which pays most of retirees' hospital costs, is in serious finan-cial trouble: the program's projected insolvency date has been moved forward to 1999 under intermediate economic assumptions, and to 1998 under more pessimistic assumptions. In such an environment, the future of employer-sponsored retiree health benefits seems far less certain than the future of pensions.

References

Charles D. Spencer and Associates, Inc. What Retiree Health Coverage and Life Insurance Cost 100 Major Firms Revealed in Spencer Survey. News Release, June 17 1988. Chicago, IL: Charles D. Spencer and Associates.

Charles D. Spencer and Associates, Inc. 1992 COBRA Survey: More Were Eligible, Fewer Elected, Employers Picked up 45% of the Bill. *Spencer's Research Reports* (July 17 1992), 329.04-1 - 329.04-6.

Chollet D. Retiree Health Insurance Benefits: Trends and Issues. *In: Retiree Health Benefits: What is the Promise?* Washington, DC: EBRI 1989: 19-36.

Clark RL, Headen, Jr. AE, and Shumaker L. Retiree Health Insurance Benefits and the Retirement Decision. Final Report to the U.S. Department of Health and Human Services, Grant No. 90-ASPE-231A, June 1992.

Cotter MC. National Practice Director for Post-Retirement Benefits. Hay/Huggins. Statement before the Select Committee on Aging, United States House of Representatives. March 1993.

Employee Benefit Research Institute (EBRI). *Fundamentals of Employee Benefit Programs.* Washington, DC: EBRI 1990.

Feldstein M, Seligman S. Pension Funding, Share Prices, and National Saving. *Journal of Finance* 1981; 36(4): 801-824.

Financial Accounting Standards Board. *Facts About FASB.* Norwalk, CT: Financial Accounting Foundation, February 14, 1990.

Hay Group. *Trends in Retiree Medical Benefits.* Philadelphia: The Hay Group, 1993.

Hewitt Associates. *1990 Survey of Retiree Medical Benefits.* Lincolnshire, IL: Hewitt Associates, Inc. 1990.

Hutchison C. Prefunding Retiree Health Benefits: An Overview of Current Alternatives and their Pros and Cons. *BNA Pension Reporter* 1991 (Dec. 19); 18(50): 2299-2308.

Landesman W. An Empirical Investigation of Pension Fund Property Rights. *The Accounting Review* 1986; 61(4): 662-691.

Lazear EP. Pensions and Deferred Benefits as Strategic Compensation. *Industrial Relations* 1990 (Spring); 29: 263-280.

Millholland P. Examining Options for Prefunding Retiree Health Benefits. *Employee Benefit Notes* 1992 (May); 13:5. Washington, DC: Employee Benefit Research Institute.

Mintz J. McDonnell Looks to United States on Health Care. *Washington Post* (Sunday, February 28 1993); A1.

Mittelstaedt F, Warshawsky M. Impact of Liabilities for Retiree Health Benefits on Share Prices. *Journal of Risk and Insurance* 1993 (March); 60(1): 13-35.

Monheit A, Schur C. *Health Insurance Coverage of Retired Persons,* DHHS Publication No. (PHS) 89-3444. National Medical Care Expenditure Survey Research Findings 2. National Center for Health Services Research and Health Care Technology Assessment. Rockville, MD: Public Health Service, September 1989.

Schiller BR, Weiss RD. Pensions and Wages: A Test for Equalizing Differences. *Review of Economics and Statistics* 1980; 62: 529-537.

Smith RS, Ehrenberg RG. Estimating Wage-Fringe Trade-Offs: Some Data Problems. *In:* Triplett JE, ed. *The Measurement of Labor Cost: Studies in Income and Wealth* 48. National Bureau of Economic Research. Chicago: University of Chicago Press; 1983: 347-367.

United States Department of Commerce. Bureau of Economic Analysis. *Survey of Current Business.* Washington, DC; July 1992.

United States General Accounting Office. *Employee Benefits: Companies' Retiree Health Liabilities Large, Advance Funding Costly.* GAO/HRD-89-51. Washington, DC; June 1989.

Warshawsky M. *The Uncertain Promise of Retiree Health Benefits: An Evaluation of Corporate Obligations.* Washington, DC: American Enterprise Institute; 1992.

Zedlewski SR. Retirees With Employment-Based Health Insurance. *In:* Turner JP, Wiatrowski WJ, Beller DJ, eds. *Trends in Health Benefits.* Washington, DC: USGPO; 1993.

Notes

1. By comparison, employer contributions to pension and profit-sharing plans in 1990 were less than one third this amount, or $52.5 billion (U.S. Department of Commerce 1992).

2. These counts exclude persons covered as a dependent of a retiree with benefits in his or her own name, as well as employed retirees whose coverage is provided by a past employer. Including these persons (but also individuals who may have coverage only as COBRA continuation), the 1987 National Medical Expenditures Survey (NMES) counted 10 million retirees with coverage from a past employer (Monheit and Schur 1989).

3. Other national estimates based on different empirical methods have produced similar estimates (Chollet 1989). Based on a sample of 1989 corporate statements, estimates produced by Warshawsky (1992) suggest that accrued liability for retiree health benefits may be somewhat higher. The difference among these estimates is related primarily to differences in assumptions about the long-term rate of inflation in health care costs.

4. FASB first commented in 1979 on disclosure of nonpension benefit liabilities in *Disclosure of Pension and Other Post-Retirement Benefit Information* (July 12, 1979). Five subsequent papers were issued related to accounting for retiree health benefits between 1981 and 1984, culminating in *Statement 81* (November 1984).

5. *FAS 81* required corporations to (1) describe the benefits and employee groups that are covered; (2) describe the accounting and funding policies related to these benefits; and (3) report as a footnote the current cost of the benefit (if distinguishable from the cost of benefits for active workers and dependents) or the combined current cost of the benefit for active and retired workers (if the firm was unable to distinguish costs for each).

6. A survey of 100 corporate annual reports for 1987 indicated that 10 percent were unable to disclose costs at all; 18 percent did not distinguish between costs for retirees and for employees (Charles D. Spencer and Associates 1988).

7. A discussion of various key cases related to retiree rights to continued benefits is provided in Chollet (1989) and in Warshawsky (1992).

8. COBRA requires employers to offer retiring workers the option to continue coverage for 18 months following retirement, or 29 months for disability retirement. Spouses and dependent children must be offered the option to continue

employer coverage for as long as 36 months, if they lose coverage as a result of an employee's eligibility for Medicare, or a retiree loses coverage as the result of sponsor bankruptcy (EBRI 1990).

9. This provision includes former active workers who separate within one year of the transfer.

10. The Internal Revenue Service also has allowed the creation of an "HSOP;" that is, an ESOP that qualifies as a money purchase pension plan and is combined with a 401(h) plan dedicated to funding retiree health benefits. Such a plan provides tax-free benefits to retirees, with allocated assets counted toward the firm's FAS 106 liability. Since approving such a plan created by Procter & Gamble, the IRS has subsequently declined to issue determination letters on other HSOPs.

11. Among current retirees with health benefits from a past employer, 33 percent paid part of the cost of benefits; 19 percent paid the full cost of coverage, with no employer contribution (Zedlewski 1993).

12. Of 2215 firms selected for study, Warshawsky (1992) discovered only 49 firms that used some form of accrual accounting for retiree health benefits; only 19 firms had any prefunding of benefits.

13. Warshawsky's (1992) estimates indicate that some firms' accrued liability for retiree health insurance is very large, averaging 31 percent of net worth and 17 percent of the market value of equity among 676 large firms in 1989. Furthermore, the variance in liability for retiree benefits relative either to net worth or to market value of equity was substantial: in that sample, employer liability for retiree health benefits ranged from zero to 38.5 times the market value of equity.

14. In 1988, only about 12 percent of retirees with health benefits (3.7 percent of all retirees aged 55 or older) reported not receiving a pension benefit as well (Clark et al. 1992).

15. FASB also determined that the relevant attribution period for retiree health (and other retiree welfare benefits) concludes at the employee's date of eligibility for benefits, rather than at the employee's expected retirement date. As a result, the accrual period for retiree health benefits may be shorter than that which the employer uses to fund pension benefits.

16. Statements made by Standard & Poor (in 1989) and by Moody (in 1990) suggest that neither believes that recognition and accounting for retiree health benefits will affect firms' credit ratings. Moody's stated position is that the credit market had already internalized these obligations, so that no further adjustment was likely.

17. In 1988, 62.5 percent of retirees aged 55 or older who had retired from a transportation, communications, or public utility firm reported receipt of retiree health benefits. This compares to 58 percent of retirees from mining firms and 30 percent of retirees overall (Clark et al. 1992).

18. Mittelstaedt and Warshawsky (1993) found that the market apparently undervalued firms' unfunded liabilities for retiree health benefits in 1986, 1987, and 1988, and, in fact, appeared to do worse in each successive year during that period. They attribute the market's failure to evaluate liabilities appropriately to the historic vagueness of firms' obligations for retiree health benefits as well as anticipation of the enactment of the since repealed Medicare Catastrophic Coverage Act which was presumed to reduce the employer cost of health benefits for Medicare- eligible retirees.

19. The attribution for retiree health insurance benefits, as required by FAS 106, terminates when the employee becomes eligible for benefits. This is shorter than the attribution period (terminating at retirement) that is allowed for recognition of pension liabilities.

20. Despite the intuition of this result, researchers generally have failed to produce consistent evidence or measures of compensating wage differentials with respect to pension benefits. This problem generally is attributed to inadequate data (Smith and Ehrenberg 1983; Schiller and Weiss 1980).

21. Employers' failure to obtain an offset in wages or other forms of compensation would in most cases induce them to reduce output and employment, all else being equal. Depending on the size of the firm or the prevalence of this behavior among firms, this result could depress wages marketwide. In this case, workers who are not directly involved in bargaining for retiree health benefits would also bear the incidence of the increased cost of current funding. I am indebted to Mark Pauly for this insight.

Commentary: Olivia S. Mitchell

Supply of and Demand for Retiree Health Insurance in the Labor Market

Voluntarily provided employee benefits are only observed in the labor market when both workers and employers desire them. A micro-economic framework suggests that employees will desire a company-sponsored benefit when (1) the price of the benefit is low, compared to other forms of compensation, and (2) workers have strong preferences for the insurance benefit as compared to earnings.

In the special case of retiree health insurance benefits, all workers may not necessarily want and/or be able to afford employer-provided, post-employment health coverage. For example, employees' desires for retiree health coverage are expected to be highest among those more likely to need the benefit, those who are most risk averse, and those who face lower prices for nonwage benefits versus cash—perhaps for tax reasons.[1]

The determination of who receives retiree benefits must also consider the employer side—who chooses to sponsor retiree health insurance plans. Compensation specialists sometimes suggest that companies offer retiree health insurance to attract and retain employees. Although this is undoubtedly true, the explanation does not tell us why some firms do not sponsor these plans. Drawing from the literature on other benefits, theory tells us that an employer will gain from offering retiree benefits if, by doing so, (1) the firm can elicit certain desirable behaviors from its workers, and (2) the advantages of providing the benefits exceed their costs (Gustman et al. 1993).

Recent studies on private pensions show that companies offer deferred compensation to induce workers to be more productive, to reduce employee turnover, and to elicit optimal retirement patterns (Gustman et

Research support was provided by the Cornell Industry and Labor Relations Center for Advanced Human Resources Studies (CAHRS) and the Pension Research Council of the The Wharton School of the University of Pennsylvania. Opinions and conclusions expressed are solely those of the author.

al. 1993). Companies that do not offer these benefits tend to be those where monitoring technology permits ready assessment of worker output, where younger workers are readily and cheaply available, where training and turnover costs are low, and/or where the production process does not require long-term workers.[2] Extending this argument to the retiree health insurance arena suggests that companies that offer these benefits do so because of their expected effects on employee behavior. Specifically, the particular level of deferred benefits should be determined by their relative price and by employees' willingness to exchange benefits for other forms of compensation.

It is difficult to disentangle the factors that affect employee demand for retiree health benefits from factors that influence companies to provide them. This is because analysts observe both sides of the labor market, working simultaneously. This simultaneity also makes it difficult to judge whether "too many" or "too few" Americans are covered, or how seriously public policymakers should respond to falling retiree health coverage rates reported over the last decade (EBRI 1988, 1991). In another benefits area—the pension field—researchers have only begun to unravel this simultaneity problem. It appears that roughly half of the last decade's downward trend in defined benefit pension coverage may be attributable to industrial employment shifts (Bloom and Freeman 1992). Whether recent retiree health insurance coverage changes also can be attributed to these overall employment shifts or whether other factors are more important is unclear, but the issue demands an urgent look in future research.

Policy Changes and Retiree Health Insurance Coverage

The simultaneity just mentioned also makes it difficult to evaluate how innovations in the policy environment can affect retiree health benefit offerings. This is especially true when the change affects employer *and* employee valuations of the benefit. This point is clarified by discussing two recent changes in the retiree health environment.

FASB Accounting for Retiree Health Insurance

Consider the recent change in retiree health benefit accounting required by the Financial Accounting Standards Board (FASB) ruling No. 106. As Chollet describes clearly in Chapter Three, this rule requires corporations offering retiree health insurance coverage to recognize the benefit promises on their balance sheets and, in addition, requires that employers accrue retiree health liabilities even before the workers covered by the plans attain vested status. An important policy question is whether these FASB rules have discouraged employers from providing retiree health benefits, because these promises are almost completely underfunded and represent an important claim against future profitability.

One strand of research measuring the FAS 106 effect takes the position that these rules will have only a small impact on the availability of retiree health insurance and on the labor market in general. In particular, if the health insurance liability had been fully recognized and allocated previously, no impact of the FASB rulings would be anticipated. Support for this position is offered by studies showing that retiree health liabilities were partially reflected in share prices of corporations that offer these plans, even before FAS 106 (Warshawsky 1992). The fact of partial capitalization suggests that further exploration of this matter is required. In particular, it is possible that other stakeholders should be considered as well, and prime candidates include the covered workers themselves. In the pension arena, for instance, workers who hold underfunded pension promises appear to be compensated partly by higher earnings (Gustman et al. 1993), and a similar pattern might be expected in the retiree health arena.[3]

The policy concern, of course, is that at least some of the recent changes in the retiree health insurance scene probably are attributable to factors other than the FASB accounting innovations and must be taken into account if we are to obtain a clear picture of the rule change on its own. These other factors are numerous, and Chollet (1994) points to many of them, including unexpectedly high medical cost inflation, cutbacks in Medicare, increasingly expensive and high-tech medical advances, and changes in laws that enhance retirees' health care claims in bankruptcy. The common element to all these changes is that they have altered the nature of the insured risk, in large part by raising the projected costs of retiree health insurance and by making it more variable. As yet, few analysts examining changes in retiree health offerings have had access to information on costs of quality-adjusted insurance benefit packages. These other factors must be taken into account when evaluating the impact of FASB changes on retiree health insurance coverage.

A different factor that may explain cutbacks in retiree offerings is the elimination of mandatory retirement in the private sector—a factor that has been underrated to say the least. A series of recent papers indicates that employers who used mandatory retirement while it was still permissible also were more likely to adopt early-out retirement incentives when mandatory retirement was outlawed (Luzadis and Mitchell 1991; Mitchell and Luzadis 1988). It appears that these firms had paid workers according to a deferred compensation profile and required retirement when earnings began to exceed productivity at the end of the contract (Lazear 1983). A compensation system like this can reduce turnover throughout the worklife, but it will not be profitable unless it also carries with it a prespecified termination-of-contract retirement date enforced by mandatory retirement. After legislation rendered mandatory retirement unenforceable, some employers used alternative human resource tools such as pensions to achieve the same departure patterns (Fields and Mitchell 1984; Mitchell 1992). In fact, early pension offerings were increased the most by employers who previously required mandatory retirement (Luzadis and Mitchell 1991). In other cases, employers might have sought to renegotiate the long-term contract by lowering older workers' pay, to retain them profitably after the now illegal mandatory retirement age.

To the extent that retiree health promises were part of a long-term contract, it follows that reducing or eliminating retiree health insurance promises can be seen as a method to reduce compensation that exceeded workers' productivity at the end of their worklives. This practice probably was concentrated among companies that had paid older workers above their market rates and, hence, had relied most heavily on mandatory retirement when it was still legal.

Of course, the FASB accounting rule changes did not occur in isolation; they were part of a larger change in the environment for older workers. Among the changes were rules that restricted the use of age in early retirement windows, Consolidated Omnibus Budget Reconciliation Act (COBRA) regulations that required continuation of benefits after retirement at relatively premium rates, and laws that protected jobs of disabled workers. Taken as a whole, these policies have limited employers' ability to manage turnover among older workers flexibly and may explain why employer commitment to retiree health benefits has suffered recently.

Several explanations are plausible for why retiree health insurance offerings have been curtailed lately. Demonstrating which of these explanations is more nearly correct will require a longitudinal study of employer pay and benefit options that covers enough workers and firms and that extends for a long enough time to offer real variability for measuring the behaviors of interest. These data are not currently available and obtaining them should be a high priority for the future (Gustman and Mitchell 1992). In the interim, it is Chollet (1994) who appears to be accurate when stating that changes in retiree health insurance promises did not occur solely because of accounting rule developments, although FAS 106 "has come at a difficult time" (p. 39).

Price Sensitivity of Retiree Health Insurance

Another area of substantial policy interest is the price sensitivity of retiree health insurance offerings, with particular reference to the benefits' tax status. The general economic principle is that workers' interests in obtaining retiree health care coverage and employers' willingness to provide these benefits depend in part on their price. Tax law, in turn, affects the extent to which benefit dollars are shielded from income and payroll taxes. Current regulations on tax-qualified prefunding of retiree health insurance are nicely summarized by Chollet (1994), who uses inferential data to conclude that regulatory limitations on 501(c)(9) and 401(h) plans have prevented tax-preferred prefunding of retiree health offerings over the last decade. In contrast, pension contributions still can be offered at tax-favored rates, so that for many employers a dollar devoted to a pension plan goes farther than a dollar set aside for post-employment health care. Public policy discussions actively debate the merits of allowing retiree health coverage to be granted tax-qualified status, but the huge size of the tax loss anticipated—$37 billion per year—ensures that the proposal meets fervent political opposition (EBRI 1991).

Despite fiscal politics, the fact remains that we do not know the price sensitivity of supply and demand for benefits in general, and for retiree health coverage in particular. This information is difficult to discover because the price of retiree health care depends in complex ways on employer-side and worker-side behavior; hence, price changes for retiree coverage can elicit unexpected outcomes.

An example of this complexity may be instructive. Consider an older worker who must chose between no health care insurance on the current job and coverage from one of two plans, one of which is a prepaid plan with little choice over physicians and the other, a fee-for-service plan that requires high costsharing for active workers. The sponsoring employer specifies that the plan option chosen during the worklife must be identical to the option carried into retirement—a rule often used to reduce adverse selection. In this example, if the worker opts for no active employee health plan (perhaps because other health insurance coverage was available through a spouse's program), then the employee would not be permitted to select retiree health care coverage if the spouse were to die. If the employee selects the prepaid plan while employed, then any choice of a fee-for-service plan after retirement would be eliminated. The point, of course, is that health care insurance purchases during the worklife can feed into prices and availability of insurance after retirement in complex ways not often well-measured by researchers. It should be noted that workers may not fully understand how retiree health consequences flow from their health care plan choice while employed, and this too is a high priority research agenda item.[4]

The issue becomes more complex if the older worker can obtain extended coverage for 18 months after retirement under COBRA legislation, by paying up to 102% of the regular premium. Because the full cost of continued health insurance probably is far greater than the premium charged under COBRA (Chollet 1994), this permits retirees to obtain a substantial amount of subsidized health care coverage. In addition, CO-BRA benefits are offered through tax-qualified health insurance plans.[5] It would be interesting to investigate who takes up COBRA coverage and to what extent the tax subsidy enhances the program's appeal. To date, however, no such analysis has been undertaken by researchers.

What this means is that evaluating the demand for retiree benefits, as well as the supply of such offerings, is made complex by an intricate menu of prices, some of which are determined endogenously and some of which are affected by tax preferences in unexpected ways. As a result, researchers do not know how price sensitive workers' desires are for retiree health insurance and, hence, how much retiree coverage would increase if plans could be pre-funded in a tax-favored way. This should receive high priority in future studies on why some firms and workers have retiree health coverage while others do not.

Conclusions

Labor market researchers seek economic explanations for observed differences in older workers' compensation patterns, as expressed in their earnings profiles as well as in their pension and retiree health insurance plan structures. This discussion highlights the need to understand better the relative importance of retiree health insurance options in the overall menu of retirement incentives available to older employees. It would also be useful to "nail down" the role of retiree health insurance in encouraging older workers to leave the workforce early, or to defer retirement from earlier to later dates.[6] Finally, research should examine differences in health care insurance options across different types of employees (e.g., depending on income, occupation, age, and service), and across different types of employers (e.g., by firm size, by technological level, and by industry). Such an investigation is required to determine how retiree health insurance plans influence employee behavior and, in turn, contribute to modern human resource policy.

Several data needs must be met if such research is to be carried out. Surveys are needed with information about the retiree health care and pension options that confront workers when they make job changes and retirement decisions. Some gaps will be filled with the new Health and Retirement Survey (HRS) funded by the National Institute on Aging, which is collecting information on pay and benefits packages as people near the end of their worklives. Such worker-side surveys are invaluable for understanding what individual retiree coverage actually is and what workers believe their coverage to be. Previous studies that have focused on pension plan features find that employees have extraordinarily imprecise notions of their retiree benefit coverage (Mitchell 1988), and it may be that knowledge of health care insurance coverage is worse than their pension knowledge. It would be informative to find out whether employee misinformation about retiree health care plans is widespread, and what "incorrect" retirement decisions are made, as a result.[7]

In addition to the worker-side data, new employer-side surveys must be developed to understand better who offers what types of retiree benefits and how these benefit strategies influence and, in turn, are influenced by sponsoring companies' economic status. Currently, few data sources exist to meet this need. One benefits information source known as the Employee Benefit Survey (EBS), devised by the United States Bureau of Labor Statistics, offers many useful insights into retiree benefit offerings, with data provided by a wide range of firms. Unfortunately, the survey omits employers who sponsor plans but who do not contribute a portion of the premium. This causes problems for analysis, since one reason employers sponsor benefit plans is to provide employees risk pooling not readily obtained by individual purchase (Gustman and Mitchell 1992). As a result, the EBS cannot be used to explore the valuable role of the employer as a risk-pooling agent.

Another important reason to collect better employer-side information is that existing sources do not link compensation and benefits data to information on profitability and other important employer-side outcomes. It has been difficult to pinpoint which specific pension and retiree health care designs improve productivity and, in turn, which corporate environments produce benefits systems with specific features. This point probably has been underrecognized in the retiree health insurance area, although it has been made in the pension context (Gustman et al. 1993). Improved and linked data sets can help establish, for example, why many employers are moving to a defined dollar retiree health care plan and how this change, in turn, affects earnings profiles, other benefits, turnover and retirement outcomes, and a host of other labor market outcomes. Data such as these also are invaluable if we are to evaluate properly the impact of changes in the regulatory environment on employer benefits offerings. For instance, proposed increases in payroll and other benefits taxes to pay for national health insurance certainly will have potent effects on earnings, employment, and the availability of employer-sponsored benefits. Better employer-side surveys collected now will allow improved evaluations of the effects of regulatory changes on health insurance plans and will provide better explanations of overall labor force trends in the future.

References

Bloom D, Freeman R. The Fall in Private Pension Coverage in the US. *American Economic Review Papers and Proceedings* 1992; 82(May): 539-545.

Chollet D J. Are Health Care Benefits Crowding out Retiree Cash Benefits? *In:* Mazo J, Rappaport AM, Schieber SJ, eds. *Providing Health Care Benefits in Retirement,* Philadelphia: Pension Research Council and the University of Pennsylvania Press, 1994.

Clark RL, Headen AE, Shumaker L. Retiree Health Insurance Benefits and the Retirement Decision. Final Report HHS Grant No. 90, ASPE 231A, June 1992.

Employee Benefit Research Institute. *Issues and Trends in Retiree Health Insurance Benefits.* Issue Brief. Washington, DC: EBRI, Nov. 1988.

Employee Benefit Research Institute. *Retiree Health Benefits: Issues of Structure, Financing, and Coverage.* Issue Brief. Washington, DC: EBRI, March 1991.

Fields GS, Mitchell OS. *Retirement, Pensions and Social Security.* Cambridge, MA: MIT Press, 1984.

Gustman A, Mitchell OS. Pensions and the US Labor Market. *In:* Bodie Z, Munnell A, eds. *Pensions and the US Economy: Sources, Uses, and Limitations of Data.* Philadelphia: Pension Research Council and the University of Pennsylvania Press, 1992: 39-87.

Gustman A, Mitchell OS, Steinmeier T. The Role of Pensions in the Labor Market. National Bureau of Economic Research Working Paper, April 1993.

Gustman A, Steinmeier T. Employer-Provided Health Insurance and Retirement Behavior. National Bureau of Economic Research Working Paper, March 1993.

Lazear E. Pensions as Severance Pay. *In:* Bodie Z, Shoven J, eds. *Financial Aspects of the US Pension System.* Chicago: University of Chicago Press, 1983: 57-89.

Luzadis RA, Mitchell OS. Explaining Pension Dynamics. *Journal of Human Resources* 1991; 26(Fall): 679-703.

Mitchell OS. Trends in Pension Benefit Formulas and Retirement Provisions. *In:* Turner J, Beller D, eds. *Trends in Pensions 1992.* Washington, DC: US Dept. of Labor, PWBA, 1992: 177-216.

Mitchell OS. Worker Knowledge of Pension Provisions. *Journal of Labor Economics* 1988; 6 (Jan): 21-39.

Mitchell OS, Luzadis RA. Changes in Pension Incentives Through Time. *Industrial and Labor Relations Review* 1988; 42(Oct): 100-108.

Warshawsky, M. *The Uncertain Promise of Retiree Health Benefits.* Washington, DC: American Enterprise Institute, 1992.

Notes

1. Other reasons for cross-sectional differences in the demand for retiree health insurance include differential bequest motives, differential forecasts of life expectancy and medical care needs, and, perhaps, different needs for self control. For a related discussion in the pension context see Gustman et al. (1993).

2. Principal/agent theory suggests that defined benefit pensions can also be used to impose additional risk on workers who otherwise might maximize short-term returns at the expense of shareholders. There is considerable debate about this theory, as summarized by Gustman et al. (1993).

3. This suggests that requiring employees to recognize accruing retiree health insurance promises before retirement will have little effect, even though vesting

in retiree health care coverage does not generally occur until the firm's early retirement age. This is because in a well-informed labor market, the option value of vesting in a retiree health plan should be reflected incrementally in earnings as the promise accrues. As a result, requiring employers to recognize the future liability in a formal manner should not be expected to change materially the worker's or the shareholder's view of the future claim, unless one or both parties was misinformed about the liability.

4. Research on employees' knowledge about pensions reveals some systematic myopia (Mitchell 1988).

5. The limited duration of COBRA benefits restricts the extent of the subsidy, but the existence of these tax-qualified and subsidized benefits should not be ignored in evaluating which workers will want retiree health insurance.

6. Recent studies have come to very different conclusions, with Gustman and Steinmeier (1993) finding that retiree health influences retirement patterns only very modestly and Clark et al. (1992) arguing for a more potent role. Both studies suffer from data problems, however, and the jury must be said to be still out.

7. Alongside the individual HRS survey will be an employer survey of health care insurance and pension offerings.

Commentary: Diana L. Murray

Dr. Deborah J. Chollet takes the position that Financial Accounting Standard (FAS) 106 and a lack of good tax preferential funding arrangements have combined to make it difficult for employers to provide retiree benefits in the same manner as in the past, and that employers will not provide retiree health benefits at the expense of retiree cash benefits. Overall, this commentary supports Dr. Chollet's basic thesis. It also is noteworthy to consider, however, that in shifting the focus of benefit cost from the benefit budget to the employer's bottom line, FAS 106 has merely accelerated the trend of controlling cost through reallocation of benefit dollars that began in the early 1980s. To illustrate this point, the comments that follow begin with an historical perspective of benefits planning during the 1980s, describe the initial reaction of employers to FAS 106, and conclude with a discussion of the current benefit issues that employers are addressing as they seek to determine the most efficient use of their benefit dollars.

Historical Perspective of Benefit Planning

During the 1970s, there was little benefit planning. Most medical plans were insured, and the birth of the Employee Retirement Income Security Act (ERISA) was just starting to have an impact. In fact, because the main function of the benefit office was primarily enrollment and bill paying, the accounting department of many companies assumed responsibility for benefit planning.

In the early 1980s, employers were hit hard by rapidly escalating health care costs and an explosion of government regulations. Benefit managers were no longer just paying bills but were forced to control health care costs at the same time that they were interpreting and implementing the changes required by TEFRA, DEFRA, ADEA, TRA '87, COBRA, OBRA, and the infamous, short-lived Section '89. Since most benefit departments were paper driven, it became extremely expensive to provide the

The author acknowledges useful discussions with Anna Rappaport.

newly required reporting data. Unfortunately, benefit dollars now had to be allocated to cover data systems, actuaries, consultants, and attorneys at the same time that medical costs were escalating.

In addition, rapid changes in the business world impacted on traditional corporate culture. The 1980s became an era of divestitures, acquisitions, closures, downsizing, globalization, decreasing numbers of unskilled manufacturing jobs, and increasing numbers of skilled technical positions. Employers and employees no longer were certain of their business future. Companies were worried about staying in business, and employees were worried about having jobs. Responding to this state of uncertainty, many employers considered replacing their current management philosophy of lifetime guaranteed benefits with a management philosophy of flexible benefit planning that could be adjusted to changing business needs. Rising medical costs, proliferating government benefit regulations in conjunction with detailed reporting requirements, and an unstable business economy forced benefit managers to review the allocation of benefit dollars. No longer were many companies willing to take the total financial risk of providing benefits.

Massive changes were underway in benefit design, with many employers making annual changes to their benefit plans. Basic/major medical plans were replaced by comprehensive plans with cost-sharing deductibles and coinsurance; insured plans were replaced by self-insured plans; utilization management, health maintenance organizations (HMOs), and preferred provider organizations (PPOs) were introduced; employees were asked to share in plan cost through monthly contributions; and most importantly, companies now reserved the right to amend or terminate their benefit plans.

Retiree cash benefits were also affected by this shift in benefit philosophy. Many employers introduced employee stock ownership plans, savings plans, and 401(k) plans. Some employers actually replaced their defined benefit plans with defined contribution plans to limit their company's financial risk. In the 1980s, benefit planning became a dynamic, everchanging process as employers assumed that benefit cost could be controlled through effective, efficient plan design.

Impact of Financial Accounting 106

In the 1980s, the responsibility for benefit planning and cost control was delegated to a company's benefit department. With the introduction of FAS 106, the high cost of providing retiree health benefits would now be highlighted as a booked expense on the company's income statement. Many employers became worried that public exposure of this escalating liability would reduce stockholder confidence in the strength of their companies. Now the command, "Do something to control cost!", came from the executive level down. Benefit planning had evolved to strategic business planning.

Determining the extent of FAS 106 liability was not easy for employers. Like the case in the 1980s, much of the data required for FAS 106 liability were unavailable. Most pre-65 retiree plans were identical to the active employee plans, and the claims data for actives and retirees were not separated. In addition, many companies administered their retiree medical plans locally at the different plant locations. Employee contributions often were collected sporadically or waived at will for particular retirees under special circumstances. Even more difficult was the task for companies with unions. Many companies had multiple union retiree medical plans, all varying in benefits and contributions based on the contract year of an employee's retirement.

At the same time that the employer, consultant, and actuary were calculating the FAS 106 liability, the employer's attorney was reviewing the summary plan descriptions and plan documents of current retirees. Many older plans implemented before the mid-1980s often expressly stated or implied that health benefits were guaranteed for life. Employers weighed the savings from amending or terminating their old retiree medical plans against the cost of potential litigation and/or adverse publicity.

Many employers have decided not to risk changing their older retiree health plans but have been reassessing benefit provisions for future retirees. In the last few years, many employers have limited coverage to pre-age 65, established employee service requirements, capped employer financial exposure, offered flexible plan choice, and implemented managed care. A few employers have terminated all future retiree health benefits and have implemented employee/employer matched savings plans to assist employees with their future retiree health expenses.

Some employers are currently amending or terminating old retiree health plans. These employers have calculated the risk and cost of changing guaranteed benefits and have determined that the cost of their FAS 106 liability is much greater than that of potential litigation. Many cases are now pending in the courts.

Allocation of Benefit Dollars: Current Issues

As stated earlier, the issuance of FAS 106 has merely focused wider attention on the cost of health benefits and accelerated a trend of cost control through benefit dollar reallocation that was begun in the 1980s. Although employers in the 1980s concentrated on the impact of federal legislation and attempted to control cost within the parameters of benefit plan structure, employers today are viewing benefits as a strategic element in the cost of doing business. Employees and their needs (i.e., "benefits") are no longer ancillary to the business; they are essential to business success. As employers look to "Workforce 2000," they are determining what is needed to maintain their "human capital," that is, to attract and retain skilled, productive employees.

Like any other business decision, cost and benefit analyses are being done to determine the most efficient allocation of employer benefit resources. Employers are reviewing their current human capital needs, assessing how well their current benefit programs address those needs, and projecting the needs of their future workforce. Employers realize that all kinds of costs are attached to doing business. Each employer must determine the correct cost/benefit balance (including the cost of retiree health) that supports business growth strategically. Listed next are a few cost factors that illustrate each employer's uniqueness in that decision-making process.

Type of Business

Employers look at what benefits their competition may be providing. Depending on the type of business and its needs, that competition could be across the street, across the country, or across the ocean. Employers who need to attract and retain specialized, highly skilled employees may have to provide a specific benefit package. On the one hand, the cost of providing special benefits may be less than the cost of a potentially volatile workforce. On the other hand, if needed workers are in large supply, then employers may decide to spend their benefit dollars elsewhere.

Business Strength

Employers are looking at their company's anticipated growth or loss in today's sluggish economy. Benefit planning that may seem strategic when the company is growing may not be prudent if the business is facing a loss. If an employer is planning a benefit strategy in isolation of current business status, then the employer may find that the strategy remains but the company does not.

Unique Business Needs

Employers make many different decisions based on the unique needs of their companies. In nonunion companies, an employer may offer a generous benefit package to discourage unionization. The rationale is that the cost of doing business in a unionized environment is more expensive than the cost of offering a benefit package larger than the company's unionized competitors.

Another important factor is public image. Many goods are sold because the buyer feels that if a company treats its employees well, the company's product must then be good. This is particularly true with businesses in small communities, where everyone knows everyone or with companies that sell brandname products. Providing good benefits becomes a cost of goods sold.

As employers begin to feel the impact of "Workforce 2000," the traditional allocation of benefit dollars may be diluted by the pressing needs of a more diverse workforce. Day care, elder care, long-term care, or flex time all may compete for a piece of the benefit pie. Given the projected workforce demographics, benefit planning may require a more individualized approach to maintain the business' human capital and to ensure its productivity.

Management Philosophy

As stated earlier, management philosophy is very important in determining the direction of benefit planning. Management philosophy ranges along a continuum, from the paternalistic company that takes care of its own to the cash-driven employer who relegates risk and costsharing to the employee. Management philosophy toward benefit planning can shift with the profitability of the business or with a change in company leadership. Seldom does an employer's management philosophy remain constant along the continuum, but, rather, management philosophy swings dynamically, in reaction to the current economic and political environments.

Administrative Ease and Cost

Administrative ease and cost are important in benefit planning. In the 1980s, employers learned that benefit administration could be extremely expensive. As benefit planning and government regulations became more entangled, administration complexity, reporting requirements, and penalties for violations likewise escalated. Benefit consultants, actuaries, and attorneys thrived at the expense of the benefit budget.

FAS 106 also increased the cost that employers must spend on benefit administration. Many employers do not want to put themselves at further risk by using the Section 420 transfer or a 401(k) plan to pay for retiree benefits. Not only do the current restrictions make these methods of paying for retiree benefits unappealing to most employers, but, perhaps more importantly, given the government's propensity for increasing its regulations and reporting requirements, many employers do not want to put themselves into a potentially vulnerable position.

Future Benefit Planning Issues

Employers are becoming increasingly unwilling to make major benefit changes, other than cutbacks, because of the uncertainty of future health benefit requirements. State legislators and members of Congress are shaking the foundations of the ERISA tree. ERISA pre-emption, which has upheld the right of self-insured employers to plan their own health benefit package, is being attacked on all sides as being discriminatory. Individual states want to regulate benefit provisions and costsharing for all health benefit plans, including those of the self-insured. The recent Americans with Disabilities Act (ADA) is raising further questions about discriminatory intent or cause in benefit design. Perhaps the most unsettling thought for employers is the future state of national health care. Most employers foresee a benefit future that is inundated with complex regulations, reporting requirements, discrimination testing, and penalties.

FAS 106 uprooted employer-provided retiree health benefits, but national health care reform may destroy it. When asked who should be responsible for providing medical coverage to retirees, many employers shake their heads and say, "Let the government do it!"

Conclusion

Are health care benefits crowding out retiree cash benefits? The issue is not so much that retiree health care benefits may or may not be crowding out retiree cash benefits but how employers will incorporate benefit planning into their companies' strategic business plans, to ensure that they stay competitive and productive in today's changing global economy.

Chapter 4
Adequacy of Employer-Sponsored Retiree Health Benefit Programs

Anna M. Rappaport and Carol H. Malone

Employer-sponsored retiree health benefits have undergone significant changes in the past ten years and have become a leading source of concern for employers. In fact, the future of health care coverage for retired employees has been threatened by many financial, demographic, medical, and legislative developments. These include the astronomical rise in the cost of medical services, recognition of the costs and liability for retiree health care, as required by Financial Accounting Standard 106 (FAS 106), increasing frequency of early retirements, and retirees who are living longer than before.

As a group, retirees usually have a greater number of health problems and, consequently, typically use more medical, hospital, and prescription drug benefits than active employees. Hence, it is far more expensive to provide health benefits for retirees than to provide health benefits for active employees. Furthermore, during the last decade, employers have seen a decline in Medicare and Medicaid reimbursement of hospital, medical, and surgical providers, a burgeoning of Medicare Secondary Payer provisions, the enactment of the Consolidated Omnibus Budget Reconciliation Act (COBRA), continuation coverage requirement and the repeal of the Medicare Catastrophic Care Act, all of which contribute to an increase in the health care costs borne by employer-sponsored plans.

This chapter examines employer-sponsored retiree health benefits in terms of the scope of coverage and the level of benefits provided, the continual growth in the cost of coverage, how employers are dealing with the health care cost dilemma, and the prospect of continued retiree health coverage in the future. In attempting to measure whether employer-sponsored retiree health benefit programs are adequate, it is important to recognize that no absolute or numerical standard exists for evaluation purposes. Instead, adequacy should be considered in terms of the employee's total retirement benefit package, in addition to the coverage provided, the design of the plan, and the level of contribution from the employer.

The chapter also examines the levels of affordability of retiree health benefits according to varying amounts of retiree contributions. The cost of retiree health benefits for employers, the recognition of these costs, and their effects on the employers' decision-making process in offering benefits also are discussed. Finally, employer retiree health plan design changes and trends are reviewed throughout the chapter.

Environment for Retiree Health

People in the United States generally obtain health care coverage through employers, a government-sponsored program, or a plan purchased directly from a health insurance company. Employer-sponsored health care coverage for active employees became a standard fringe benefit in the United States during the early 1950s, when the economy was bouncing back after World War II. Health care benefits for retirees evolved, however, as more of an afterthought to pension benefits and were considered, for the most part, as a goodwill gesture and an inexpensive addition to the total retirement package. In 1974, when the Employee Retirement Income Security Act (ERISA) was enacted, significant restrictions were placed on an employer's ability to take away previously promised pension benefits; however, no similar restrictions were imposed on health benefit promises. Recently, however, the astronomical rise in health care costs and the lack of access to and affordability of nonemployer-sponsored, individual health care coverage for employees younger than age 65 have made the continuation of health benefits for retirees as essential as pension benefits.

Employers originally provided health plans to retirees to ease the transition from employment to retirement. Eligibility for a majority of the plans established during the 1950s and 1960s generally was based on pension plan eligibility, regardless of the retiree's age or years of service. The benefit levels of most plans usually were continuations of the active employee plans. Upon Medicare eligibility, employers, for the most part, continued to cover whatever Medicare did not. Many employers paid the full cost of retiree health coverage because of the reasonable cost of benefits at the time and the difficulty in collecting premiums from retirees. In addition, many of these plans had first-dollar coverage for hospital and surgical services with little or no retiree/dependent cost-sharing requirements. Changes in workplace demographics, rising health care costs, government-sponsored health programs, and new financial accounting standards for retiree health liabilities have permanently changed the nature of employer-sponsored retiree health care coverage for retirees of the future.

Demographic and Labor Force Context

The population in the United States is getting older; the near-elderly, that is those persons aged 55 to 64, represented approximately 9 percent of the total population in 1990. By 2020, this group is projected to expand to 14 percent of the total population. Those persons over the age of 65 represented 9.2 percent of the American population in 1990 and are expected to account for almost 24 percent of the population by 2030, as the baby boomers age (U.S. Dept. of Commerce,1992).

According to recent data from the U.S. Department of Labor (DOL), the labor force participation rate for males aged 55 to 64 has decreased from 89.5 percent in 1948 to 66.9 percent in 1991 (DOL 1992). Data for the past eight years indicate that the participation rates for this group have leveled off at approximately 67 percent. In addition, the Bureau of the Census estimates that by the year 2000 nearly 35 million people in the United States will be 65 years of age or older, an increase of 12 percent from 31.2 million in 1980 (U.S. Dept. of Commerce 1989). The ratio of elderly to working age persons (aged 18-64) will increase from 1 to 5 in 1985 to 1 to 3 in 2025, hence fewer workers will be supporting a larger number of retirees (EBRI 1992). Both non-Medicare- and Medicare-eligible retiree populations are increasing in numbers and as a percentage of those age groups.

In addition to these projected increases in the total numbers of retired persons over the next decade, retirees also are living longer today and will require some form of basic or supplemental health benefits (before and after Medicare eligibility) for an even longer time than two or more decades ago. For example, in 1960, male life expectancy in the United States at age 60 was 15.8 years, whereas, in 1990, it was 18.6 years. Female life expectancy at age 60 in 1960 was 19.5 years, whereas, in 1990, it was 22.7 years (OECD 1992). Data also indicate that older persons are living longer and are sicker in these later years (Crimmins 1991). Hence, the demand for and use of health services are rising in direct proportion to the decreased mortality rates for the elderly.

Furthermore, the ratio of active to retired employees in 1965 was 15 to 1, whereas the ratio today for many companies/industries is approximately 3 to 4 employees for each eligible retiree. In fact, the current ratio for some older industrialized companies is closer to three retirees for every active employee. Several factors contribute to the changing balance in many companies in the numbers of active to retired employees. These include

- Demographic shifts;
- Growth of retirement plans—making retirement affordable;
- Downsizing of older, well-established companies—with retirees being;
- survivors of workforces that once were much larger;
- Growing popularity of early retirement windows—these provide incentives for certain employees to retire earlier rather than later.

Because demographic trends, downsizing, and early retirement windows are likely to continue throughout the 1990s and beyond, the active-to-retired employee ratio is not likely to improve. As the so-called "baby boomers" age, demographics will become an increasingly more important factor.

Scope of Coverage Provided

Large, mature employers, such as utilities, the mining industry, construction, manufacturing, the energy/petroleum industry, banks, and insurance companies, tend to sponsor retiree health coverage. The relatively young age of other employers, such as retailers, colleges, and universities, seems to determine whether retiree health coverage is provided. Employers with unionized workforces are also more likely to provide retiree health coverage than nonunionized companies. In addition, health coverage for retirees is common among public employers. Coverage is much less common, however, in the health care industry and among middle-sized employers, and it is rare among small employers.

Although only an estimated 4 percent of all companies in the United States provide retiree health coverage, about one third of all private sector employees work for companies that cover retirees in their health plans, according to recent estimates from the U.S. General Accounting Office (GAO 1991). Among retirees who receive health benefits from a past employer, 62 percent had worked in companies with more than 1000 employees, and 76 percent had worked in companies with more than 100 employees (see Table 4.1) (EBRI 1991).

According to GAO estimates, approximately 32 million people are currently enrolled in employer-sponsored plans that provide health benefits for retirees. The most recent data indicate that in 1989, of the 23.7 million retirees, more than 9 million had retiree medical coverage through an employer-sponsored plan (GAO 1991). Within this group, an estimated 3 million retirees were under age 65. Health benefits are especially important to the early retiree because most of them are not yet eligible for Medicare benefits.

TABLE 4.1   Retirees Receiving Health Coverage from Employers, by Firm Size and Industry: August 1988 [a]

Firm Size and Industry	Covered by Own Employer Plan
Total (thousands)	10,358
Firm Size	
< 20	3.7%
20 - 99	5.8
100 - 249	5.1
250 - 499	4.3
500 - 999	4.8
1000 or more	61.8
Do not know/no response	14.5
Industry	
Private	54.1
Government	
Federal	16.4
State and local	19.4
Self-employed	1.3
Unemployed	*
Do not know/no response	8.7
*Less than 0.5% of total	

[a] *Source:* Employee Benefit Research Institute tabulations of the August 1988 Current Population Survey. This universe consists of all persons aged 40 and over in the U.S. civilian noninstitutionalized population living in households.

Early Retirees

Early retirees (aged 55 to 64) who receive private pension and/or Social Security income are more likely to have employer-sponsored health insurance (52.9 percent) than those who do not (36.8 percent) (U.S. Dept. of Commerce 1986). Among early retirees, there is a decrease in health coverage provided by former employers, from 70.2 percent before retirement to 54.2 percent after retirement (Rogowski and Karoly 1992). This drop tends to be larger for retirees aged 62 to 64 than for those aged 55 to 61, perhaps because of the increasing number of early retirement packages offered today that usually include a promise of continued health coverage and the reluctance of those employees without coverage to retire at early ages.

Post-65 Retirees

For retirees over the age of 65, insurance patterns differ considerably from the under 65 age group, because Medicare eligibility begins at age 65. Most retirees over the age of 65 have Medicare coverage, although only 15 percent of retirees have coverage solely through Medicare, and the remainder (84 percent) have a plan that supplements Medicare (Rogowski and Karoly 1992). Of the 84 percent of Medicare-eligible people with more than one source of coverage, approximately 41.4 percent have purchased private coverage; 33.6 percent have coverage through an employer; 5 percent have coverage through a spouse's employer; and 3.8 percent are entitled to Medicaid (Rogowski and Karoly 1992). A small number of post-65 retirees (0.8 percent) who are not eligible for Medicare only have employment-related coverage (Rogowski and Karoly 1992). In the United States, fewer than 1 percent of retirees over the age of 65 have no health coverage at all.

Uninsured Retirees

The probability of becoming uninsured after retirement is generally related to the type of insurance coverage a person has before retirement. Approximately 5.4 percent of retirees become uninsured shortly after they retire (Rogowski and Karoly 1992). Early retirees who have private insurance (not employer-sponsored) before they retire are the most likely to become uninsured. Even with COBRA continuation coverage availability, some early retirees do not continue their employer-based coverage when they retire. This may be related to the high cost of purchasing health insurance coverage, whether private or employer-sponsored, on a retirement income. Those persons who have insurance coverage through their spouse before they retire are the least likely to become uninsured.

Coverage Trends

Although millions of workers and retirees today have or are eligible for employer-sponsored retiree health benefits, the employer's role in providing these benefits is changing. As a result of the FAS 106 liability, the increasing numbers of retirees, and the escalating cost of retiree health care, many employers either are reducing or terminating retiree health benefits. The Employee Benefit Research Institute (EBRI) reported in August 1992 that the percentage of employees under age 65 eligible for wholly employer-financed retiree coverage fell from 53 percent in 1988 to 45 percent in 1989 (EBRI #128 1992). Furthermore, the number of companies that provide retiree health benefits continues to slip, falling below half to 49 percent in 1992 from 54 percent in 1990. The GAO found that wholly employer-financed coverage for those aged 65 and over fell from 55 percent to 47 percent between 1990 and 1992 (GAO 1991).

Although the most severe employer reaction to the high cost of covering retirees, as well as the FAS 106 liability, is simply to terminate health benefits for future retirees, a 1992 survey of 2000 employers by William M. Mercer, Incorporated showed that only 2 percent of both large and small employers actually plan to cancel retiree health care benefits altogether (William M. Mercer Companies, Inc. 1992). The Mercer study also found that only 7 percent of the large employers and 5 percent of the small employers surveyed plan to cancel these benefits for future retirees.

Workers who already have retired are far better able in most cases to maintain benefits than soon-to-retire or younger workers. Most employers are hesitant to alter the benefits given current retirees but ask active employees to shoulder more of the rising cost of health care for both active and retired persons. Concerns about litigation are a key factor in the reluctance to change coverage for existing retirees. Legal developments during 1992 and 1993 have indicated more willingness on the part of employers and employees to take aggressive positions in this regard. (Specific examples are discussed later in this chapter.) In general, however, the analysis shows significant gaps in coverage. The current system seems to be failing in its efforts to serve substantial segments of the retired population.

Levels of Benefits Provided

A retiree medical plan can be viewed as having two components—the structure and design of the medical benefits payable and the eligibility pattern and method of costsharing. The structure and design of the medical benefits often follow the employer's health plan for active employees, at least for those retirees not yet eligible for Medicare. The eligibility pattern and method of costsharing usually follow the structure of the pension plan. In contemplating issues that relate to retiree health, the former is viewed primarily as "health-benefit-related" and the second as "retirement-benefit-related". The section that follows discusses the structure of retiree health benefits and their costs relative to levels of pension benefits.

Before Medicare Eligibility

Benefits for pre-Medicare eligibles typically follow the same plan as the active employee medical plan, but they have retiree contributions that are considerably higher than the employee contributions required of active employees. The U.S. Department of Labor's survey, "Employee Benefits in Medium and Large Firms, 1989" indicates that 79 percent of retirees under age 65 have no change in coverage at retirement and before age 65, and 72 percent have no change after age 65 (DOL 1990). This survey covers employers that have over 100 employees.

Retiree medical plans often differ from the medical plan for active employees in the way that costs are shared between the employer and the employee. Cost sharing includes contributions, deductibles, and copayments. Many companies have increased their cost sharing for retirees in the last few years.

In addition, the DOL survey of benefits in medium and large firms showed the following cost sharing features for retirees enrolled in health plans for 1989 (DOL 1990):

- 97 percent of participants were in plans with coinsurance;
- 83 percent of participants were in plans with an out-of-pocket limit;
- 80 percent of participants were in plans with annual deductibles.

Individual out-of-pocket limits for retirees were as follows:

Under $500	13 percent
$500 - $749	12 percent
$750 - $999	12 percent
$1000 - $1249	25 percent
$1250 and up	22 percent
No limit	16 percent

A typical indemnity plan today may pay 70 to 75 percent of eligible charges for an average claimant.

After Medicare Eligibility

Several different employer-sponsored benefit plans are available that coordinate with Medicare, and there are three common methods of Medicare "integration." These methods include a carve-out, an exclusion, and a traditional coordination plan. Under a carve-out plan, the retiree gets the same benefit from the plan and Medicare (in total) as would have been paid before Medicare eligibility. Under an exclusion plan, the benefits paid by Medicare are excluded, and the plan formula is applied to the balance of the charges. Under a traditional coordination of benefits provision, the benefits are determined as if there is no Medicare, but the total payments from the plan and Medicare generally are limited to 100 percent of the total charges.

TABLE 4.2   Retiree Health Insurance Costs Compared to Pension Benefits: Benefit if 1.25% of Final Average Earnings per Year of Service[a]

Pay Level	Period of Service				
	10	15	20	30	35
	Annual Benefit at Age 65 Based on Formula				
$ 20,000	$ 2500	$ 3750	$ 5000	$ 7500	$ 8750
40,000	5000	7500	10,000	15,000	17,500
60,000	7500	11,250	15,000	22,500	26,250
80,000	10,000	15,000	20,000	30,000	35,000
100,000	12,500	18,750	25,000	37,500	43,750
	Annual Benefit at Age 55 Assuming 50% Reduction				
$ 20,000	$ 1250	$ 1875	$ 2500	$ 3750	$ 4375
40,000	2500	3750	5000	7500	8750
60,000	3750	5625	7500	11,250	13,125
80,000	5000	7500	10,000	15,000	17,500
100,000	6250	9375	12,500	18,750	21,875

[a] *Source:* Authors' calculation.

TABLE 4.3   Value of Retiree Health Insurance: Assume Couple Covered[a]

Pre-65 in 1992	$8000
Post-65	$2000
Rate of Annual Increase 10%	

Pay Level	Health Benefit as a Percentage of Pension				
	Period of Service				
	10	15	20	30	35
	Benefit at Age 65 in 1992				
$ 20,000	80%	53%	40%	27%	23%
40,000	40	27	20	13	11
60,000	27	18	13	9	8
80,000	20	13	10	7	6
100,000	16	11	8	5	5
	Benefit at Age 55 in 1992				
$ 20,000	640%	427%	320%	213%	183%
40,000	320	213	160	107	91
60,000	213	142	107	71	61
80,000	160	107	80	53	46
100,000	128	85	64	43	37

[a] *Source:* Authors' calculation.

TABLE 4.4   Value of Retiree Health Insurance: Assume Retiree Pays for 50% of Health Benefit Contribution as Percentage of Pension[a]

Pay Level	Period of Service				
	10	15	20	30	35
	Benefit at Age 65 in 1992				
$ 20,000	40%	27%	20%	13%	11%
40,000	20	13	10	7	6
60,000	13	9	7	4	4
80,000	10	7	5	3	3
100,000	8	5	4	3	2
	Benefit at Age 55 in 1992				
$ 20,000	320%	213%	160%	107%	91%
40,000	160	107	80	53	46
60,000	107	71	53	36	30
80,000	80	53	40	27	23
100,000	64	43	32	21	18

[a] *Source:* Authors' calculation.

TABLE 4.5   Value of Retiree Health Insurance Benefit as a Percentage of Pension Benefit[a]

Pay Level	Period of Service				
	10	15	20	30	35
	Benefit at Age 65 in 1997				
$ 20,000	129%	86%	64%	43%	37%
40,000	64	43	32	21	18
60,000	43	29	21	14	12
80,000	32	21	16	11	9
100,000	26	17	13	9	7
	Benefit at Age 55 in 1997				
$ 20,000	1031%	687%	515%	344%	294%
40,000	515	344	258	172	147
60,000	344	229	172	115	98
80,000	258	172	129	86	74
100,000	206	137	103	69	59

[a] *Source:* Authors' calculation.

TABLE 4.6   Value of Retiree Health Insurance: Assume Retiree Pays for 50% of Health Benefit Contribution as Percentage of Pension[a]

Pay Level	Period of Service				
	10	15	20	30	35
	Benefit at Age 65 in 1992				
$ 20,000	64%	43%	32%	21%	18%
40,000	32	21	16	11	9
60,000	21	14	11	7	6
80,000	16	11	8	5	5
100,000	13	9	6	4	4
	Benefit at Age 55 in 1992				
$ 20,000	515%	344%	258%	172%	147%
40,000	258	172	129	86	74
60,000	172	115	86	57	49
80,000	129	86	64	43	37
100,000	103	69	52	34	29

[a]*Source:* Authors' calculation.

Another plan is the Medicare supplement. Under this design, the benefits are scheduled and designated to fill in for expenses not covered by Medicare. Federal law regulates Medicare supplemental (also called *Medigap*) insurance plans sold on an individual and group basis (plans not sponsored by employers). Medigap insurance plans must fit one of ten defined benefit plans established by federal law.

Relationship to Pension Benefit Levels

Pension benefits are calculated and compared to retiree health benefit values in Tables 4.2 - 4.6, which help determine whether retiree health benefits, if heavily paid for by the retiree, are affordable. For this analysis, a final average pay plan with a benefit equal to 1.25 percent of final average earnings has been assumed. This is a fairly generous plan, but not the most generous offered. The DOL study of employee benefits in medium and large firms shows replacement ratios from the private plan only as follows:

Years	Sample Plan: Percent of Final Average Earnings	Average Replacement Ratios 1989 DOL Study, Percent of Final Pay
10	12.50%	9.8%- 12.1%
15	18.75%	14.8%- 17.6%
20	25.00%	19.8%- 23.4%
30	37.50%	33.3%- 39.5%

Source: U.S. Department of Labor (1990), Table 85.

The DOL results vary by pay level. The range is shown for the data for all participants. The results also vary by type of employee. These replacement ratios are comparable to that for the sample plan shown in Tables 4.2 - 4.6. The sample plan results should be reduced by about 6 percent to be percentages of final pay. For example, 12.5 percent of final average earnings is equal to about 11.8 percent of final earnings. For purposes of this analysis, the 1.25 percent plan is a good representation of the average for employees in medium and large firms, as reflected in the 1989 survey.

For the sample plan, benefits are shown at age 65 and at age 55, assuming that at age 55, a 50 percent reduction in the pension occurs to reflect the fact that benefits will be paid for ten years longer than they would have been had they started at age 65. Benefits are shown for five different pay levels and several service periods and do not include Social Security. At age 55, under this plan, an employee with 30 years service would have income replacement of under 20 percent of final average earnings, so that the cash income does not support retirement even with a drastic reduction in living standard. People who retire at age 55 must have other income sources and assets or accept a drastic reduction in living standard.

Retiree health was assumed to be worth $8000 in 1992 for a couple both under age 65, and $2000 in 1992 for a couple both over age 65. Medicare reflects the difference. Costs are assumed to increase 10 percent per year, considerably more than recent Consumer Price Index (CPI) increases and considerably less than medical costs increases under many current medical plans. Pensions are assumed to be level dollar amounts, but some employers will offer ad-hoc increases.

The value of retiree health is compared to the pension in 1992 and 1997 in Table 4.6, and contributions are calculated as a percentage of the pension benefit if the retiree is required to pay 50 percent of the value of the retiree health benefit (considerably more than the contributions required in most plans today). At the 50-percent contribution level, the benefit is clearly not affordable at age 55, except for longer service and higher pay levels. Retirement would be feasible only if other substantial assets existed, or if the retiree or some other family member has current earnings and/or employment that provides benefits. Retirement may still require a major change in lifestyle.

Significant contributions to retiree health will make retirement at earlier ages considerably more difficult for most retirees. Pension benefit levels for hourly employees generally are lower and the situation will be considerably worse. The impact of significant retiree health contributions for early retiree medical is likely to be postponement of retirement to age 65 in many cases, and to at least age 60-62 in other cases.

Employers Without Plans

Considering all the costs and liabilities associated with retiree health, it might seem that companies not offering such plans would be happy. The situation, however, is more complex. In fact, many such companies are wondering what to do, because the absence of plans is a major barrier to early retirement. Some companies are finding that employees cannot afford to retire without access to coverage (particularly those aged under 65 years), and although they would prefer not to provide coverage, they are concerned about the impact on their business of having employees unable to retire. It is unclear at this point what strategies might be adopted on a widespread basis.

Trends in Plan Design

A retiree health plan can be thought of as a medical plan and a retirement benefit. Until the last five years, virtually all the attention paid to these benefits was on the medical benefit itself, but more recently an equal, if not greater, focus has been on the retirement-related issues of cost sharing, how benefits are earned over time, and who gets them.

TABLE 4.7   Results of Mercer Survey: Popularity of Approaches to Manage Retiree Health Benefit Costs[a]

Action	For Existing Retirees	For Future Retirees	For Both Groups	Total
Raised retiree contributions	5%	18%	25%	48%
Increased deductible or copay	5	12	27	44
Used managed care techniques	3	6	29	38
Tightened eligibility	1	19	9	29
Capped employer contributions	2	11	10	23
Changed Medicare integration	2	4	13	19
Used a defined dollar approach	-	8	5	13
Canceled benefits	-	9	3	12
Reduced lifetime benefit cap	1	2	4	7

[a]Survey findings demonstrate that the most popular way of managing retiree medical liabilities is to increase the portion of costs borne by retirees. Almost half (48%) the 780 respondents have raised retiree contributions and about the same number (44%) have implemented a higher deductible or copayment in their plans. The least popular cost-management approach was to reduce the lifetime limit on benefits payable under the plan —only 7% said they had done so. Although only 12% said they had canceled benefits for either existing or future retirees, the prevalence of this approach increased from 1991, when only 1% of 902 respondents said they had stopped providing retiree medical benefits.

Various surveys have shown that employers have reduced coverage for retiree benefit plans. A 1992 Mercer survey indicates the nature of some of these reductions (see Table 4.7). In general, the survey found that

- Until 1992, reductions in benefits were most often for future retirees;
- A few employers have dropped coverage entirely;
- Many employers have adopted programs that might be called "holding actions." Adoption of a "cap," or maximum, on what the plan will pay for a retiree's coverage is common.

Cost and Cost Recognition of Employer-Provided Retiree Health Benefits

Basis for Cost Recognition

Costs are accounted for in profit and loss statements according to accounting rules published by the Financial Accounting Standards Board (FASB). FAS 106, effective for most employers' 1993 fiscal year, requires that a change in accounting be made for other post-retirement employee benefits (OPEB) from the pay-as-you-go (cash basis) method to the accrual method, to reflect the liability of the benefit earned. As a result, employers now are required to accrue post-retirement benefit obligations as an expense from the time an employee is hired until benefit eligibility. Post-retirement benefits are typically health care plans, life insurance, and, sometimes, long-term care benefits. Furthermore, FASB permitted employers to adopt one of two transition methods to recognize their FAS 106 obligation. Employers either could recognize their accumulated liabilities immediately on a one-time basis in 1993, or they could amortize the cost attributed to past periods over a maximum 20-year period.

Effects of FAS 106 on Employer Profits

Although FAS 106 does not increase an employer's long-term cost of providing post-retirement benefits or require that funds be set aside to pay for future benefits, it does require employers to account for the cost much earlier. This change will reduce reported net operating income and earnings per share for employers. Some forecasters suggest that the new accounting method could reduce the pre-tax profits and net worth of large American employers by about 10 percent.

Much larger estimates of the effect of FAS 106 on employer earnings and net worth have been reported. For example, Wein (1992) reports that FAS 106 will have an earnings impact in 1993 of about $1.00 per share for the Standard & Poors 500 companies. That report also identifies a number of other companies for which an even greater impact is predicted.

A major accounting firm surveyed annual report disclosures of 64 public companies that adopted FAS 106 early (before 1993) (Ernst and Young 1992). For these companies, FAS 106 (or OPEB) costs varied from less than 1 percent to nearly 5 percent of revenues. For companies that recognize the obligation immediately, the effect on pre-tax income and net worth was, on average, reduced by 28 percent and 8 percent, respectively.

Present Value of Liability

According to estimates by the GAO, the present value of private employers' liabilities for current post-retirement benefits, as of 1991, was approximately $296 billion (GAO 1991). It is this amount that employers will be required to recognize in their financial statements with the adoption of FAS 106. About $93 billion of this amount is owed for current retirees and covered dependents, and an estimated $203 billion is the accrued liability for current employees and covered dependents, according to the GAO. To begin prefunding this accrued liability, companies would have had to contribute an estimated $42 billion in 1991—about four times their pay-as-you-go costs. Estimates of the total employer accrued liability for retired workers' health benefits vary from $300 to $400 billion (EBRI 1991).

The total toll on American corporate profits is expected to be a record for any accounting rule, with the liability as high as $1 trillion (Berton and Brennan 1992). Hardest hit will be businesses that are unionized, labor-intensive, low in employee turnover, and high in the ratio of retirees to active employees. For example, the Big 3 American automobile makers spent on average $1086 per vehicle in 1990 for health care coverage compared to $475 for Japanese automobile manufacturers who build cars in the United States. American car makers have complained for many years that their high health care costs have affected their ability to compete on an international basis. Ford, General Motors (GM), and Chrysler also cite the fact that their foreign competitors all have some form of national health coverage.

In February 1993, GM announced that it was taking a one-time $21 billion charge for FAS 106 and an annual charge of $1.4 billion a year on an indefinite basis to account for future unfunded post-retirement medical liabilities. Other companies with older workers and generous health plans, like Ford Motors, AT&T, and IBM, have also announced liabilities for post-retirement medical benefits in the billions of dollars.

Financial Impact

Many studies have attempted to measure the financial impact of implementing FAS106 on employer plans. A William M. Mercer, Incorporated survey (1992) of recent retiree health valuations shows that employer costs will increase by the following multiples when FAS 106 is adopted:

- For highly mature companies (those with fewer than two active employees per retiree), 3.5 times;
- For mature companies (those with two to six active employees per retiree), 7.0 times;
- For less mature companies (those with more than six active employees per retiree), 13.5 times.

This study also showed the average cost per active employee in 179 actuarial valuations performed by William M. Mercer consultants:

Pay-as-you-go cost	$528
EPBO	$24,785
APBO	$11,927
Expense	$2097

The pay-as-you-go cost is the amount needed to pay benefits to current retirees, or, if the plan is insured, the premium costs needed to cover current retirees for one year. The EPBO (expected post-retirement benefit obligation) is the present value (including discount for interest, terminations in employment, and so forth) of lifetime retiree health benefits per employee determined at the time of the valuation. Hence, if an employer had exactly average results and wants to set aside enough money today to cover these benefits for the existing workforce, approximately $25,000 would be needed for each employee. The APBO (accumulated post-retirement benefit obligation) is the portion of the EPBO attributable to past periods by the cost-spreading method prescribed in the accounting rules set forth in FAS 106.

Finally, the expense is the amount that will be booked on average, assuming that employers spread out (or amortize) the amounts charged to past periods. Many employers have chosen not to amortize this amount because future earnings will be greater if the amount is recognized in a single year. In that situation, the annual average expense is reduced to $1495 per active employee. For an employer with a $30,000 average pay amount, the expense is 7 percent of pay if there is amortization of APBO, and 5 percent of pay if the APBO is recognized immediately rather than amortized.

Cost Information

Most current post-retirement cost data are based on estimates from surveys conducted by employee benefit, accounting, and actuarial consulting firms and the GAO. Most employers have focused their attention on their health benefit plan expenses because they represent the largest post-retirement expense. In particular, employers are reviewing the actuarial assumptions regarding health care cost projections, levels of participation in the retiree plan, health service utilization rates, age at retirement, mortality rates, employee turnover rates, and rates of marriage.

Much of the more recent retiree health plan data are incomplete due to a number of employer health plan reporting inconsistencies. Some of these inconsistencies include a failure to differentiate retiree health plan cost data from active plan data and a widespread lack of separate pre-65 retiree versus post-65 retiree information. In some cases, it has been difficult determining the actual numbers of retirees and covered dependents in the plan and their related claims cost and utilization information.

For example, a 1992 study of 226 Fortune 500 companies found that only 99 of the surveyed firms reported cost information on post-retirement benefits, and this data combined health care benefits with life insurance benefits (Tang and Langsam 1992). The total 1990 post-retirement benefit cost for these firms was $4.23 billion. The top eight employers with the largest post-retirement costs in 1990, according to the study, were

General Motors	$1200 million
Ford	$ 582 million
Chrysler	$ 266 million
Textron	$ 236 million
DuPont	$ 216 million
Honeywell	$ 158 million
Rockwell International	$ 142 million
Navistar	$ 123 million

When attempting to determine the cost per retiree receiving health benefits, this study found that data on the specific numbers of retirees, for the most part, have not been available in annual financial reports. Instead, the study calculated the 1990 cost of post-retirement benefits per active employee and found that the costs vary widely by employer. Navistar had the highest post-retirement cost per active employee at $8742. Navistar, which had more than 40,000 retirees as of 1990, reduced its active employee population from 96,000 in the 1980s to 14,000 workers by 1992. In July 1992, the Chicago-based truckmaker asked a federal district court for permission to cut health benefits by $90 million for current retirees, including those represented by the United Auto Workers (UAW).

The UAW challenged Navistar's right to adopt certain retiree health benefits outside the collective bargaining process. Navistar and the UAW announced an agreement in late December 1992 that included an increase in retiree contributions, deductibles, and copayments. In addition, Navistar reportedly agreed to issue at least 255 million new shares of common stock to be held in a newly formed trust for future retiree health benefits. In April 1993, a federal judge gave preliminary approval to their proposed settlement to modify Navistar retiree's health benefits. Final approval of the plan is expected to be granted after further court hearings.

Employer Payments for Retiree Health Coverage

The GAO estimates that private employers paid $9 billion for health care benefits for retirees and their dependents in 1988 and that costs have increased an average of more than 20 percent a year since then. The GAO also reports that, in general, employers that offer coverage to their retirees have higher total health care costs. A survey of medium- and large-sized employers found that the provision of retiree health benefits represented 14 percent of total employer health benefit plan costs (GAO 1992). In the communications and utilities industries (employers that traditionally tend to have rich benefit plans), retiree health expenses represent over 20 percent of total health costs each year. In contrast, health services or technical/professional service firms (employers that have less generous benefit plans) report that retiree health costs consume 6 percent of overall health care costs.

In terms of employers' total payroll costs, one benefits consulting firm estimates that after FAS 106 is fully implemented, the median annual health expense for retirees, as reported on profit and loss statements, will increase from the current 1.1 percent of payroll to approximately 6.25 percent (Hewitt Associates 1990).

Employer Cost Variation

Not surprisingly, many surveys have indicated that retiree health care costs vary by employer. For example, 11 percent of employers surveyed in 1990 reported that health care costs per retiree were under $1000 whereas 16 percent noted costs in excess of $3000 per retiree (Foster Higgins 1991).

Variation among employers for retiree health care costs occurs for many reasons: the benefit plan design; the number of employees expected to reach retirement age; the age of retirees and their dependents; the number of retirees under the age of 65; and the size and geographic location of the employer.

As expected, employers that offer a generous health benefit plan to retirees tend to have the largest retiree health costs. This is certainly the case among the medium- to large-sized employers with collectively bargained workers. Historically, they have been known to offer very generous health benefits to salaried and hourly employees alike. Many of these plans have similar deductibles and coinsurance levels for early retirees and for active employees. Employers that do not implement an increase in required costsharing or a reduction in benefits, especially for the under age-65 group, are likely to experience substantial health care cost increases yearly for their covered retiree population.

In addition, the number of employees expected to reach retirement age greatly affects the level of an employer's retiree health costs. For example, manufacturing firms have twice as many retired plan participants as wholesale/retail firms (GAO 1991). In general, retailers experience higher rates of employee turnover than other employers and, as a result, have much lower retiree health costs.

The age spread of participants in the retiree health plan also has a direct effect on an employer's retiree health costs. The greater the number of early retirees not yet eligible for Medicare, the greater the level of retiree health costs, especially for employers whose pre-65 retiree plan is similar to the active employee plan, because Medicare pays for the majority of acute health care benefits for retirees 65 years of age and older.

Available evidence suggests that it costs employers 35 to 60 percent more to provide health benefits for retirees not yet eligible for Medicare, as compared to active employees of the same age, because employees under the age of 65 often retire because they or a dependent covered under an employer plan are ill (Hay Group 1993). Other consultants believe that as much as 40 percent of the cost of retiree health comes from early retirement; however, this varies according to the employee's reason for retirement. Recent insurance industry estimates indicate that the median annual cost for insured plans that cover retirees under age 65 was $2246 per retiree/dependent, compared with $1033-$1372 per retiree/dependent older than 65 and eligible for Medicare benefits in 1990. Costs also tend to increase for both the under and over age-65 retiree groups (according to the size of the employer, by geographic location, and by cost-sharing provisions).

Dealing with Cost Increases

Trends in Employer-Sponsored Plans

Even with skyrocketing medical cost inflation, an increasing number of retirees, and the FAS 106 requirements, only a handful of large employers actually have terminated or plan to terminate retiree health benefits.

Many, however, have changed their retiree medical plans in some way. United Dominion Industries and First City Bancorporation are examples of two employers that have terminated retiree medical plans: United Dominion discontinued benefits in 1988 at the end of a bargaining agreement, and First City canceled benefits effective January 1991.

Other employers, such as McDonnell Douglas and Unisys, have announced that their company-funded retiree medical plans for all current and future nonunion retirees will change to plans that are fully funded by retirees. Although McDonnell Douglas is providing its retirees with a one-time taxable pension supplement to assist in paying these premiums, the company is guaranteeing group retiree health plan coverage availability only through the end of 1996. Please note, however, that McDonnell Douglas retirees have filed a class action suit in Los Angeles to prevent these changes. In December 1992, the court refused to issue a preliminary injunction that would have prevented McDonnell Douglas from imposing the premium requirements on the retirees; however, the court urged the retirees to pursue their claim. In addition, eight separate groups of Unisys retirees have filed class action suits against Unisys to prevent it from proceeding with its plan.

Bankers Trust terminated benefits for future retirees, except for employees who were over the age of 40 on January 1, 1990. Another employer, Boise Cascade, will provide coverage only for retirees over the age of 65.

Far more common are employers like Green Bay Packaging and Media General that no longer offer or subsidize retiree medical benefits for employees hired after a certain date. El Paso Natural Gas Company, like other employers, recently announced its plan to eliminate retiree medical contributions for employees that retire after a certain date. Please note that the U.S. Court of Appeals for the Fifth Circuit ruled on March 25, 1993 that El Paso's unilateral cut-off did not violate ERISA (Wise v. El Paso Natural Gas Company, 1993).

In general, although most employers want to continue offering retiree medical benefits, most are seeking ways to slow down or limit not only the growth rate of their retiree health costs but also their future liability. Employers are doing this in a number of ways and often are using one or more of the following methods:

- Changing the health benefit plan design;
- Increasing contribution amounts required of employees;
- Switching from a defined benefit to a defined contribution plan;
- Changing eligibility criteria;
- Using managed care and flexible benefit plans;

- Offering a catastrophic plan and/or a long-term care plan instead of a more comprehensive plan.

Although many employers are maintaining traditional retiree medical plans, a growing number are reducing benefit levels and increasing the contribution amounts required of current and future retirees. Many employers now require retirees to pay the entire cost of certain benefits such as prescription drugs, dental, vision, or hearing, and some employers are eliminating such benefits altogether. Sundstrand, for example, eliminated dental benefits for future retirees, effective 1992. Also, UOP, a joint venture between Allied-Signal and Union Carbide, eliminated its prescription drug benefit for retirees and replaced it with an annual $500 medical reimbursement account.

General Motors announced medical plan changes and an increase in cost-sharing for salaried retirees, effective in 1994. General Motors retirees will now have a greater selection of managed care programs but will have to share a greater portion of the cost of both the health plan and prescription drug coverage. In addition, Unilever employees who retired after 1987 can now choose between a low- or a high-option medical plan. Benefits are reduced under both plans for retirees with fewer than 25 years of service. Unilever retirees are not required to contribute to the lower option plan, and cost-sharing for the higher option plan depends on the retiree's years of service.

The method by which the employer's retiree health plan integrates with Medicare for retirees over age 65 also will have a tremendous influence on plan costs. For example, per retiree costs reportedly were 12 percent lower among employers using a nonduplicative carve-out approach when integrating their covered retiree benefits with Medicare benefits. Under the Medicare carve-out method, the employer calculates regular plan benefits, assuming that Medicare does not exist. The Medicare payment is then subtracted from the employers' calculated amount and the employer pays the difference. The Medicare-eligible retiree's combined benefit is then the same as the company-provided benefits for retirees not eligible for Medicare.

Campbell Soup, for example, which previously had paid 80 percent of any covered expense that Medicare did not pay, implemented a carve-out plan for coordinating benefits with Medicare. Under this approach, Medicare's payment plus Campbell Soup's Medicare supplemental plan does not exceed 80 percent of their pre-65 plan approved amount. The utility Central and South West Services Inc. also switched to a Medicare carve-out plan and replaced their indemnity drug plan with a managed prescription drug program.

In addition to benefit plan changes, most employers now require retirees to share more, or, in some cases, all the cost of the retiree health plan. One consulting firm found that about one third of employers that modified their retiree health plans in 1990 and 1991 imposed higher retiree contribution requirements. It is estimated that requiring retirees to pay a higher deductible, share more of the costs, or be limited to a maximum dollar amount of benefit can cut as much as 12.5 percent of post-retirement costs.

One employer, DuPont, is planning to reduce retiree health benefits for current and former employees and their dependents starting in January 1994. DuPont will split with the retirees any health care cost increases that occur after January 1997. Equifax and Sears also require health plan contributions from current retirees. Another employer, Ball Corporation, has announced that it no longer will make retiree health contributions for salaried employees hired after 1989. Yet another employer, Morgan Stanley, subsidizes retiree health coverage for people hired after 1988 at 4 percent of plan costs for each year of service, to a maximum of 25 years.

Many employers are switching from a defined benefit approach to a defined dollar approach by capping their contributions to the cost of retiree health care at some predetermined level. General Electric, Keebler, Maersk, and Westinghouse, for example, all have capped the amount they will pay for the cost of current and/or future coverage for retirees. Some defined dollar benefit plans place a cap on annual health payments based on years of employment. The Bank of Boston, for example, provides a defined dollar plan whereby the retiree receives a $500 credit for each year of service, starting at age 40, up to a maximum of 20 years, or $10,000.

Employer plans that restrict eligibility for retiree health coverage might include those that govern the age of employees and the years of service to be eligible initially, the age at which employees stop being eligible, and whether and for how long spouses and other dependents are covered. Southeast Banking Corporation, for example, set their retiree health contribution at $125 per retiree per month, with no subsidy for spouse coverage. Sundstrand makes no contribution toward health care benefits for retirees once they reach the age of 80.

Many employers also are disengaging pension eligibility from retiree health benefits. Other employers are finding that by changing plan eligibility, they can reduce their accounting liability considerably because they may not have to book a liability for retiree health care for all employees from the date of hire.

A growing number of employers are enhancing the managed care plans offered to retirees. For example, GM plans to expand their Preferred Provider Organization (PPO) and Health Maintenance Organization (HMO) retiree health options. For post-65 people, some HMOs coordinate with or replace Medicare and provide a greater level of benefits than a Medigap plan. Although these Medicare HMOs generally limit enrollment to individuals, both employers and retirees also can save money on Medicare HMO risk plans. In addition, a new PPO type of Medicare supplement—Medicare SELECT—has been implemented. Some employers are even offering a choice of several flexible benefit plan options.

Flexible compensation packages allow workers to choose from among various pension and welfare benefits. The number of flex plan credits that retirees receive will apply toward their coverage options and will be based on their age at retirement and years of service. Offering multiple medical plan options allows retirees to select a plan within their financial limits. Employers can use flexible benefit plan options and pricing strategies to promote lower cost plans. For example, many employers provide a lower subsidy for the higher cost health plan options.

One employer, Pillsbury, implemented a retiree flex plan for employees who retired after 1986. To qualify for the plan, retirees must have at least 10 years of service and be at least 55 years old. Pillsbury retirees receive credits worth $1400 for each year of service (up to a maximum of 30 years, or $42,000). At retirement the employee decides how the lump sum is to be allocated annually. Retirees then can use the credit to purchase medical, dental, or life insurance and/or to establish a reimbursement account.

Finally, providing a relatively inexpensive catastrophic plan is another way that employers can limit their retiree health liabilities. Employers can subsidize coverage based on years of service and provide more coverage to employees with longer service. Many employers give retirees the option of electing an additional level of coverage that requires significant employee contributions. For example, Johnson and Johnson replaced their basic/major medical plan for salaried employees with a $1000 deductible and a $3000 out-of-pocket maximum catastrophic comprehensive plan.

Dealing with Catastrophic Illness

The catastrophic illness issues are different for pre-65 and post-65 coverage. Pre-65, there is no Medicare coverage available (except for certain disabled persons and those with end-stage renal disease), but Medicare is available after age 65. Pre-65, the issues are similar to active employee issues, except that the nature and incidence of various illnesses differ by age.

The typical employer plan has a lifetime maximum benefit of from $250,000 to $1,000,000. A few plans have lower maximums, particularly for retirees. A lower maximum applies to some employer plans, but, for most employer plans, the overall maximum is generally not a problem.

The major issues in terms of coverage for catastrophic illness are the overall maximum amount, mental illness, prescription drugs, and long-term care.

Long-Term Care

Typically, long-term care is not covered in employer plans, nor is it covered under the Medicare program to any significant extent. Long-term health care is a major issue for an aging population.

Long-term care is financed largely by the individual and Medicaid, with each paying nearly half the cost. In the past, it usually was required that the individual spend down assets to be eligible for Medicaid (leaving the surviving spouse impoverished and without assets). There is a growing trend at the state level to modify such requirements. Development of a financing system for long-term care is, however, a future issue and will need to be addressed in the months and years to come.

Cost of Terminal Illness

As technology has opened up new treatment alternatives, the cost of terminal illness has become an increasingly difficult issue, and the application of resources in the event of terminal illness creates a number of questions. Lester Thurow in *Head to Head,* (page 170), summarizes the issue from an economist's point of view:

Consider the conventional "do-no-harm" rule for deciding when medical treatment should be stopped. If every treatment is carried to the point where its negative side effects become worse than the original effects of the disease, doctors prescribe treatments far beyond the rational economic stopping rule (marginal costs should equal marginal benefits) and run up huge costs in situations where few benefits are to be expected— more than one third of all U.S. medical costs are incurred in the last year of life.

In the past, employing every available procedure to the point where it actively began to harm the patient did not cost very much, since there weren't many expensive technologies to be employed in most illnesses. But when such technologies arise and give doctors and their patients a lot of expensive technological options with submarginal payoffs, the old stopping rule can become a very expensive decision rule that can no longer be afforded.

From a social point of view, resources are being allocated to expensive, highly technical treatments when primary care often is not available to people who need it.

A recent article in the Journal of the American Medical Association (JAMA) provides insight into the costs and results of intensive care for terminal cancer patients (Shapiro et al. 1993). The authors concluded that the majority of patients with solid tumors and hematologic cancers admitted to the intensive care unit die before discharge, or, if they survive the hospital admission, they spend a minimal amount of time at home before dying. They found that the potential for survival of these patients was poor once they became critically ill. They recommend that physicians treating patients with these diseases should discuss potential outcomes with the family, including the possibility of withdrawing life-support therapy. The cost per year of life gained for their study group was $189,339. The study also examined the effect of hospice care on hospitalization. The authors note that patients not enrolled in hospice care spent 23 of their last days in the hospital and received only four days of home health care visits. In contrast, those enrolled in hospice care spent only eight of their last 50 days in the hospital. The aggregate effect of these decisions is a material factor in health care costs. The JAMA article indicates that $62 billion of the $809 billion of the estimated 1992 health care spending in the United States were dedicated to the intensive care unit.

It seems clear that this is not a problem of retiree health plans per se, but, rather, a problem of the medical system in general and of the decisions that will be made without treatment. The impact of this issue on retiree health benefit plans, however, is significant.

Future Prospects for Retiree Health

The new accounting rules for retiree health are effective for most employers in 1993, and, as of late 1992, it remained to be seen how this will affect the way in which employers manage their plans. Until late 1992, many major employers had reduced benefits primarily through increased costsharing, but relatively few had eliminated benefits altogether. For the most part, changes affected future retirees only. As indicated earlier, several prominent employers have announced new programs that limit the period during which they will provide retiree health coverage.

As of early 1993, the situation was transitional at best; it may be several years before stabilization occurs and it becomes apparent just which policies will prevail among employers. Other employers have been swapping company payments for retiree health for increased cash retirement benefits, either through defined benefit or defined contribution plans.

Depending on the perspective, the current structure can be viewed either as a success or failure. On the success side, many retirees receive benefits that are generally adequate and important to their personal security in retirement. On the failure side, many employers have no plans or else the plans have weaknesses, such as

- Lack of coverage for people who leave before early retirement age;
- Future cost sharing that may make plans unaffordable;
- Plans that generally are subject to unilateral changes;
- Plans that usually are not prefunded so that benefits depend on the ability of the employer to pay.

Demographics

The issues that relate to retiree health benefits will only get worse in the next century as the age structure of the population becomes considerably older and periods of retirement lengthen (unless retirement ages change drastically). These changes were discussed in a previous Pension Research Council publication (Bodie and Munnell 1992). What is not discussed here directly is that many forces point to uncertainty with regard to future retirement ages. Given current retirement ages and projected increases in life expectancy, employer costs for retiree health will continue to increase and represent a great burden on companies.

Public Policy/National Health Reform

A key question with regard to retiree health coverage is the future role of the federal government. Presently, the federal government provides health benefits to retirees in the form of Medicare, which covers virtually all Americans after age 65; federal funding also partially supports Medicaid, which provides additional benefits to the medically indigent and funds about 50 percent of long-term care benefits.

Currently in the United States, approximately 38 million Americans have no health insurance. Health benefits for these Americans is a major priority for the Clinton administration, which has announced a blueprint for overhauling the American health care system. Hillary Rodham Clinton and the White House Task Force on Health Care Reform have endorsed a concept of health care delivery called managed competition. Under this system, most people would purchase health insurance from large HMO-like managed care networks that would compete for customers in a given region. In addition, a federally created board would set up non-profit insurance purchasing organizations to bargain with networks of providers for the most favorable rates.

A major issue in the health reform debate is the ongoing role of employers in providing health benefits for employees. Under two of the three managed competition proposals that have gotten major attention, the employer continues to play a major role. The employer may well be mandated to offer health coverage. It is unclear, however, how such a policy would affect retirees. If the employer is required to provide coverage to active employees, would the mandate extend to retirement? If the health benefit system is tied to employment, must it also extend to retirement?

Exactly how retiree health benefits, Medicare, or even Medicaid would be changed by the reform legislation remains to be seen. As a result of the current uncertainty in Washington, many employers prefer to consider "holding actions" that limit their retiree health liability as much as possible but, at the same time, preserve their future options. The "cap" and "defined-dollar" benefits provide a way to do this, with the "cap" being more popular at this time.

Legislative Activity

The linkage of employment to health care benefit availability has and will continue to be debated by members of Congress, the White House, and health care policy experts. In March 1993, the U.S. Senate Committee on Labor and Human Resources, Subcommittee on Labor, held hearings on the erosion of employer-sponsored retiree health benefits and the impact on workers and businesses. Many of the employers that testified before the Committee placed the blame squarely on FAS 106, the ever escalating cost of health care, and the lack of national health insurance. In addition, the subcommittee was reminded that employer retiree health plans are covered by ERISA. Unlike pension benefits, ERISA does not mandate that employers provide for the accrual, vesting, and funding of their retiree health liabilities. ERISA does indicate, however, that employers that promise lifetime benefits must provide lifetime benefits. As a result, Subcommittee Chairmen Senators Howard Metzenbaum (D-OH) and Donald Riegle (D-MI) may introduce legislation to protect retiree health benefits.

Continuation Coverage Under COBRA

Under current law, employers are required to continue health benefits coverage for at least 18 months to retirees who lose it at a rate equal to 102 percent of the average cost. This is required under the continuation coverage statute of the Consolidated Omnibus Reconciliation Act (COBRA) of 1985. Proposals have been made to lengthen the period of continuation coverage to Medicare eligibility, although this has not been discussed recently. That is one possible solution to the access problem.

Note, however, that this still would cost employers significant amounts if COBRA rates are determined as at present. For an average employer group, the COBRA rates, in general, are approximately 40 percent of the average cost for an early retiree group. This is primarily because of differences in age. The ratio can be lower if a large number of early retirees are in poor health.

The future of COBRA is tied to the national health reform debate. Under one proposal, which decouples health coverage from employment, COBRA continuation coverage disappears.

Coverage Sold to Individuals/Groups

Federal and state legislation regulate insurance sold to supplement Medicare. Good policies are available to individuals or through organized programs like that offered by the AARP, but only to those people who are Medicare eligible. Virtually no market exists for individual coverage for retirees not yet eligible for Medicare.

It is likely that many employers will discontinue offering post-65 coverage and encourage employees to buy a Medicare supplemental policy on their own. Some employers may offer a retiree subsidy for the payment (or partial payment) of premiums under this arrangement. The retiree premium plan and increases in cash pension benefits are forms of such a subsidy.

Tie to Medicare-Eligibility Ages

Social Security retirement ages for full benefits have been legislated to increase to age 67 for those born after 1960, but, presently, no plans are on the table to increase the Medicare eligibility age beyond 65. Proposals have been made to reduce the Medicare eligibility age to 60, but this also seems unlikely in light of the federal budget deficit.

If Medicare eligibility were reduced to age 60, it seems likely that many employers would no longer sponsor retiree health benefit coverage and would encourage employees to buy supplemental coverage on their own. This idea may resurface in discussions about national health reform.

Underlying Inflationary Structure

Health care costs have risen much more rapidly than costs in general so that health care represents a constantly escalating percentage of the gross national product (GNP). Employer plan costs have risen even faster than health care costs generally and present employers with increasingly difficult issues. This is also a major issue at the national level.

It seems clear that health care cost increases must be brought under control, but it is not clear how to accomplish that goal. If costs cannot be brought under control, then employer-sponsored coverage will decline markedly and become less common. The same forces also will serve to put pressure on nonemployer-sponsored plans.

Conclusion

The adequacy of employer-sponsored retiree health coverage, an issue that considers the concerns of people who have coverage and evaluates the levels of coverage available, is the main focus of this chapter. As indicated earlier, adequacy is clearly deteriorating. The number of people who have retiree health coverage is dropping, so that the employer role in retiree coverage is no longer a straightforward one. The level of coverage for those who have it has been adequate historically, but the design changes made recently are calling such adequacy into question for many current and future retirees.

The adequacy of the level of coverage also is a function of the contributions required and the total retirement benefit package. Pension levels for many retirees are not good enough to pay for the fair value of their coverage. Substantial concerns abound about the level of total retirement benefits. If employer support for medical coverage is unavailable, then people generally will not be able to retire until they are eligible either for Medicare or for other subsidized coverage.

A number of challenges and concerns have been presented here. A key question is whether employers will have a continuing role in providing adequate health care coverage. Whereas this chapter sets forth some of the challenges to be addressed if employers are to continue to support retiree health needs, a companion chapter in this book by G. Lawrence Atkins investigates the employer's role more closely.

References

Berton L, Brennan R J. New Medical Benefits Accounting Rule Seen Wounding Profits, Hurting Shares. *Wall Street Journal.* April 22, 1992; C1.

Bodie Z, Munnell A, eds. *Pensions and the Economy: Sources, Uses, and Limitations of Data.* Philadelphia: University of Pennsylvania Press and the Pension Research Council, 1992.

Crimmins EM. Trends in Health Among the American Population. *In:* Rappaport AM, Schieber SJ, eds. *Demography and Retirement: The Twenty-first Century.* Westport, CT: Praeger Publishers in cooperation with the Pension Research Council, 1993.

Employee Benefit Research Institute. *Issue Brief Number 112. Retiree Health Benefits: Issues of Structure, Financing and Coverage.* Washington, DC: March 1991.

Employee Benefit Research Institute. *Issue Brief Number 128. Features of Employer-*

Sponsored Health Plans. Washington, DC: August 1992.

Employee Benefit Research Institute. *Issue Brief Number 132. Public Opinion on Health, Retirement, and Other Employee Benefits.* Washington, DC: December 1992.

Ernst and Young. Information Release: Survey of Postretirement Benefits Other Than Pensions – FASB #106. New York City: August 3, 1992.

Foster Higgins. *1991 Survey on Retiree Health.* New York City: 1992.

Hay Group. Trends in Retiree Medical Benefits—A Survey. Philadelphia: February 1993.

Hewitt Associates. Statement of Dallas Salisbury, President, Employee Benefit Research Institute, before the Subcommittee on Health, Ways and Means Committee, U.S. House of Representatives, Hearing on Retiree Health Care. Washington, DC: November 1991.

William M. Mercer Companies, Incorporated. *1992 Survey of Retiree Health Benefits: Postretirement Health Valuations Clearinghouse.* New York, NY: March, 1992.

Organization for Economic Cooperation and Development. Health File Data 1992. New York,NY: 1992.

Rogowski J, Karoly L. Study 10: Retirement and Health Insurance Coverage. *Health Benefits and the Workforce.* Washington, DC: U.S. Department of Labor, Pension, and Welfare Benefits Administration, 1992; 125

Shapiro DV, Studnicki J, Bradham DD, Wolff P, Jarrett A. Intensive Care, Survival and Expense of Treating Critically Ill Cancer Patients. *Journal of the American Medical Association.* February 10, 1993; 783-786.

Tang R, Langsam SA. Disclosure of Postretirement Benefits by Fortune 500 Companies. *Employee Benefits Journal.* December 1992; 38-43.

Thurow, L. *Head to Head.* New York: William Morrow & Company, 1992;170.

U.S. Department of Commerce, Bureau of the Census. *Projections of the United States by Age, Sex and Race: 1988 to 2080.* Current Population Reports, Series P-25, No. 1018. Washington, DC: 1989.

U.S. Department of Commerce, Bureau of the Census. *Population of the United States by Age, Sex, Race and Hispanic Origin: 1992 to 2050.* Washington, DC: October 1992.

U.S. Department of Commerce, Bureau of the Census. *Survey of Income and Program Participation.* Full Panel Micordata Research File. Technical Documentation 1986. Prepared by the Data User Services Division, Bureau of the Census. Washington, DC: 1990.

U.S. Department of Labor, Bureau of Labor Statistics. *Employee Benefits in Medium and Large Firms, 1989.* Washington, DC: June 1990; 67.

U.S. Department of Labor, Bureau of Labor Statistics. *Labstat Series Report: Labor Force Participation Rate — Civilian Population 55-64 years: Male.* Washington, DC: December 7, 1992.

U.S. General Accounting Office. Retiree Health: Company-Sponsored Plans Facing Increased Costs and Liabilities GAO/T-HRD-91-25. Statement given before the House Subcommittee on Ways and Means. May 6, 1991.

U.S. General Accounting Office. Employer-Based Health Insurance: High Costs, Wide Variation Threaten System. GAO/HRD-92-125. September 1992.

Wien, BR. *Sorting Out FAS 106.* New York City: Morgan Stanley and Company, November 1992.

Wise V. El Paso Natural Gas Company [CCA-5, March 25, 1993].

Commentary: William S. Custer

Retiree Health Coverage

Retiree health coverage represents two separate benefits for employees. The first is that retiree health benefits are deferred income, and the second is that these benefits offer employees access to a risk pool that is, to health insurance at group rates. This combination makes the adequacy of retiree health benefits difficult to assess.

The second benefit is especially important. Access to health insurance at group rates gives retirees an implicit subsidy. Older persons are more likely to need health care services and, thus, cost more to insure. If these people were to purchase coverage outside a group, early retirees would face premiums that would reflect their higher use of health care services. In a group, the premiums reflect the average costs of the group. If that group includes active workers, then those younger participants subsidize health insurance coverage for retirees. Essentially, Medicare eligibility provides the same subsidy that group coverage provides retirees under the age of 65, except that younger workers subsidize the health benefits of over-65 retirees through the payroll tax, as do employer-sponsored retiree health benefits.

To determine the adequacy of retiree health benefits requires a point of view. It is obvious from Chapter Four, by Rappaport and Malone, that the adequacy of retiree health benefits depends on the distance that workers are from retirement, the degree of risk aversion, employee self-assessment of future health risks, and the rate at which future income is discounted. From this position, younger workers may not place much value on retiree health benefits and would rather not forego other portions of total compensation to receive such benefits. Conversely, workers nearing retirement may value retiree health benefits highly.

How are the costs of providing retiree health benefits distributed? Simple economic theory suggests that the workers bear the costs of providing any noncash benefit, and that they would agree to accept noncash rather than cash compensation in situations where employers provide goods or services at a cost lower than what the individual could purchase alone. The tax code obviously affects the relative prices of goods purchased by individuals, compared to goods purchased through an employer, and also affects the provision of noncash benefits. In the case of health benefits, adverse selection makes group purchases less expensive than individual ones. Employees, therefore, are willing to receive some of their compensation in the form of health benefits rather than in cash. The tax code further encourages that choice by excluding the employer's contribution to health benefits from the employee's taxable income. Similarly, the tax code and the employer's greater access to capital markets encourage the allocation of a portion of total compensation as income deferred until retirement.[1]

As discussed earlier, employees are likely to differ in the value that they place on these benefits, but employers are limited in their ability to alter benefits to match individual preferences, because employees would lose the advantages of group purchases.[2] How employers determine the level of health benefits appropriate to their workforce (or desired workforce) is interesting. One possibility is that the level of health benefits is determined by the preferences of the median employee or, in collectively bargained plans, by the median union member, where the median is determined over all employees weighted by their influence within the organization. To the extent that the median employee is likely to be older, the level of health benefits, and especially retiree health benefits, may be greater than younger workers prefer.

From the point of view of the younger worker, if retiree health benefits are too high, then who actually bears the costs? Employment-based retiree health benefits have not generally been prefunded. To the extent that retirees are included in the same risk pool as active workers for purchasing or providing health benefits, younger workers then may face higher costs for health benefits. Seventy-five percent of early retirees who have retiree health coverage participate in the same plan as active workers (KPMG Peat Marwick 1992), who may wish that less of their total compensation went to retiree health benefits.

As previously stated, older workers nearing retirement are likely to view the adequacy of retiree health benefits in a different light than active workers. The access to group purchasing of health insurance benefits is important in evaluating the adequacy of total retirement income. Moreover, the employer contribution to that benefit is excluded from taxable income in retirement, whereas other sources of retirement income are tax deferred.

There may be a systematic sorting of workers related to noncash compensation in general and to retiree health benefits in particular. Larger employers can exploit economies of scale in administration. They also have more market power and present a larger risk pool for providing health benefits than smaller employers. They thus are able to offer benefits at lower costs than smaller employers, to the extent that retiree health benefits today are almost exclusively provided by larger employers.

Employee Reactions

The responses of employers to health care cost inflation and to FAS 106 are varied, but a common thread has been the desire to separate the two portions of the retiree health benefit. That is, if employers reduce, or "cap," the deferred income portion of the retiree health benefit, then they effectively reduce or limit their liabilities under FAS 106. Employers also can increase retirement income through various vehicles that preserve the tax-deferred status of that income. The difference to retirees is that they must now purchase health benefits with after-tax dollars.

Conclusion

From society's point of view, employment-based retiree health benefits are clearly inadequate: only about one third of retirees receive health benefits from a former employer. Most proposals for health care reform would extend coverage to those early retirees who presently do not have coverage. Many proposals, and particularly managed competition proposals, essentially would provide retirees with access to a risk pool, but they advocate that coverage be paid with after-tax income. Most proposals would provide tax credits or deductions for lower income retirees. In other words, these proposals also separate the provision of health care benefits from retirement income. The adequacy of retiree health benefits then would depend on the composition of the risk pool that retirees can access and the adequacy of their retirement income.

In Chapter Four, Rappaport and Malone expressly state that to determine the adequacy of employment-based retiree health benefits is a subjective exercise. The authors stress, however, that it is important to view health benefits in the context of total retirement income. Employment-based retiree health benefits have contributed to that income in two ways: the employer contribution to the purchase of health benefits that is excluded from taxation, and the access to the risk pool that allows retiree coverage to be subsidized by younger workers. Health care cost inflation and new accounting rules have created a breach in these arenas, however, and health care reform seems likely to exacerbate that trend. Whether employment-based retiree health benefits are sufficient is likely to hinge almost completely on the adequacy of the individual retiree's income.

Reference

KPMG Peat Marwick. Survey on Retiree Health Benefits. Washington DC: 1992.

Notes

1. The story is not that simple. Employers face a heterogeneous workforce and use benefits as a means of attracting workers with the most productive work characteristics.

2. This is more of a factor in the provision of health benefits than in retirement income, where the combination of a core pension plan and various savings plans gives employees relatively more flexibility in allocating total compensation.

Commentary: Paul B. Grant

Current Status

Based on the rapidly growing number of retirees, increasing life expectancy in the United States, and the need for health care coverage after retirement, it is not out of line to look at employer-provided health care coverage as a growth industry. The population is aging, Americans are retiring earlier, and those persons contemplating retirement are realizing that the ability to pay for their ongoing health care is as important as food and shelter.

Rather than a growth industry, however, retiree health care might now be considered an industry in turmoil and one even in decline. Two major factors contribute to this state: the impacts of continually and rapidly rising costs for health care, and the Financial Accounting Standards Board regulation (FAS 106) that decrees that employers must accrue the liabilities for the benefits promised to retirees.

The result has been that many firms either have made reductions in the coverage they offer retirees and/or employees, or they are seriously considering doing so. One recent study of Fortune 200 firms found that about 85 per cent of companies believe that their plans are targeted for change, with most employers feeling that more of the costs for health care must be shifted to retirees. A majority of employers foresee cutbacks in the benefits being offered (Goeppinger and Dobbelaere 1993).

It is hard to imagine that any firm would establish a new retiree health care program today. Effectively, the field appears to be closed. The evidence, much of it painfully reported in the national media, strongly suggests that firms will seek to reduce of even terminate their obligations. Those who recall the terminations of thousands of defined benefit pension plans after the passage of the Employee Retirement Insurance Security Act (ERISA) will relate to that.

In addition, it is important to remember that this trend strongly suggests that few among the majority of Americans now employed by firms that do not now offer any retiree health coverage are likely to be offered such coverage in the foreseeable future. The question of how adequate employer-sponsored retiree health plans are may be addressed first by noting that such total coverage is not available in any form to most workers today. Only about one third of American workers are employed by firms that offer sufficient health benefit programs for retired employers and for their dependents (GAO 1991).

Most studies indicate that existing retiree health care programs are offered only by larger firms (see Chapter Four), where it is not unusual for one or more programs to exist. The incidence of retiree health care benefits falls precipitously with smaller firms. The problem is that when no pension or other retirement program is available to older employees of smaller firms, how do they then afford health care coverage in retirement? Must the choice be one of medicine or food?

Medicare

It probably would be unnecessary to discuss the adequacy of employer-sponsored retiree health care programs if Medicare provided comprehensive health care for retirees. Many people believe that this was the intention when Medicare was enacted in 1965. The same cost pressures that have led to this particular discussion of employer-sponsored retiree health care, however, also have bedeviled Medicare. Within a few years after passage, it became necessary to increase participant premiums and to reduce coverages in the Medicare program, a trend that has continued. In fact, one of the annual rites of government has been the announcement that the premium for Medicare B has been increased for the next year, as have the various deductibles for hospitalization.

Even so, Medicare was deficient in its coverage from the start. An attempt to extend its benefits in 1988, with the passage of the Catastrophic Protection Act, failed when angry older people, who would have had to pay for the improved benefits, persuaded Congress to repeal the legislation before it became effective.

Medicare does not provide coverage for out-of-hospital prescription drugs, whose costs are rising faster than any other area of health care (EBRI 1992). Nor does it provide for long-term care, an often bankrupting but rapidly growing health care problem. Hospital and other health care costs that also are not covered by Medicare continue to rise. It could be said, ironically, that Medicare is causing many of the problems that are forcing employers to look more closely at the need to reduce health care coverage.

Early Retirement

For many years, there has been a tendency to retire before age 65, a trend exacerbated by company-inspired early retirement programs designed to encourage older workers to step aside (GAO 1985). Given the fact that, except in a few cases, Medicare is not available until age 65 and that individual health insurance policies for older people are very expensive, workers contemplating retirement are loathe to make the break without assurance of continued health care coverage.

Most employers have provided early retirees with continuation of the same coverage that the individual enjoyed when employed, at least until Medicare eligibility would kick in. Yet, the health care costs of older persons continue to rise rapidly. Such costs for a 60-year-old active employee, for example, may be as much as four times those for a 25-year-old active employee. Many companies are discovering that the health care component of the retirement package offered in early retirement programs is far more expensive than imagined. Similarly, costs of the continuing coverage for dependents of former employers often are surprisingly high.

Current Reactions to Spiraling Costs

For at least a generation, there has been concern over the cost of providing health care to employees. Employers and others have pointed to annual double-digit increases in costs and have said that something had to be done to control the cost spiral. And a large number of "somethings" have been attempted, to relatively little avail. Government-protected oligopolies have continued to act in the same way that they are prone to act: that is, prices continue to rise.

The desire to slow rapidly rising health care costs led to cutbacks in health care provided by employers in the 1980s. That trend has continued and is now being observed in the area of retiree health care. Some firms simply are terminating their retiree health care plans, a cruel fate for those retirees who had expected to receive continued coverage and had built that into their retirement plans. In many cases, angry retirees have reacted by suing, claiming that the former employer had made a lifetime promise. Although kindly, elderly lower court judges may find merit in these claims, recent decisions, at least on the appellate level, have largely favored the companies. (See, for example, Senn v. United Dominion Industries, Inc., C.A. No. 90-3100 [CCA - 7, January 8, 1992]; Boyer v. Douglas Components Corp., No. 91-2098 [CCA - 6, February 18, 1992]; and Wise v. El Paso Natural Gas [CCA - 5, March 25, 1993]).

Several lawsuits are pending, including some that affect Unisys and General Motors. Whether there will be sufficient interest on the U.S. Supreme Court to inspire a definitive statement on the issue is not clear;

but, with the growing numbers of appellate court decisions largely leaning in the same way, the issue already may be settled. In a situation where a firm has clearly reserved for itself the right to terminate or modify benefit plans, the company may well prevail if it chooses to reduce or eliminate coverage.

Although some firms have terminated plans altogether, others are reducing or eliminating coverage for current or future employees. Still other firms are instituting or increasing contributions for retirees and for their dependents, designing other cost-sharing methods, and, in other ways, attempting to shift costs to the employees. One company, AAR, the parent of American Airlines, has instituted employee contributions during employees' active years (Amoroso 1991).

Controversy also is growing over whether the final employer should bear the full burden of providing ongoing retiree health care. With regard to retirement income, firms generally accept no obligation to provide fully a pension or an annuity that a person might need – companies generally accept the obligation only to provide benefits based on the period of time that the employee worked for them. Employers are asking if it would not make more sense to prorate the retirement health obligation in a similar way.

All these modifications to retiree health care plans result in a lessening of the protection afforded retirees, through greater cost to the retiree, reduced overall coverage, or a combination of the two. In effect, they reduce the adequacy of the employer's commitment.

Some firms are turning to cost-control measures recently introduced for active employees with satisfactory results. More emphasis is being given to participation in health maintenance organizations (HMOs), preferred provider organizations (PPOs), and managed care. Flexible benefit plans, with coverage options open to retirees, also may be used. In one area, managed care for prescription drugs, substantial savings appear possible.

In any question of adequacy of benefits, it is clear that reducing them or increasing their costs raises questions. And the chart prepared by Rappaport and Malone for their presentation in Chapter Four demonstrates that retiree health care costs are important to the total retirement income of most people. In fact, for those retiring at lower income and pension levels, retiree health care may constitute a large part of total retirement income. Deprive people of such coverage and they may have to make choices between eating and taking a needed drug.

Uncertainty of Retiree Health Benefits

In any discussion on adequacy of retiree health care benefits, the question of uncertainty should be considered. In the area of retirement, it long has been advocated that people plan for the event. Popular pre-retirement programs sometimes suggest that planning should begin when workers are in their early 50s. With today's muddled health care world, however, how can anyone plan adequately for the future? In an environment where companies are known for phasing out or terminating their retiree health care programs (or adding new restrictions to them), enough uncertainty exists that few people can feel confident about retirement or feel free to enjoy a company health care program for their lifetime. Retirement is thought of as a time of peace, a time to enjoy the fruits of earlier labors. Now, this image is clouded by increasing financial uncertainty.

Unless an employee contemplating early retirement is convinced that health care coverage will continue at least until Medicare eligibility, how can a rational choice be made? Lacking the safety net of Medicare, such a person is exceedingly vulnerable. Because many workers recently have opted to retire early, in part because of continued health care coverage provisions, will uncertainty now slow this trend?

Additional Considerations

As industry began to prepare for FAS 106, studies were initiated to evaluate the impact that the new accounting rule would have on existing health care plans. In many cases, analysts discovered that they could obtain only incomplete and often inconsistent data. As Rappaport and Malone indicate, many participants' records were not coded in ways that would provide useful data.

Only recently have meaningful data about health care costs been isolated. Before the last 10 to 15 years, it was possible to isolate individual cases and aggregate claim amounts, but little data were available to study health care experience by gender, age, diagnostic classification, or in other ways that might have been useful. This has been changing, but only slowly.

It is now clear that the aggregate data available for so many years tended to obscure some important facts. New information is contributing to an evolving debate over treatments that do not affect life expectancy, do not improve the quality of life, and so forth. When former Chicago Bear football coach Mike Ditka was asked how hard his team had to work, or what he himself was willing to contribute, he would answer, "Whatever it takes." And that appears to have been a guiding principle for health care in the United States for many years, regardless of the cost/benefit analysis that might be used.

The recent Medicare emphasis that about one third of Medicare expenditures for retirees are incurred in the last year of life will add to the debate. Is this really the most efficient use of scarce resources? It is logical to expect that plans may refuse to pay costs associated solely with pro-longing life. To many, it is clear that the national crisis over health care eventually will result in far more quotas and rationing than exist today. What better place to start than with the elderly, on whom large sums are expended solely to prolong life with no demonstration of improving or even maintaining its quality.

Many investigators have been watching the experiment in Oregon, where coverage may not be provided for procedures that do not contrib-ute to a societally approved goal. Perhaps the day will come when the examining physician will determine that the cost/benefit analysis will not support additional treatment and simply makes the patient comfortable. The hospice industry almost certainly will greatly increase in size and scope.

The problems already described are likely to worsen. There is no rea-son to anticipate a slowing of the inventions, innovations, new drugs, and so on that have contributed to the recent great advances in health care. Even with a national health scheme that may downplay expenditures in the laboratory, however, support for continued research funding in such critical areas as AIDs, cancer, and other major killers must be anticipated. And the private sector may be expected to fund research into diabetes, multiple sclerosis, and many other serious problems. Based on experi-ence, all these improvements surely will lead to longer life but also to sharply higher costs.

Long-Term Care

A cruel irony of life has been the health care industry's ability to assist in prolonging life beyond society's ability to provide long-term care. Soci-etal changes have left no one at home to tend the elderly: changes in attitudes leave people unwilling to do so today. As a result, long-term care facilities have proliferated.

Many people are not aware that Medicare does not provide coverage for long-term care. The Medicaid program that does offer such coverage originally required that a person spend down assets until a spouse often was left destitute. Although some states have changed this regulation recently, the provision of such care still results in poverty for some survi-vors. Less admirably, it encourages fraud as people attempt to hide as-sets.

Little insurance protection is available for long-term care, although the field is growing. A few firms have experimented with such programs for employees and their families, usually on an employee-pay-all basis. Experience apparently has been mixed. With possibly one fourth of the population expected to spend some time in nursing homes, however, there is little question that long-term care needs are not being met.

Conclusion

Federal protection is being reduced, firms are being forced to terminate or reduce the coverage that they offer, and, in both instances, higher costs are being pushed onto retirees. Often, the retirees were never prepared for the possibility that health care protection would be reduced or eliminated. Consideration of the adequacy of available future health care may well impact the decision to retire at all.

Considering that retiree health care is part of the overall retirement package, these reductions in coverage and increases in costs directly affect the overall standard of living that a retiree can anticipate.

References

Amoroso V. Retiree Medical Liabilities: Problems and Solutions. *Employee Benefits Journal.* September 1991; 3-4.
Boyer v. Douglas Components Corp., No. 91-2098 [CCA - 6, February 18, 1992].
Employee Benefits Research Institute. Prescription Drugs: Coverage, Costs and Quality. *Issue Brief* No. 122. January 1992; 4.
Goeppinger K, Dobbelaere A. The Future of Corporate Health Benefits, 1993: A National Report. Chicago: Business Publications, 1993; 8.
Senn v. United Dominion Industries, Inc. C.A. No. 90-3100 [CCA - 7, January 8, 1992]
U.S. General Accounting Office. Retiree Health: Company-Sponsored Plans Facing Increased Costs and Liabilities. GAO/T-HRD-91-25. Statement given before the House Subcommittee on Ways and Means. May 6, 1991; 13.
U.S. General Accounting Office. Retirement Before Age 65 Is a Growing Trend in the Private Sector. GAO/HRD-85-81. Report to the Chairman, Subcommittee on Civil Service, Post Office and General Services, Committee on Governmental Affairs, United States Senate. July 15, 1985; 5-9.
Wise v. El Paso Natural Gas Company [CCA - 5, March 25, 1993].

Chapter 5
The Employer Role in Financing Health Care for Retirees

G. Lawrence Atkins

The growing pressure on employers who finance health benefits for retirees is evidence of an emerging conflict over the responsibility for financing the health care of older Americans. Modifications in the employer commitment for retiree health, in combination with government cuts in Medicare, are gradually shifting the burden of costs to retirees. The long-term solution is not to protect retirees by shoring up the employer role, because that role already has expanded far beyond the dimensions envisioned by most employers when retiree health benefits were first adopted. The trend now is toward a reduction in that role. It is more likely that comprehensive health care reform will set forces in motion to encourage and enable employers to restructure and reduce the role they now play.

In many ways, the crisis that has emerged, particularly the conflicts now being played out in the courts between retirees and former employers, results from a clash of management and worker expectations. What workers want and need in the way of health benefits in retirement is most likely not what management intended or what is realistic over the long term. By the same token, the benefits that employers could provide easily would not be adequate for the long-term needs of retirees.

For decades, these differences in expectations went largely unnoticed. Then, in the late 1970s and early 1980s, a series of recessions forced widespread corporate downsizing, aggressive early retirement incentives, and, in some industries, a dramatic increase in the number of retirees per active worker. These things all placed a tremendous burden on the remaining productive capacity. At the same time, a continuous 5-to-6-percent real annual growth in health care costs, lengthening lifespans for retirees, and Medicare reductions that shifted costs to employer plans helped make rising retiree health costs noticeable for employers. On top of this trend, an increase in corporate merger and acquisition activity and bankruptcies of large corporations highlighted the high costs, lack of funding, and benefit insecurity of retiree health.

The final straw has been the financial accounting standard on post-retirement benefits (FAS 106), effective January 1993. FAS 106 requires employers to account on the corporate balance sheet for projected health liabilities for retired and active workers, offset by any assets reserved for their use. Their resulting awareness of the immensity of these long-term obligations has moved many employers to reduce or eliminate the promise to active workers and to limit the benefit for retirees. Although most employers remain committed to these benefits in some form, an opportunity to contain or reduce the long-run obligation in the context of overall reform inevitably will precipitate widespread changes.

The gap between the expectations of retirees who have employer health benefits and the employer's limited capacity to meet these expectations raises important questions about the wisdom of attaching retiree health benefits to employment. Success by employers in limiting their share of the future retirement health burden, however, will not reduce the overall burden itself. The residual costs will have to be met in the future, either from the limited retirement incomes of future retirees or from government funding. These large redistributional questions are the crux of the retiree health financing issue to be tackled in the health care reform debate.

Role of Retiree Health in Financing Care

Employer-provided benefits are an important part of the financing of health care for retirees overall, but they play a more significant role for pre-Medicare-aged retirees than for those persons enrolled in Medicare. For substantial subgroups of retirees, employer-provided benefits are the major source of health care financing. The importance of retiree health benefits to various groups of retirees is a function of the extent of coverage and the level of financing.

Retiree Health Coverage

Roughly half of all retirees in the United States have some employer-provided retiree health coverage, according to data from the 1987 National Medical Expenditure Survey (NMES). Employer-provided coverage is the second leading source of health insurance coverage for retirees, after Medicare. In 1987, of the 22 million retirees aged 55 and older, 38 percent had coverage from a former employer, another 10 percent had coverage through a spouse's employment-related plan, and 32 percent purchased individual coverage, whereas 19 percent had no private coverage (see Table 5.1) (Monheit and Schur 1989).

Early retirees rely most on employer-based coverage. According to NMES, employment-related health benefits were the dominant source of coverage of the 5.5 million retirees aged 55-64 in 1987: 51 percent were covered as policyholders and 17 percent as dependents under an employer plan; only 16 percent had individual coverage; whereas another 16 percent were without private coverage (Monheit and Schur 1989).

TABLE 5.1   Health Insurance Coverage of Retirees Aged 55 and Older: 1987[a]

		Sources of Private Health Insurance Coverage (Percent of Total Retirees)			
Age	Number of Retirees (millions)	Employment-Related (Policyholder)	Employment-Related (Dependent)	Other Private Coverage	No Private Coverage
55-59	1.7	50.1	20.6	11.2	18.1
60-64	3.8	51.9	15.0	17.5	15.6
65-69	5.2	40.3	11.1	29.7	19.0
70-74	4.8	37.1	7.6	38.7	16.6
75+	6.4	28.1	4.9	43.5	23.6
55-64	5.5	51.3	16.7	15.6	16.4
65+	16.5	34.6	7.7	37.7	20.1
Total	22.0	38.8	9.9	32.1	19.1

[a]*Source:* Monheit A, Schur C. *Health Insurance Coverage of Retired Persons,* National Medical Expenditure Survey Research Findings 2. National Center for Health Services Research and Health Care Technology Assessment. (DHHS Publication No. (PHS) 89-3444.) Rockville, MD: U.S. Public Health Service. September 1989; see Table 2.

More recent data analyzed by the Employee Benefits Research Institute (EBRI) from the Census Bureau's 1992 Current Population Survey (CPS) show some decline in employer-provided coverage for early retirees aged 55-64. Of the 3 million retirees that EBRI counts in this age group, 42 percent have direct employer-provided insurance, 17 percent have coverage through a spouse's employer, and 18 percent have purchased private coverage (see Table 5.2) (Foley 1993).

Retirees aged 65 and older were more likely to purchase an individual Medigap policy than to be covered under an employer plan. Of the 24 million Medicare beneficiaries who no longer were working in 1987, 41 percent had private policies that were not employment related, 25 percent had no insurance, and only 21 percent had their own employment-related coverage, whereas 12 percent had employment-related coverage through a spouse, and 2.4 percent had coverage as an active worker (see Table 5.3) (Monheit and Schur 1989).

The EBRI estimates from the 1992 CPS survey show a similar pattern for the 65 and older population but indicate some erosion in employer

TABLE 5.2   Health Insurance Coverage of the Population Aged 55-64 in 1991[a]

Age 55-64 by Work Status	Total (millions)	Employer Coverage (Self)	Employer Coverage (Spouse)	Sources of Private Health Insurance Coverage (Percent of Total in Age Group)				
				Other Private	Total Public	Medicaid	No Health Insurance
Working	13.0	61.2	13.5	12.1	7.6	1.3	10.8
Retired	3.0	41.7	17.1	17.7	24.8	4.3	11.8
Other Activity/ Could not find work	5.1	8.1	33.5	15.2	38.7	18.5	16.0
Total	21.1	45.7	18.6	13.6	17.4	5.8	12.4

[a]Source: Foley J. Sources of Health Insurance and Characteristics of the Uninsured. Analysis of the March 1992 Current Population Survey. Special Report SR-16 and Issue Brief Number 133. Washington, DC: Employee Benefit Research Institute. January 1993; see Table 24.

TABLE 5.3   Private Health Insurance Coverage of the Population Aged 65 and Older Who Have Medicare in 1987[a]

Age	Number of Persons with Medicare (millions)	Sources of Private Health Insurance Coverage (Percent of Total in Age Group)						
		Retiree	Employment-Related Coverage			Other Private Medicaid	No Private Insurance
			Dependent of Retiree	Active Worker	Dependent of Active Public		
65-69	8.9	23.2	12.6	5.8	2.6	33.0	22.7
70-74	7.4	23.8	11.9	1.1	0.8	41.3	21.1
75+	10.8	16.3	7.8	0.5	0.6	46.3	28.5
Total	27.1	20.6	10.5	2.4	1.3	40.6	24.6

Source: Monheit A, Schur C. Health Insurance Coverage of Retired Persons. National Medical Expenditure Survey Research Findings 2. National Center for Health Services Research and Health Care Technology Assessment. (DHHS Publication No. (PHS) 89-3444.) Rockville, MD: U.S. Public Health Service. September 1989; see Table 5.

TABLE 5.4   Private Health Insurance Coverage of the Population aged 65+ 1991[a,b]

	Total (millions)	Sources of Health Insurance Coverage (Percent of Total in Age Group – Duplicated Counts)					
		Employer Coverage	Other Private	Medicare	Medicaid	Champus/ VA	No Health Insurance
Age 65+	30.6	33.1	34.7	96.0	9.5	3.8	0.9

[a] *Source:* Foley, J. *Sources of Health Insurance and Characteristics of the Uninsured.* Analysis of the March 1992 Current Population Survey. Special Report SR-16 and Issue Brief Number 133. Washington, DC: Employee Benefit Research Institute. January 1993; see Table 1.

	Total (millions)	Sources of Health Insurance Coverage[b] (Percent of Total in Age Group – Author's Unduplicated Estimates)						
		Medicare Only	Medicare plus Employer	Medicare plus Other Private	Medicare plus Medicaid /Champus	Private Insurance Only	Medicaid/ Champus /VA Only	No Health Insurance
Age 65+	30.6	22.5	29.2	32.1	12.2	2.7	0.4	0.9

[b] *Source:* Author's estimates from J. Foley, EBRI Issue Brief Number 133; Tables 1 and 5.

coverage for this age group as well. Of the 30 million persons aged 65 and older in 1992, 29 percent had group health insurance in addition to Medicare (compared to 34 percent in the 1987 survey), 32 percent had private individual insurance in addition to Medicare, and 35 percent had Medicare only or Medicare and Medicaid (see Table 5.4: Foley 1993 and author's estimates).

Retiree Health Financing

Employer plans provide a varying proportion of total financing for health care to early retirees and Medicare-eligible retirees. Because payments from employer plans for health care services are broken out by age group but not by employment status, it is difficult to distinguish employer plan payments for services to early retirees from those to active workers. Employer plans are the most significant source of health care payment for the older population (aged 55-64), because over half (55 percent) of this population is still in the labor force, and the majority of those retired have employer-provided health benefits as the primary payer and no Medicare coverage. Among this age group, the primary source of payment for 66 percent of the hospital discharges in 1987 and 48 percent of the physician office visits in 1985 was private insurance (Blue Cross, prepaid plans, or other commercial insurance), most of it, presumably, employer-provided. By contrast, among those aged 65 and older, private insurance was the primary source of payment for only four percent of hospital discharges and 31 percent of physician office visits (see Tables 5.5 and 5.6) (Van Nostrand et al. 1993). For this age group, private insurance in total accounts for less than 10 percent of personal health expenditures in 1987. Most private spending by those aged 65 and over is not from insurance but, rather, through out-of-pocket payments, largely for long-term care. Nearly 60 percent of private spending for the elderly is for nursing homes and other care, almost all uninsured (Senate Committee on Aging 1991).

Although employer plans are a significant source of acute care financing for early retirees, they play a minor role for Medicare enrollees. As a group, retirees rely much less heavily on employer-provided benefits than other groups because, at best, only half of retirees are covered, and Medicare dominates hospital and physician payments for those 65 aged and older. Individuals and families already bear a substantial out-of-pocket burden for retiree health care, and, with shrinking coverage from employer-based plans, this self-financing of care by the elderly is likely to increase.

TABLE 5.5   Hospital Discharges for Persons Aged 55 and Older by Principal Source of Payment, 1987[a]

Age	Total Discharges (millions)	Expected Principal Source of Payment (Percent of Total Discharges)						
		Medicare	Medicaid	Blue Cross/ Blue Shield	Other Commercial Insurance	Workers Compensation	Self-Pay	Other or No Charge
55-64	4.0	16.1	6.5	25.4	40.5	1.5	5.2	4.8
65+	10.4	93.4	0.9	1.1	3.0	0.7	0.5	0.4

[a]Source: Van Nostrand JF, Furner SE, Suzman R, eds. Health Data on Older Americans: United States, 1992. Washington, DC: U.S. Public Health Service, National Center for Health Statistics. 1993. Vital Statistics 3(27):219; see Table 6.

TABLE 5.6   Physician Office Visits by Persons Aged 55 and Older by Principal Source of Payment, 1987[a]

Age	Total Visits (millions)	Expected Principal Source of Payment (Percent of Total Visits)					
		Medicare	Medicaid	Blue Cross/ Blue Shield	Other Commercial Insurance	Prepaid Plan	Self-Pay
55-64	75.0	9.2	5.4	17.3	22.8	7.5	48.1
65+	130.5	71.4	8.2	15.4	10.2	4.9	32.7

[a]Source: Van Nostrand JF, Furner SE, Suzman R, eds. Health Data on Older Americans: United States, 1992. Washington, DC: U.S. Public Health Service, National Center for Health Statistics. 1993 Vital Statistics 3(27):220; see Table 7.

Rationale for an Employer Role

Origins of Retiree Health

In its early years, the rationale for employer-based retiree health benefits was that it was a simple benefit to provide with few reasons not to provide it. It was a benefit that emerged, largely without design or intent, through the collective bargaining over benefits in the 1950s and 1960s. In the context of providing early retirement pensions, the extension of the active workers' health insurance into retirement was viewed as an important benefit for retirees, and one that cost the employer little or nothing. Medical benefits were often viewed by employers as a "throwaway" in collective bargaining, because the cost was such a small portion of total compensation (Kelly 1985). With relatively few retirees, comparatively small health benefit costs, and a philosophy that American manufacturing would dominate world markets forever, the idea of financing retiree health from future income seemed reasonable. The employer obligation became even less significant with the enactment of Medicare in 1965. Until the early 1980s, employers rarely even measured or cared about the separate cost of the medical benefits provided for retirees.

For workers, the implied promise of lifetime health benefits, particularly until Medicare eligibility, became an increasingly important aspect of retirement security. Highly skilled workers who were in demand and had become most sophisticated about benefits were aware of health benefits in their retirement package, and large companies in established industries were willing to provide such benefits to attract and retain talented workers (Abrahams 1993). With the growing use of age-rated and experience-rated insurance premiums, the opportunity for a worker to continue in the employers' group indefinitely became increasingly important. The idea of lifetime coverage under an affordable policy without regard to the worker's or spouse's current or future health conditions provided peace of mind for workers who were near retirement. For early retirees, health benefits could be worth more than the pension, and, for many, the availability of retiree health benefits was a significant or even deciding factor in the decision to take early retirement (McIntyre 1993).

Employers adopted retiree health benefits because they needed them to make their retirement packages work, because they helped in collective bargaining, because they were attractive to labor in competitive labor markets, and because the costs were rarely significant—a few retirees were simply continued in their health plan. The benefit was viewed as an extension of the health benefit in a world of relatively low-cost health benefits. Had it been viewed properly and valued as a retirement benefit, it might never have been adopted, particularly with its original design.

General Rationale for Retirement Benefits

The logic for connecting retiree health benefits with employment is related to the logic for financing any retirement benefits through work. Because the phenomenon of retirement is viewed in industrial society as a consequence of work, it is appropriate to connect the income for retirement to the productive output of work.

That retirement benefits are employment-based means several things. First, they are "earnings related" to protect workers against the loss of their earning capacity. With widespread industrialization in the early twentieth century and the separation of workers from control over the means of production, workers could be involuntarily severed from their jobs, lose all capacity to generate income, and become public wards. Taking a small portion of the returns from production to guarantee income security was viewed as a reasonable way to reduce the public burden and to improve the worker's security and productivity on the job.

Second, retirement benefits are employment based in that they are financed through labor productivity. The justification for tapping returns on labor to pay for retirement traditionally takes one of two forms. Under the "human depreciation" concept that was advanced by the labor movement, the cost of maintaining the worker during *and* after the active working life was viewed as a cost of production. Human capital that was depleted through use should be depreciated by putting aside small amounts of money (in the form of health and retirement benefits) toward its maintenance and eventual replacement. In effect, the worker was owed a secure retirement in exchange for having been worn out. Under the "deferred wage theory," workers who otherwise would be unable to save for their own retirements could collectively forego cash wages during their active working life to finance retirement (McGill 1984).

Third, retirement benefits are employment based in that they can serve as tools for employers in meeting objectives for labor supply and productivity. Pensions often have been designed to attract and retain skilled labor in competitive labor markets, to reduce turnover, and to reward loyal employees. Because turnover is costly to employers, the benefits of a more productive and more stable workforce offset the added costs and then some of the pensions (Lazear 1982; Blinder 1982).

Pension and retiree health benefits also have been used to encourage and enable older workers to retire, to create openings for younger workers, and to increase overall productivity. Many established pension programs, including Social Security and the Federal Civil Service Retirement System, had their origins in efforts to reduce the number of "superannuated" workers. Recently, pension and health benefits have been offered to younger populations of older workers to induce early retirement, particularly during downsizing. The use of attractive benefits to encourage early retirement has grown as various overt forms of forced retirement, such as mandatory retirement ages, have been blocked through amendments to the Age Discrimination in Employment Act.

Weaknesses in the Rationale for Retirement Benefits

The rationale for any employer-based retirement benefit is based on conflicting objectives that reduce the capacity of the system to finance retirement and raise questions about the wisdom of an employment-based system. Linking benefits to specific employers and periods of employment furthers the labor supply goals of employers at the expense of the retirement income goals of workers and society. At the one extreme, labor supply goals would be best served by a benefit that vested only at retirement and was related purely to length of service with the last employer. At the other extreme, retirement income is best provided through a program like Social Security that relates benefits solely to lifetime earnings and is unaffected by anomalies in employment history.

This conflict has been increasingly resolved, especially since the enactment of the Employee Retirement Income Security Act of 1974 (ERISA), through legislation to strengthen the delivery of retirement income benefits. Employers have been forced to accrue pensions more evenly over a working career, to minimize disparities in pension benefits between low- and high-paid workers, to vest benefits earlier in the working career, to fund vested benefits fully, and to provide some degree of portability of benefits for workers who leave and go to another job. Employers have found that their flexibility to construct retirement income packages that favor loyal employees or highly compensated employees has become increasingly constrained, and, as a consequence, they have tended to reduce their commitment to traditional forms of retirement benefits.

The linkage of retirement benefits with specific employers causes a poor distribution in both benefits and costs. Retiree benefits are distributed on the basis of employment history rather than on lifetime earnings or needs. The employment relationship produces deficiencies in coverage, vesting, benefit delivery, and equity in outcome not found in a public program such as Social Security, which bases benefits on lifetime earnings without regard to employer and distributes costs equitably among employers as a function of total compensation.

Without prefunding, the retiree who no longer makes a productive contribution to the employer must be financed from the productive output of active workers, and that financing must continue over the retiree's remaining life, regardless of the employer's profitability during that time. Costs of financing old age are distributed as a function of each employer's workforce demographics rather than as a function of labor productivity. Where an employer's retirees outnumber active workers, where an employer's output is insufficient to finance the benefits, or where an employer ceases to operate, it may become impossible to finance the benefits.

Weaknesses of Retiree Health as an Employer Benefit

The rationale for retiree health as a retirement benefit is even weaker. Essentially, retiree health is an unreformed pre-ERISA benefit that meets neither the employee's retirement income goals nor the employer's labor supply goals. It was not conceived as a stand-alone retirement benefit but evolved, instead, from an indefinite extension of an active worker's health benefit into retirement. It many ways, it resembles a severance benefit more than a retirement benefit.

In the past, its weakness as a retirement benefit has been that it often accrued entirely upon eligibility for a pension, and indiscriminately provided full benefits to short-service workers who reach retirement, sometimes depriving long-service workers of benefits if they left the job before retirement. Because retirement was the only test, the responsibility and cost of a retiree's health care were borne fully by the last employer. At the same time, the benefit had the same value for all employees unrelated to compensation or length of service, thus long- and short-service retiring employees received equal benefits, weakening the benefit's value as a tool to encourage worker loyalty.

Recently, some employers have modified their retiree health benefits to relate them more directly to their labor supply goals. A survey released in 1992 by A. Foster Higgins indicated that 11 percent of the 2409 employers surveyed had tightened their eligibility for retiree health benefits in the previous two years (e.g., by relating benefits to years of service), and another 10 percent were planning to do so by 1994 (Foster Higgins 1992). Another survey by the Wyatt Company found that 20 of the top 50 industrial companies in the United States restrict coverage based on age, length of service, date of hire, date of retirement, or some other factor (The Wyatt Company 1992).

Poor Distribution of the Financial Burden

Retirement income benefits can be rationalized for the employment relationship by accruing and funding them over the worker's active life and, thus, relating their cost to the active worker's productivity. Retiree health expenses, however, are realized only after the worker retires. Although the FAS 106 accounting rules require that liability be accounted for on an accrual basis over the worker's active life, the actual cash outlay for retiree health is rarely prefunded. In this way, the cash outlay remains a post-retirement expense. As a consequence, companies' costs in relation to active worker compensation are entirely a function of the ratio of retirees to active workers. Those companies that have young workers and few retirees, either temporarily as start-up companies or permanently because of the nature of their employment, devote only a small portion of compensation to retiree health costs. Those companies that have high ratios of retirees to active workers, either because of the natural aging of their workforce or a reduction in force combined with aggressive early retirement programs, devote substantial portions of compensation to retiree health costs.

Retiree health therefore is something that makes the least sense as an employee benefit. Companies that have the greatest responsibility for providing the benefit often are least able to. It is easy for companies to promise substantial retiree health benefits when they have few retirees. At the time when retirees begin to receive benefits, however, some companies may become unable to deliver them. Financially troubled companies often are left with huge retiree health costs as a result of downsizing and end up bearing these costs on a reduced productive base. Companies with large numbers of retirees may be driven to bankruptcy by the burden of unfunded pension and severance benefits combined with retiree health benefits. In the end, the companies either reduce or eliminate these benefits in the process of restructuring.

No particular social purpose can be served in distributing these costs unevenly across companies. If the intent is to finance retirement on the productive output of the economy, then to clump retiree health costs in the segment of the economy that has the oldest or most financially insecure companies is counterproductive. In effect, the present system finances retirement disproportionately through the manufacturing base, particularly through the core-industry manufacturing base that recently has been forced to downsize so substantially, with little impact on retail and service industries that now provide few or no retiree health benefits.

To the extent that the uneven distribution of total health costs across industries and types of employers impairs the international competitiveness of some American manufacturing industries, retiree health costs can be considered a compounding factor. Whether high health benefit costs have contributed to a lack of competitiveness or whether the lack of competitiveness has contributed to high health benefit costs is controversial. At least one school of thought holds that large manufacturing companies that matured in earlier decades in a protected domestic market showed little resistance at that time to providing elaborate and expensive health benefits for workers, because the costs could be passed on easily to consumers in markets where an oligopoly of suppliers controlled prices. The introduction of these companies into highly competitive world markets in the late 1970s and 1980s highlighted these health obligations—particularly retiree health—as a substantial irreducible factor in the cost of production. Other industries that always were in competitive world markets, and those that were in highly competitive domestic markets, never acquired these benefit obligations to begin with (Brailer et al. 1991). In any case, the net effect has been to place a tremendous burden on American manufacturers that must find ways to become more competitive in current markets.

Unpredictability of Costs

Funding health benefits over the worker's active life would be nearly impossible for most employers today because the value and costs of the benefits are constantly changing and are largely unpredictable. Although FAS 106 has established conventions to set values on liabilities (for accounting purposes only), these conventions may no longer relate to the factors that now drive actual expenses.

To begin with, the precise scope of benefits is influenced by a conflict between retirees' and employers' perceptions of the benefit. Retirees see the benefit in terms of coverage of medical treatment, whereas employers view it in terms of the costs of care. A static benefit for retirees is one that continues to cover a specified set of conditions and treatments at the current nominal level of copayments and deductibles. Contrary to this, employers view this definition of benefits as dynamic—as a package that increases in real value over time not only as the cost of treatment increases but also as the nature and quality of treatment grow. New and more elaborate medical procedures are added or substituted for earlier forms of treatment and, as more effective and less risky procedures are developed, a greater proportion of patients can be treated. All this expansion in treatment eventually is encompassed within the existing definitions of coverage.

Employers would prefer a commitment that provides a set amount of real value over time. As the real value and cost of the package increase, employers feel justified in raising the costsharing in the plan to offset some of the growing value. In fact, most employers—even those who adopt substantial cost sharing features—continue to finance most of the cost and value increases in the plan. Most employers will adjust deductibles and copayments for inflation in an effort to maintain the real value of the existing costsharing. Even when they undertake more aggressive efforts to add new premiums or increase other costsharing for more than inflation, employers still are unlikely to allocate an equal share of the cost increases to retirees.

Even without this conflict over the scope of the benefits, other aspects of retiree health make it difficult to prefund the benefit accurately. Like any cash benefit, health care costs in the distant future are difficult to predict. In addition to this normal uncertainty, there is the added one of trying to predict changes in health conditions and treatments. Where benefits are coordinated with Medicare, the potential for substantial unpredictable changes in that program add another dimension of uncertainty. For individuals who split their working careers among a number of employers, it is impossible to subdivide the health benefit to enable portions of it to accrue through separate employers without first converting it to a cash equivalent. Finally, because the benefit is never vested by statute, it can, in certain circumstances, be reduced or eliminated legally, making it difficult to predict the liabilities and, therefore, making it inefficient to prefund.

The consequence of not accruing and not prefunding the benefit over a workers' active career is that all actual expense is borne once workers retire and continues to be borne as long as the retiree remains alive, even though the liabilities may have been accounted for previously under FAS 106. This structure provides neither the predictability that the employer needs nor the security that employees and retirees need. Employers already have begun to resolve this problem by limiting their liability. Retirees are likely to respond with greater pressure to guarantee coverage. It is only a matter of time before this growing conflict forces a radical change in the employer-provided retiree health benefit.

Options for Restructuring the Employer Role

Employers are wrestling with the uncertain future costs of retiree health benefits, the need to manage liabilities, and, to the extent that it is still necessary, the need to deal with FAS 106. Those who have significant liabilities have a strong incentive to limit them either by redistribution to other employers or by transfer to retirees. Employees and retirees are looking for some assurance that the benefit (or something of equal value) will be there in the future, no matter what their health status, so that their health care bills can be paid. The health care reform process now under way offers the best hope for restructuring responsibilities and costs.

For most employers, the problem with retiree health costs is not the annual expense but the size of the future liability and the resultant impact on corporate balance sheets. Although health care is the most rapidly growing input cost, it still is not a significant one for most employers, compared to other compensation costs. Chamber of Commerce data show that, on an expense basis in 1990, active workers' medical benefits were only a little over seven percent of payroll on average in 1990 (a little over eight percent for manufacturers), or $2358 per worker, and retiree medical benefits were only one percent of payroll (almost one-and-one-half percent for manufacturers), or $323 per worker (Piacentini and Foley 1992). Unlike expenses, however, liabilities may be significant compared to company assets or equity. Retiree medical liabilities, according to a Hay-Huggins survey of FAS 106 liabilities of 300 companies, may average almost seven times the company's annual pay-as-you-go expense (Hay Group 1992). In fact, for three percent of the companies surveyed, FAS 106 liabilities were reported to be at least 20 times their annual costs.

Redistributing the Retiree Burden

The poor distribution for payment of the retiree health benefit is the most significant issue for some employers. The redistribution of this burden, however, is a zero sum game for employers as a group. Employers with large retiree health liabilities will benefit from any opportunity to shift toward broad-based financing. Employers with few or no retiree health liabilities could be at a substantial disadvantage with such a shift. Although various approaches to refinancing retiree health benefits would have different distributional results, all refinancing schemes, whether based on new or higher taxes or on community-rated insurance premiums, inherently tax those people who do not provide the benefits now so that others who do provide benefits can be relieved of the burden.

The problem is that although a large number of employers have significant FAS 106 retiree health liabilities in relation to their net worth, the majority of employers either have more manageable liabilities or have no liabilities at all. In fact, most employers now provide no financing for retiree health. An estimated 57 percent of medium and large private firms, 42 percent of state and local governments, and 83 percent of small private establishments provide no retirement health benefits or require that retirees pay the entire cost (Piacentini and Foley 1992). For this reason, redistribution will be difficult politically.

In the end, only a limited number of ways can effectively redistribute the burden: payroll tax financing that spreads the cost in relation to overall compensation rather than linking it to the demographics of an individual employer's workforce; or community-based ratings that spread the cost equitably among all premium payers rather than associating costs with the health risk of the individual.

Payroll Tax Options

Payroll tax proposals focus on expanding Medicare, either by lowering the age of eligibility to cover early retirees or by expanding the scope of benefits for those age 65 and older, to eliminate Medigap coverage. One proposal to lower Medicare eligibility to age 60 (H.R.3205) was introduced in the 102nd Congress by House Ways and Means Chairman Dan Rostenkowski. Under this proposal, everyone aged 60 to 64, whether retired or employed, would become eligible for Medicare benefits, with the expansion in eligibility financed by an increase of 0.2 percent (from 1.45 percent to 1.65 percent) in the HI payroll tax rate for employers and employees.

The proposal would have several advantages for employers, with significant early retiree health costs. It would shift a portion of the retiree health costs to the Medicare tax and, by spreading this portion across all employers, would reduce the competitive disadvantage for employers with benefits. By converting a portion of the retiree health obligation to a tax, it also would reduce the amount of liability that had to be offset by assets or that had to be booked under FAS 106. Employers would receive support for the pre-65 health plan participants—working and retired. The extent of support for workers would be substantially lower than that for retirees, because Medicare would probably act only as a secondary payer for workers.

To the extent that the proposal provided federal subsidies for health benefits for early retirees, it could encourage employers to offer early retirement incentives. It also would skew *the subsidies* to companies that had pledged expensive health benefits to gain the productivity improvements associated with downsizing and would skew *the costs* to companies that had avoided taking on the burden in the first place. In this way, the federal government might reward inefficient labor practices and other industrial inefficiencies and penalize the very companies that have operated the most efficiently.

Another approach to expanding Medicare is to improve the benefit for those who already are eligible. This proposal would resemble the Medicare Catastrophic Coverage Act provisions enacted in 1988 and repealed in 1989. Specifically, it would expand the scope of benefits for those who are aged 65 and older, with the intention of providing full coverage under Medicare and eliminating the employer's obligation for retirees once they reach age 65. The Medicare Catastrophic Coverage Act provided employers with a windfall by financing the new benefits entirely through Medicare premium and tax increases for the elderly. An alternative would be to use an increase in the Medicare payroll tax to finance all or part of the expansion and then redistribute retiree health costs among employers, regardless of their share of retirees.

Eliminating company obligations for post-65 health benefits would enable employers to focus exclusively on early retirement benefits, which usually are more directly under the employer's control and are related to the employer's own workforce needs and decisionmaking. The fact that the benefits would be time limited (granted only to age 65) would make the total cost of the benefit more predictable in that the unknown factors—life expectancy and the uncertainty of future Medicare benefits— would be removed from the equation and the time horizon for estimates could be shortened. In addition, the affordability of the benefits could be tied more directly to the employer's larger decisions about early retirement packages.

Proposals for Pooling and Community Rating

Proposals to restructure the insurance market—to pool health risk better or to have community-rated premiums—offer opportunities to redistribute the burden of retiree health costs. Proposals considered by President Clinton's Health Care Task Force for health insurance purchasing cooperatives (or health alliances) suggest community rating to pool health risk and to reduce adverse selection incentives. These prospects, however, raise a number of questions about the financing of health care for pre- and post-65 retirees.

To implement health alliances like those designed by the Jackson Hole Group that merely provide affordable individual and small group coverage could easily prompt a wholesale abandonment of employer-provided retiree health benefits for today's active workers. Because the health alliance would guarantee insurance at an affordable community-rated premium to individuals with no regard for health risk, retirees then could be assured of obtaining adequate health benefits through the health alliance and no longer would have to depend solely on the coverage available through the employer's group. Employers could substitute a supplemental pension benefit calculated to pay health alliance premiums, assuming that pension benefits could be increased sufficiently under the tax code limits on contributions and benefits. Although employers might be reluctant to terminate current retirees' health coverage for legal reasons, there would be little reason to continue promising retiree health coverage to active workers. It is most likely that retirees would lose value in the conversion from health to pension benefits, because pensions would be unlikely to match or keep pace with health alliance premiums. Employers would benefit from the ability to prefund this pension obligation and to manage its liabilities.

Although the Health Alliance would be attractive to employers as a way to manage their retiree costs better, it would not necessarily reduce those costs. For the health alliance to actually reduce an employer's retiree costs it would have to do three things: use community-rated or modified community-rated premiums to redistribute the retiree burden to employers with younger workers and to others in the community; offer a standard benefit below the level of current retiree benefits to share a greater portion of the cost with retirees themselves; and slow the rate of growth in future health care costs.

Community rating is a highly controversial aspect in the health alliance proposal. Community rating that included older workers and retirees in the rating pool could be expected to raise premiums substantially for low-risk individuals and groups that have benefited for many years from experience-rated premiums. Small employers currently insured and anticipating lower premiums from the development of health alliances could find that community-rated premiums actually were higher. Employers forced to sponsor health benefits for the first time could find these premiums to be well beyond their economic reach. Federal subsidies for small employers that financed premiums in excess of a specified threshold ultimately would transfer some portion of the added cost of retirees to the federal budget.

To the extent that employers continued to make contributions, retirees or employers themselves could be required to pay a portion of the cost differential through modified community ratings that based premiums on age or other demographic or risk factors. Employers that chose to "buy" their retirees into the health alliance might be required to pay an age-adjusted premium. This also would have to apply to older individuals not in groups, to prevent employers from terminating retiree health coverage and letting their retirees purchase coverage as individuals. Employers that chose to pay modified community-based rates would still realize savings from recharacterizing the benefit as a cash benefit with prefunding, from the greater costsharing in the health alliance standard benefit, and from any of the health alliance's administrative savings or cost-containment successes. They would not realize as much benefit, however, from a redistribution of the health care costs attributed to their active worker/retiree ratio.

The main impediment to redistribution of the retiree health burden is the reluctance of lower risk groups, younger individuals, and employers without substantial retiree health costs to pay higher premiums to offset costs of early retirement programs adopted voluntarily by employers with larger retiree health burdens.

Managing Liabilities Without Redistribution

Even if no significant redistribution of costs occurs, many questions remain for employers who will need to cope with this liability in the future—particularly for those who continue to provide benefits for currently active workers. First, the liability will need to become more predictable and manageable. Employers are now attempting to tame their retiree health liabilities (1) by converting the current open-ended health benefit to a predictable and measurable cash benefit; (2) by accruing the benefit over a working life or at least relating the benefit to the employee's length of service; and/or (3) by increasing retirees' costsharing. Second, employers will need some way to offset retiree health liabilities with tax-favored assets. Again, by converting the liabilities to cash obligations, it becomes easier to prefund the benefit through a pension program, given that contributions for employees will not exceed the IRS section 415 limits on tax-favored contributions and benefits.

Trade-Offs for Retirees

To convert retiree health obligations to cash results in many trade-offs for retirees. Retirees are at a disadvantage in that cash benefits, which tend to be static and maintain a nominal value over time, are rarely adequate enough to replace health benefits, which are dynamic and grow in both nominal and real terms. For retirees to avoid a substantial loss from this exchange, they need to have increased or indexed cash payments. Cash benefits need to be increased more to compensate for the loss of tax credits as the tax-free health benefit is converted to taxable cash. Retirees can gain some advantage from the conversion to cash benefits, however. To the extent that cash benefits can be accrued over the working life, can be vested and prefunded, and can be more portable than health benefits, retirees may find that, on balance, they receive more security and fungibility of the benefit, even if the cash value is not equivalent to the health benefit value.

Who Should Pay for Retirees?

The question of who should pay for retiree health care was answered partially in 1965 when Medicare was enacted to spread the hospital and physician expenses for the elderly equitably (as a percentage of compensation) across the productive output of the country. The Medicare act acknowledged the difficulties that the elderly encountered in financing this cost through private insurance or other private retirement vehicles—but it went only part way. Medicare left almost half of the expenses for the post-65 and over population uncovered, the most significant being prescription drugs and long-term care, and it never addressed the costs of health care for younger retirees. The holes in Medicare are plugged by the elderly and by their families, by employer-provided and individual early retirement, by Medigap insurance policies, and by Medicaid, a federally funded program for those people who have no resources. This patchwork of coverage and costsharing places burdens on employers and individuals, however, and seems temporary at best.

Recently, soaring projections of future health care costs have made it even more difficult to resolve the question of who should pay for retirees. Long-term care costs have moved beyond the economic reach of most families, impoverishing large numbers of the elderly and placing an increasing strain on the ailing Medicaid program that already finances more than 40 percent of nursing home expenses. Prescription drug costs are consuming growing portions of the budgets of the chronically ill elderly, and employer-provided retiree health programs have come under increasing scrutiny from their sponsors as rising costs and projections of liabilities have begun to affect the financial health of many large corporations. Although Medicare expansion may seem the most equitable way to finance these costs, within a decade Medicare will be unable to finance its current package of benefits on its prevailing tax rate, and any congressional enthusiasm for Medicare expansion has been dampened severely by the painful repeal of the Medicare catastrophic benefit soon after its enactment. In short, no sector of the economy seems prepared to step forward to cover the growing gap in health care financing for retirees. In this context, what is the proper role for employers?

Early Retirement

The strongest case for employers to finance health benefits is to make them available in early retirement packages. In the absence of accessible and affordable individual insurance for older persons, the ability to continue in the employer's group can be worth more to an early retiree than the pension benefit. The health benefit is a necessary element in a package that makes early retirement attractive to an older worker. It also enables employers to reduce capacity in a humane way.

More significantly, from a national policy perspective, early retirement is viewed as a convenience to the employer that runs counter to the public good. It is inappropriate to finance early retirement through public funds, because able-bodied workers are removed prematurely from the workforce, the tax base is reduced, and the demand for public benefits is consequently increased. As a device used to lower the cost of production for a specific firm, the entire cost of early retirement should be financed through the productivity of that firm and not by its competitors.

The problem with early retirement health benefits is that they have been overvalued by retirees and undervalued by employers. Retirees who act on the offer of health benefits assume that these benefits will continue throughout retirement. The fact that employers do not vest or fund the benefits and reserve the right to modify or terminate them in the future adds an element of risk that retirees often discount in their calculations. At the same time, when firms calculate the cost of a reduction in force or a plant shutdown, they rarely account for the true cost of the future stream of health benefits that they pledge in early retirement packages. This undervaluation has contributed to shutdowns, downsizing, and early retirement offerings that have cost companies far more than they have saved.

If employers are to continue to finance early retirement health benefits, these valuation issues need to be addressed. On the one hand, promised benefits should be vested at the time that the promise is conveyed. On the other hand, if the benefits are promised as part of a package of deferred compensation, then they should accrue and vest over the working life and become portable with the worker. If they are part of a severance package and accrue fully at the moment when a worker becomes eligible for retirement, then they should vest fully at that point as well.

With vesting comes funding. Without funding, vesting becomes hollow, to be met through creditors' claims in bankruptcy. Without vesting, prefunding has no purpose, because the benefits may never become payable. This combination of events can be made manageable if the early retirement health benefit is treated as severance and is earned, vested, and fully funded at the employee's retirement. In the context of health alliances that could provide affordable insurance for early retirees, the alternative is to convert the promise of health benefits to a cash commitment and then allow it to accrue and fund it over the working life. As a cash benefit, early retirement would be earned, regardless of whether a worker retired early, and could be used to purchase health insurance or could be deferred for other retirement uses.

Medicare Supplementation

The case for employer financing for normal retirement health benefits is not as strong as that for early retirement benefits. From a public policy perspective, normal retirement is a societal phenomenon and not unique to specific employers. A stronger case, therefore, exists for spreading the health costs associated with normal retirement equitably across society's total productive base. To the extent that the public sector draws a limit on its commitment and chooses to split the cost of health care with retirees (through limitations in Medicare coverage or copayments) to meet their other retirement goals, employers may find it necessary to ensure that future retirees have sufficient incomes to pay these out-of-pocket health costs. More appropriately, this begins to resemble a retirement income obligation, not a promise of health benefits. Nonetheless, two significant problems arise when retirement income approaches are used to prefund out-of-pocket health expenses: it is difficult to anticipate the scope of out-of-pocket expenses that the Medicare policy will leave to retirees in the distant future, and, it is difficult to provide a cash benefit that can be indexed adequately to pay rising health care premiums over a retired lifetime. As of early 1993, most conversions of retiree health benefits to cash obligations have left the retirees responsible for any increases above current health care costs.

Controlling costs in private plans or Medicare by shifting growing portions of the costs to retirees and their families is not a viable way to finance retiree health over the long run. This long-term reduction in health coverage will leave future retirement incomes more vulnerable and less valuable, reducing the incentives that employers can offer to make retirement attractive, and increasing popular pressure for an expanded public role in financing health care for retirees.

Given the limited number of retirees aged 65 and older who are covered under employer plans, and given the uncertainties about the adequacy of future employer coverage, an expansion of Medicare coverage along the lines of the repealed Medicare catastrophic package may be appropriate. The failure of this legislation lay in its reliance on the elderly to "self-finance" the expanded coverage, because the catastrophic coverage was not sufficiently valuable on an individual basis to justify the high premiums that some individuals were required to pay. In addition, for retirees who already had employer coverage, the catastrophic act transferred the employer cost to them and gave employers a windfall without giving retirees the added retirement income needed to meet this cost. A more successful expansion of Medicare would be financed in part through a payroll tax or some other method that would capture a portion of the employer's retiree health contributions. Any payroll-tax-financed expansion of Medicare will have to be conditioned, however, on successful efforts to control rising health care costs.

Long-Term Care Financing

The financing of long-term care is a unique and complex problem that has, to date, defied all rational solutions. Although some employers have chosen to organize private group insurance for long-term care that employees may purchase, as yet, no widespread employer interest has been seen in financing long-term care for retirees. For one thing, long-term care expenses are too far removed from the retirement age for the offer of long-term care coverage to operate as a strong inducement for retirement. The costs of long-term care also are high and uncertain and, in the past, have been immune to efforts to control costs, particularly through traditional coverage limitation approaches.

The case against long-term care as an employer-financed benefit is also based on the complexity of the long-term care benefit. Long-term care is one part health services, one part housing, one part custodial services, one part protection of assets for spouses left in the community, and one part estate preservation for heirs. A persuasive rationale for the accumulation of assets over a working life is to prepare for the possibility of substantial long-term care costs late in life. The availability of Medicaid for those who consume their assets on long-term care insures against errors in estimating the amount of assets needed. In this context, long-term care insurance functions to protect those accumulated assets, to support a spouse who still lives in the community, to support the return of the patient to community living after a nursing home stay, or to provide for surviving children. In addition, long-term care insurance can help to finance home-based health care, because there is little such coverage now in Medicaid or Medicare, where home care is preferred over institutionalization. The difficulty in prefunding long-term care needs is that the nature of these needs varies so much for individuals, depending on circumstances that cannot be predicted. It may be more efficient to meet these needs through specific forms of insurance (e.g., for estate preservation) or through general retirement savings (e.g., for supported housing) than to try to meet them all in one package. At least some of these needs (e.g., nursing home or home health care) may be so prevalent at advanced ages and so expensive to meet that some form of social insurance, along with universal coverage and broad financing, would be a better solution.

Conclusion

No simple answer is available to the questions of who should pay for retirees or what the employer's role should be in financing retiree health. In general it makes sense to apply employer financing to where it relates best to the employer's labor force needs. Because employers are somewhat responsible for early retirement and because some employers need to preserve flexibility in managing their workforce, early retirement health benefits should remain their responsibility. Employers should remain free to decide whether or not to provide early retirement benefits; however, those employers choosing to offer early retirment benefits should be obligated to fund or otherwise commit to providing the promised package. With the emergence of health alliances or other forms of market reform, employers should be able to convert the benefit to a cash payment sufficient for the individual retiree to purchase health coverage through the health alliance. To make this commitment manageable, the benefit promise should be time limited until the retiree becomes eligible for Medicare.

Over time, the employer's responsibility for health benefits for retirees aged 65 and older should be phased out and Medicare's package of acute benefits should be expanded to eliminate the need for Medigap plans. To the extent that this expansion is financed through payroll taxes, it simply will replace employer and retiree financing that now comes through retiree health plans. It is inevitable, however, that costsharing with retirees will grow over time as the population ages in the next century. Today's workers should have greater opportunities for employer-financed and self-financed retirement income savings, to prepare for the higher out-of-pocket health costs they will face in the future.

References

Abrahams T. Retiree from McDonnell Douglas. Testimony given before the Select Committee on Aging, U.S. House of Representatives. March 3, 1993.

Blinder AS. Private Pensions and Public Pensions: Theory and Fact. Working Paper No. 902. Cambridge: National Bureau of Economic Research. June 1982.

Brailer D, Hirth R, Kroch E, Landon B, Pauly M, Pierskala W. The Impact of Health Care Spending on United States Industry. The Wharton School, University of Pennsylvania. November 8, 1991.

Foley J. *Sources of Health Insurance and Characteristics of the Uninsured.* Analysis of the March 1992 Current Population Survey. Special Report SR-16 and Issue Brief Number 133. Washington, DC: Employee Benefit Research Institute. January 1993.

Foster Higgins. *1991 Foster Higgins Retiree Health Care Survey.* Princeton: Foster Higgins, 1992.

Hay Group. *Trends in Retiree Medical Benefits.* Philadelphia: Hay/Huggins, 1992.

Kelly P. Welfare Benefit Plans in Corporate Acquisitions and Dispositions. *Real Property, Probate and Trust Journal.* 20:1045; 1985.

Lazear EP. Severance Pay, Pensions, and Efficient Mobility. Working Paper No. 854. Cambridge: National Bureau of Economic Research, 1982.

McGill D. *Fundamentals of Private Pensions,* 5th ed. Homewood, IL: Richard D. Irwin, Inc. 1984.

McIntyre V. Retiree from Unisys Corporation. Testimony given before the Select Committee on Aging, U.S. House of Representatives. March 3, 1993.

Monheit A, Schur C. *Health Insurance Coverage of Retired Persons.* National Medical Expenditure Survey, Research Findings 2. National Center for Health Services Research and Health Care Technology Assessment (DHHS Publication No. (PHS) 89-3444). Rockville, MD: U.S. Public Health Service. September, 1989.

Piacentini JS, Foley JD. *EBRI Databook on Employee Benefits,* 2nd ed. Washington, DC: Employee Benefit Research Institute, 1992.

U.S. Senate. Special Committee on Aging. *Aging America: Trends and Projections,* 1991 ed. Washington, DC: GPO, 1992.

Van Nostrand JF, Furmer SE, Suzman R, eds. *Health Data on Older Americans: United States, 1992.* Washington, DC: U.S. Public Health Service, National Center for Health Statistics. *Vital and Health Statistics,* Series 3, No. 27; January, 1993.

Commentary: Donald C. Snyder

In Chapter Five, G. Lawrence Atkins looks at the rationale for employers to provide retiree health benefits as an employment-based benefit. As an add-on to pensions (to facilitate early retirement programs), these benefits

- Protect workers at retirement;
- Attract and retain workers;
- Act as early retirement incentives.

Atkins concludes that the cost of the current system is not a reasonable burden for a company to bear. He correctly points out that one major problem with the current financing of these benefits is that today's retirees receive benefits from today's workers. These are not prefunded (vested) benefits. A second problem is that a single benefit is given to all workers. It is not based on pay or service at retirement. A third problem is that companies pay uneven amounts and many retirees are uncovered. As companies age and fail, these benefits are being reduced. As a result, retiree health coverage is no longer a secure benefit, neither legally nor morally. A fourth problem is that costs are growing and are unpredictable. The liabilities for these benefits have been highlighted by the Financial Accounting Standards Board's new accounting standard, FAS 106. In light of these conditions, Atkins then proposes some broad policy approaches to restructure the employer's role in providing retiree health benefits.

Background

Historically, many large employers offered retirees health benefits in the 1950s (most plans also provided spouse benefits). In total, these companies probably provided health benefits to the bulk of the 38 percent of

Opinions and conclusions expressed are solely those of the author.

retirees who had health insurance in 1965, as cited by Greer and Hillman in Chapter Seven. It is important to note that when Medicare was passed in 1965, these companies received a large windfall savings; their retiree health benefit plans became "Medigap" (second-payer) programs. So, proposals to lower the Medicare eligibility age, and the accompanying savings, are not unprecedented. Early retiree costs were unaffected by the passage of Medicare in 1965.

As Atkins points out, costs for providing retiree health benefits are low because companies sponsor group policies. These group plans have a much higher value to retirees, however, because individual policy costs are so high. In addition, retirees value this benefit so highly because many individuals who have pre-existing medical conditions could not purchase health insurance.

Retiree health benefits are valuable not only because of the absolute savings to retirees but also because health care is a high-cost expenditure relative to the modest pensions and Social Security income that most retirees receive. Prescription drugs, a high and ongoing expense for many people, can be a significant drain on disposable income. In addition, Medicare benefits have been cut periodically, shifting costs to company sponsors and to retirees. This past history of cuts in Medicare raises the question of just how secure these benefits really are.

Company Costs and Liabilities

Pay-as-you-go costs, accrued liability, and prefunding costs are large for American companies. As of 1993, it is estimated that pay-as-you-go costs for companies already are near $14 billion and 63 percent is for early retirees (author's estimate). The liability for the future stream of benefit payments is $412 billion, and prefunding costs would be around $46 billion (author's estimate).

Recent health care proposals would lower the Medicare eligibility age from 65 to 60. If the Medicare age were lowered, then the pay-as-you-go amount would fall by $5 billion (35 percent), funding costs would fall by $6 billion (17 percent), and liabilities would fall by $123 billion (30 percent). Of this, the liability for current retirees of $155 billion would fall to $119 billion (23 percent) and the liability for active workers of $257 billion would fall to $170 billion (34 percent) (author's estimates). Although these numbers are large, in the aggregate they are modest, compared to corporate profits and assets.

Atkins posits that employers got into this cost and liability situation blindly, found the costs to be unacceptably high, and, consequently, have taken actions to reduce or eliminate these benefits. In this way, companies can reduce their cost/liability exposure. They are free to reduce or eliminate these benefits if they have reserved the right to do so. As the U.S. Government Accounting Office (GAO 1991) has reported, many companies appear to be reducing retiree health benefits, using FAS 106 as an excuse.

It should be noted that FAS 106 does not impact cash flows; it only involves a bookkeeping entry. Many companies making changes to their plans do not have extraordinary numbers of retirees but are reducing health coverage or expenses for active worker plans, which recently has included retirees as well. Current data (see Chapter Four, Table 4.7 in this book) show that retiree plans are now targeted specifically for reductions in benefit coverage or for increases in the costs borne by retirees. These benefits therefore are not secure and have become less so in recent years.

In one sense, this is a puzzling situation because corporations have enjoyed a "pension-funding holiday" as their pension plans have become fully funded. It would seem that more expensive health benefits would be affordable as pension contributions have fallen.

Proposed Reforms

Atkins has proposed a split in responsibility for early-and normal-aged (65 and over) retirees. He proposes that employers pay for retiree health benefits until the Medicare eligibility age of 65. From that point on, the public plan would be responsible. The proposal fits Atkins' description of retiree health benefits as an employment-related benefit, that is, one that serves to attract and retain workers and to enhance early retirement incentives. As Medicare is constituted today, however, it generally is viewed as an inadequate medical benefit package. If Medicare is enhanced, then provision of an early retiree health benefit would seem to be reasonable for business sponsors. How secure, though, would post-age-65 health coverage be? The Medicare promise is not a secure one, and this approach of having no company benefits over age 65 would remove one layer of protection that current retirees now have against further changes.

Atkins' premise that employers should abandon those persons over age 65 is not feasible under the current health care system. Even though companies are cutting retiree health benefits, some benefits are still needed to supplement Medicare. And if the public benefits are cut rather than enhanced, then down the road company plans could pick up some of the lost benefits, by paying for those benefits that Medicare does not support (e.g., prescription drugs and long-term care).

Atkins' proposal covers one important need. Early retirees are especially burdened if they retire from a company that offers no retiree health benefits. If the Medicare age is not lowered, then one way to cover early retirees would be through a COBRA-like extension of benefits up to age 65. This approach, to let employees buy into the active worker plan when they retire, has precedent in multiemployer plans. In 1988, 13 percent of plans offered a retiree health benefit plan with 100 percent of costs paid by the retiree. Of the remaining plans, 38 percent paid all costs, and 49 percent shared the cost with retirees. This COBRA-like extension fits in with Atkins' proposal and would appeal to retirees under the age of 65 who are not covered by a company-sponsored group health plan.

Conclusion

Atkins concludes that today's workers should prepare to bear a larger share of medical expenses in their retirement. This is not a pleasant message, but one that is on target and includes a warning that workers certainly should not overlook in their pre-retirement financial planning.

References

Snyder D. Corporate Retiree Health Benefits Threatened by Financial Pressures. *Review of Business.* 14(2): 1992; 14-17.
Snyder D, Eckert W, Packard M. Multiemployer Health Plan Statistics Show High Costs to Retirees. *Benefits Law Journal* 4 (3): 1991; 367-381.
Thompson L, Snyder D. Employers' Accounting for Postretirement Benefits Other Than Pensions. Statement to FASB, Nov. 3, 1990. Washington, DC: Financial Accounting Standards Board, 1990.
U. S. General Accounting Office. *Employee Benefits: Companies Retiree Health Liabilities Large, Even With Medicare Catastrophic Insurance Savings* (June 14, 1989 - GAO/T-HRD-90-29). Washington, DC: GAO, 1989.
U. S. General Accounting Office. *Retiree Health: Company-Sponsored Plans Facing Increased Costs and Liabilities.* (May 6, 1991 - GAO/T-HRD-91-25). Washington, DC: GAO, 1991.
U. S. General Accounting Office. *Retiree Health Liability Large, Advance Funding Costly.* (June, 1989 - GAO/HRD-89-51). Washington, DC: GAO, 1989.
U. S. General Accounting Office. *Significant Reductions in Corporate Retiree Health Liabilities if Medicare Eligibility Age Lowered to 60.* Testimony prepared for the ERISA Advisory Council, April 28, 1992. Washington, DC: GAO, 1992.

Chapter 6
Long-Term Prospects for Medicare and the Delivery of Retiree Health Benefits

Mark V. Pauly

This chapter presents the challenges in planning health care benefits in retirement posed by the necessity to coordinate those same benefits with Medicare coverage and by the likelihood that the form, extent, and eligibility for coverage provided through the compulsory public Medicare program will change over the long term.[1] The exercise necessarily involves some projection, although not formal estimation, of future Medicare coverage and benefit payments. Predicting that future requires three assumptions. One assumption involves demographics, the rate at which populations grow at different ages and the likely incidence and prevalence of disease among these groups. It is relatively easy to predict future changes in this factor. The second assumption involves the level and rate of change of medical costs or technology. This factor is more difficult to predict, although the annual growth in real health care spending per capita in the United States has moved within a relatively narrow band of four to five percent over decades. The third assumption is the most problematic: What will future Medicare benefit packages include? Will health care reform eliminate Medicare as a separate program and will it, potentially, substitute other kinds of public or mandated coverage for people who retire before the current age of Medicare eligibility? Indeed, one key question is whether long-term prospects of private retiree health benefits will need to be examined.

This chapter posits that private retiree health insurance will continue in the foreseeable future. The basis for this idea is built on projections for Medicare as embodied in current law. The main purpose, however, is to investigate alternative strategies for Medicare and then relate them to the form of health care reform and to private decisions related to retiree benefits. It is difficult enough, as economists and actuaries know all too well, to predict future medical costs with precision; as noted already, however, it is not that difficult to make a rough guess. Predicting what outcomes will arise from an economic system, even one as complex and atypical as the market for medical care, is child's play compared to predicting what the political process will yield over more than thirty-five years.

Indeed, the Clinton health reform package, initially proposed at the end of September, 1993, has (as of this writing) already been modified in important ways. It seems reasonable, therefore, to consider strategies alternative to those in the current Clinton proposal since modifications are virtually certain to continue to be possible.

This chapter also describes possible options for Medicare, without purporting to predict that Medicare policy will move in a particular way. At times, the temptation is to declare what may happen, or, more to the point, what is preferred for Medicare, but the task here is simply to discuss the rationale behind various models of Medicare care reform. It then will be left to the reader to estimate the length of time it will take before policy change is adopted.

Current Cost Projections for Medicare

It has become clear that something must change with Medicare because the current benefit and tax structure for Medicare is no longer fiscally sustainable. Medicare policy needs to be changed from its current form, either in terms of coverage or in terms of Medicare financing, because the Medicare Part A trust fund will be drawn down to zero within the next decade under current law. In addition, the retiree premium for Part B coverage is likely to skyrocket. Once again, the fundamental conclusion is that Medicare has to change.

The part of current Medicare coverage in which the time bomb can be heard ticking and in which the clock is easily observable, is Part A, the section that pays for inpatient hospital bills. Medicare Part A is financed by payroll taxes imposed directly on employees and on the employer's payroll expenditures. These tax receipts then go into a trust fund. At the end of fiscal 1992, the trust fund for Part A had a balance of $121 billion. As Table 6.1 shows, however, the Congressional Budget Office (CBO) expects that balance to erode very rapidly, beginning in fiscal year 1995. Detailed estimates on the components of spending are not available beyond 1998, but the CBO and the actuaries of the Health Care Financing Administration (HCFA) predict that, given current law, the trust fund will be exhausted by approximately the year 2000.

The accounting basis for the problem is simple enough. Ever since the last attempt to "cure" the problem of Part A by raising tax rates, rev-

TABLE 6.1 Medicare Trust Fund: Part A[a]

Outlays by Fiscal Year, in Billions of Dollars	1992	1993	1994	1995	1996	1997	1998
Part A: Hospital Insurance (HI)							
A. Total HI Outlays	82	91.2	102.4	113.8	125.2	138.8	148.6
Annual Growth Rate		11.3%	12.3%	11.2%	10.0%	9.2%	8.7%
Hospitals	68.9	74.4	81.6	89.8	98.4	107.5	116.9
Annual Growth Rate		7.8%	9.7%	10.0%	9.8%	9.2%	8.7%
PPS Hospitals	59.5	63.6	69.3	75.8	82	88.6	94.9
PPS External Hospitals	9.4	10.7	12.3	14.1	18.4	19	22
Hospices	0.8	1	1.2	1.4	1.8	1.8	2
Annual Growth Rate		21.9%	19.8%	17.8%	14.9%	13.8%	14.0%
Home Health	7.1	9.8	12.4	14.7	16.7	18.5	20.2
Annual Growth Rate		37.8%	27.2%	18.7%	13.9%	11.0%	9.3%
Skilled Nursing Facilities	3.7	4.7	5.7	6.4	6.9	7.4	7.9
Annual Growth Rate		28.5%	20.1%	12.8%	8.4%	6.8%	6.4%
Other Part A:	0.3	0.2	0.3	0.2	0.2	0.2	0.2
Annual Growth Rate		-19.8%	0.9%	-2.7%	-2.8%	-9.7%	0.0%
Administration							
(Subject to Appropriation)	1.2	1.2	1.3	1.3	1.4	1.4	1.5
Annual Growth Rate		2.9%	5.0%	4.0%	4.5%	4.0%	3.9%
B. General Part A Information							
Indirect Teaching Payments	3.2	3.4	3.7	4	4.4	4.7	8
Direct Medical							
Education Payments	1.3	1.3	1.3	1.3	1.5	1.5	1.5
Disproportionate Share Payments	2.3	2.4	2.6	2.9	3.1	3.4	3.8
Inpatient Capital Payments	7.2	8.2	9.2	10.3	11.4	12.5	13.8
HI Trust Fund Income	92.9	98	101.8	106.6	111	114.2	116.8
HI Trust Fund Surplus	10.9	6.8	-0.8	-7.2	-14.2	-22.5	-31.8
HI Trust Fund Balance EOY	120.6	127.4	126.7	119.5	105.2	82.7	50.8
Other Part A Data:							
HI Deductible in CY $	$862	$876	$712	$752	$792	$832	$872
Part A FY Enrollment							
(in millions)	34.4	35.1	38.8	36.4	37	37.5	38
PPS Market Basket Increase FY%	4.4%	4.1%	4.1%	4.2%	4.1%	4.0%	3.8%
PPS Update Factor (avg.)	3.0%	2.3%	4.3%	4.5%	4.1%	4.0%	3.8%
Monthly Premium in CY $	$192	$221	$243	$256	$288	$310	$333
Premium Receipts	0.4	0.6	0.7	0.7	0.8	0.9	0.9

[a]*Source:* Congressional Budget Office. Human Resources Cost Estimation Unit. Budget Analysis Division, 1993.

Table 6.2 Medicare Trust Fund: Part B[a]

Outlays by Fiscal Year, in Billions of Dollars	1992	1993	1994	1995	1996	1997	1998
Part B: Supplementary Medical Insurance (SMI)							
A. Total SMI Outlays	50.3	58	57.3	77.7	88.5	100.3	113.4
Annual Growth Rate		15.4%	16.0%	15.4%	14.0%	13.3%	13.0%
Physicians	26.7	31.4	36.6	41.9	46.7	51.8	57.2
Annual Growth Rate		9.4%	15.8%	14.4%	11.5%	10.8%	10.5%
DME and P&O Suppliers	1.7	2	2.3	2.6	2.8	3.3	3.8
Annual Growth Rate		14.4%	13.2%	13.8%	14.1%	14.1%	14.0%
Laboratories (Independent) [b]	1.5	1.8	2.2	2.7	3.4	4.1	5
Annual Growth Rate		17.8%	22.7%	23.0%	22.8%	22.8%	22.4%
Outpatient Hospital	10.6	12.4	14.8	17.4	20.5	24	27.9
Annual Growth Rate		16.7%	18.0%	18.8%	18.4%	18.9%	16.1%
Group Practice Plans and HMOs	3.8	4.5	5.4	6.5	7.7	9.2	10.8
Annual Growth Rate		19.8%	20.8%	19.4%	18.9%	18.8%	18.2%
Other Part B:	2.3	4.3	4.4	4.8	5.4	6	6.6
Administration							
(Subject to Appropriation)	1.7	1.6	1.7	1.8	1.9	1.9	2.0
Annual Growth Rate		-2.3	5.2%	4.5%	4.2%	4.0%	3.3%
B. General Part B Information							
SMI Deductibles (In Dollars)	$100	$100	$100	$100	$100	$100	$100
MEI Update (Calendar Year)	3.1%	2.7%	2.6%	2.7%	2.8%	2.8%	2.8%
Physician Update (Calendar Year)	1.9%	1.4%	8.9%	1.6%	0.3%	-0.1%	-0.2%
Laboratory Update (Calendar Year)	2.0%	2.0%	3.0%	2.7%	2.7%	2.7%	2.8%
DME Update (Calendar Year)	2.3%	3.1%	2.9%	2.7%	2.7%	2.7%	2.7%
C. Premium Information							
Monthly Premium (In Dollars)	$31.80	$36.50	$41.10	$46.10	$47.30	$48.60	$50.00
Premium Receipts	12.7	14.6	16.8	19.1	20.3	21.1	22
FY Enrollment (In Millions)	33.6	34.3	34.9	35.6	36	36.6	36.9
Total Medicare Disbursements	132.3	149.2	186.7	191.5	213.8	237.1	262
Total Function 570 – Medicare (Disbursement Net of Premiums)	119.1	134.1	152.3	171.6	192.6	215.1	238.1

[a]*Source:* Congressional Budget Office. Human Resources Cost Estimation Unit. Budget Analysis Division, 1993.
[b]Laboratory services are also provided by physicians and outpatient hospitals. Spending for these services is included in the appropriate provider category.

enues collected at those tax rates have grown less rapidly than outlays. Indeed, in the CBO projections, outlays are forecasted to grow at 11 percent per year and revenues at only 6 percent. The fundamental message is simple and straightforward but difficult to accept. Either the rate of growth of outlays in Part A must be slowed to approximately the rate of growth in covered payrolls, or the country is in for a neverending pattern of increases in the Part A tax rate. The most important driving force behind the growth of expenditures is not the growth in enrollment, nor is it the shift in the age composition of Medicare beneficiaries toward older ages; instead, it is the growth in the benefits per beneficiary of a given age.

Are there any messages from the patterns of growth in revenues that might be used to suggest probable future Medicare Part A policy? Probably the most interesting piece of information in Table 6.1 is the projection that the largest single item of Part A expenditures, payments for hospital care, will grow least rapidly. Although their growth rate still exceeds that of trust fund income, hospital outlays for inpatient care in some years grow at rates that closely approximate the rate of growth in income. Moreover, as noted at the bottom of Table 6.1, the increase in Part A payments related to higher payments per unit of hospital care, as measured by the Prospective Payment System (PPS) market basket, generally is lower than outlays. Because the effect of enrollment growth and demographic change alone add about 2 percent per year to Medicare outlays, it follows that if no change had occurred in the volume or composition of Part A services, then fiscal stability could have been achieved, or nearly so.

There has been growth, however, in the volume of admissions for people over 65 years old and a shift in the mix of admissions toward more expensive diagnosis groups. The net impact of this shift is to cause hospital inpatient spending to grow somewhat more rapidly than trust fund income. Table 6.1 contains another important message. The growth of nonhospital-inpatient services has greatly influenced the increase in Part A outlays. In particular, rapid growth in benefits for home health care and skilled nursing facilities has fueled about one half the excess of growth in outlays over income. That growth in those two benefits doubtless was caused in part by relaxing restrictions and increasing the generosity of those benefits, as dictated by Congress. It is not just the change in benefits that accounts for this acceleration but, rather, the fact that benefits were extended to services that naturally grow at rapid rates.

Part B of Medicare is financed, for the most part, on a pay-as-you-go basis, with approximately 25 percent from premiums paid for by the elderly and about 75 percent paid for from general federal revenues. As Table 6.2 indicates, the growth rate in Part B outlays has been substantially greater than that in Part A. In fact, by the year 2000, Part B outlays will be very close to Part A outlays in terms of total magnitude. All the components of Part B outlays grow rapidly, although physician expense grows least rapidly, and the largest single item of growth is that related to outpatient hospital care. In the case of these services, the difference between the addition to outlays caused by the adjustments for inflation and the rate of growth in total outlays is even more stark. As a rough approximation, growth in volume and intensity is projected to comprise about three quarters of the growth in spending per capita. Even a substantial shortfall between the caps associated with the Medicare economic index measure of input prices for doctor's services and the update permitted for physician payments is not sufficient to slow the growth in total Part B spending.[2]

The overall picture for Medicare Parts A and B underscores the growing need for increased income, either in the form of premiums or taxes. The Part A trust fund serves to convert a system that otherwise might have succeeded with smooth and continuous tax increases to one that is discontinuous, but the overall message is the same as in Part B: if the growth in outlays is not slowed below the projected amount, then taxes to pay for the Medicare program will have to be increased continuously and substantially.

The most recent estimate of the long-term costs implied by the provisions of current law indicates that those costs will be much higher in the first quarter of the 21st century unless the rate of growth in Medicare spending drops substantially below its long-term trend. The Technical Advisory Panel to the Advisory Council on Social Security provided estimates of the equivalent tax burden for the two parts of Medicare and for Social Security in the year 2020. In these calculations, the Medicare Part B program is treated as if it were financed by a tax on payrolls in the same way as are Medicare Part A and Old Age Survivors and Disability Insurance (OASDI). Table 6.3 shows the estimated tax rate for several situations. For all scenarios that assume a growth in expenditure anywhere close to historical trends, that tax on earnings for Medicare and Social Security alone is substantial, and usually greater than 30 percent. The only assumption that will yield tax rates close to the current revenue is one that includes a rate of growth much lower than has ever been seen, and, implicitly, elimination of cost-increasing quality improvements in the medical services reimbursed by Medicare.

Although current Medicare policy needs no changes in the short run, at least as far as the Medicare program alone is concerned, although not necessarily in terms of the overall federal budget, eventually, change must occur in one of two aspects: Either the Medicare program must find substantial new financing or some change from the long-term trend must

occur that will reduce the rate of growth in Medicare outlays per beneficiary or the number of beneficiaries.

TABLE 6.3 Health Care Projections, 2020[a]

Projection	Real Growth Rate	Health Expenditures as % of GNP	OASDI and Medicare (HI and SMI) as % of Taxable Payroll in 2020
1	4.7 Last 10-year trend	36	NA
2	4.3 Long-term trend	31.5	31.6
3	3.1 Significant slowing	22.7	26.5
4	1.4 Dramatic curtailment	13.7	16[b]

[a] *Source:* Advisory Council on Social Security. *Income Security and Health Care: Economic Implications 1991-2020: An Expert Panel Report to the Advisory Council on Social Security.* Washington, DC: December, 1991; 72, 76.
[b] Author's estimates

Reform Options

The next section of this chapter deals with options for the so-called "Medicare reform." It is clear that Medicare cannot continue to do business as
usual. But what are the options needed to avoid bankruptcy of the trust
fund or the spectacular tax increases that otherwise might occur?

Raising Payroll Taxes

The most obvious option for preserving Medicare's fiscal stability is to
change taxes on payrolls from the levels in current law to the higher levels needed to finance the forecasted growth in expenditure. Such a tax
would have to be two-and-one half times as high as the current one and
would not only create substantially higher premiums (paid by the elderly
for Part B) but also general revenue taxes (for Part B).

Although it now seems impossible to finance Medicare expenditure
growth entirely through payroll taxes, it is certainly possible to imagine
that taxes will be increased to solve at least part of the financial problem.
The most likely way to increase the tax is to remove the upper limit on
earnings subject to payroll taxation. It might even be conceivable that
the extra taxes collected from applying the same tax rate to earnings
above the current limit could be used entirely for Medicare, rather than

for the better funded OASDI program. Such ideas already have been discussed in some political circles. President Clinton recently proposed the removal of the upper limit on Part A taxes as a method of overall deficit reduction, not specifically for trust fund solvency.

Further expansion of the base of the Medicare tax might also be considered. The tax could be extended to income from sources other than earnings, and efforts might be made to identify currently unreported wage income and taxes. A politically more attractive solution, although one that makes little economic sense, is to apply additional taxes to the employer's share of the Medicare tax, leaving the employee's share untouched. From an economic view, payroll taxes exert an influence on worker wages regardless of who pays for them, but it may be cosmetically desirable to levy the tax on the employer rather than on the employee. Finally, some increase in tax rates is not out of the question, although it would be surprising if the payroll tax would rise much above a combined rate of 17 or 18 percent.

If some other source of tax financing is to be used to underwrite current Medicare benefits, then the policymaker's favorite tax probably is a value added tax (VAT), or national sales tax. This has the advantage over the federal income tax of having fewer loop holes but, at the same time, does not tax savings or interest on savings and, therefore, does not depress economic growth to the same extent as an income tax. The real issue for the VAT is its political salability, which has been and continues to be open to serious question.

There is one other possible vehicle for justifying a tax increase. It is possible that, by adding additional benefits to the Medicare package, which, in themselves, would potentially generate support for higher taxes, the actual amount of tax increase could be greater than what would be needed to pay for the new benefits alone. For example, even with taxes just set sufficiently high enough to pay for the additional drug expenses, adding drug benefits might help solve the program's financial problems if the consumption of drugs actually causes a reduction in the cost of other Medicare services. This is theoretically possible; some drugs do have substantial "cost offsets" in terms of reduced hospitalization or use of physician services. The likelihood of substantial additional revenue being generated by this route, however, looks small.

A halfway step between raising taxes and cutting benefits is to increase the nontax portion of Medicare revenues, that is the Part B premium. There is an historical case for doing so. Originally, the split of Part B funding between premiums and general tax revenues was to be approximately equal, but the premium share eventually fell below 25 percent (because premiums were indexed to the cost of living) and has been brought back to the 25-percent level. Even a small increase in the share, to 30 percent, is estimated by the CBO to save substantial amounts ($30 billion over five years) (CBO 1993). There would be a higher cost for Medicaid, which picks up the Part B premium for the poor elderly. The CBO also estimates that raising the Part B premium (through an income tax surcharge) to 100 percent of costs for elderly individuals or couples with taxable incomes above $100,000 could add another $18 billion.

Substituting Private Benefits

A second strategy for reducing outlays is to require that private insurers or some other private payers underwrite services that otherwise would be covered by Medicare. Laws that require private insurers to be the first payer for Medicare eligibles who also get employment-based private coverage represents one example of this strategy, although the continued decline in the number of persons over age 65 who work suggests that this approach will not make a serious dent in Medicare's problems. This provision saves only about $1 billion per year in Medicare costs (CBO 1993). Moreover, the requirement that employers be primary payers for employed Medicare beneficiaries is about to expire in late 1995.

There is one alternative, however, that could potentially make an enormous difference. It is possible to require that employers or individuals purchase Medigap-type coverage to replace some Medicare coverage. With the majority of elderly obviously willing to pay substantial amounts for Medigap supplemental coverage, it might be tempting for budget-balancers to link reductions in the scope of Medicare's benefit, especially for elderly who are not low income, to requirements or subsidies to bring about replacement funding through private Medigap policies. For example, various tax subsidies, such as tax breaks for funded retiree benefits, might be linked to a requirement that such benefits replace payments that Medicare otherwise would have made.

Linking subsidies to Medigap coverage for purchasing substitute benefits could turn out to be a bargain for the Medicare program. Such an advantage would seem to arise, however, from misperception rather than from true financial or consumer benefit. Perhaps clever design of a subsidy tied to the purchaser's willingness to cover former Medicare benefits might work.

It seems likely that such a program would be limited to the non-poor elderly and might proceed by limitations in the scope of Medicare benefits or by increases in the extent of costsharing. On the benefits side, for example, the home health benefit or the skilled nursing facility benefit might be withdrawn, but individuals could be encouraged to purchase private insurance to cover nursing home care.

It is also possible that the government might mandate that employers purchase post-retirement Medigap policies for their current workers that are more generous than existing policies and that contain some substitute coverage. Given the current tumult over health care reform and the difficulties of proceeding with a modest program, such a mandate does not seem likely now. If employer mandates are part of reform and if they work reasonably well, there may be a demand to replace Medicare coverage for current workers with mandated employer-provided, post-retirement health benefits. From an economic viewpoint, such a mandate is equivalent to financing the substituted portion of Medicare through a head tax, because, as noted already, the incidence of employer-paid wage supplements falls on workers in the form of lower (cash) wages. The difficulty that politicians and ordinary people have in grasping this fact makes mandated employer coverage ideal for politicians bent on using a fast shuffle to solve fiscal dilemmas.

Reducing Benefits

An alternative strategy to requiring or subsidizing private substitute benefits is for Medicare simply to cut its level of benefits to retirees unilaterally, perhaps hoping that people will fill in with private coverage. Such a strategy is politically dangerous but will yield a larger net fiscal benefit.

The most subtle vehicle for cutting Medicare benefits is to raise the age at which individuals are eligible for benefits. With the passage of federal laws that prohibit forced retirement and that permit people to continue working past age 65, there is a social basis for arguing that the age for Medicare eligibility should be extended. In addition, the increase in life expectancy that has occurred since World War II has meant that the number of years for which people over 65 will collect Medicare and OASDI benefits has grown substantially. If the intent of these social insurance programs was to provide a safety net for a certain number of years before death, then the increase in life expectancy suggests that the eligibility age should be increased.

The main problem with this strategy is that, despite the changes in laws about forced retirement and despite the increases in life expectancy, the general trend has been for people to retire earlier. The fact that they could work longer has not had much of an impact on actual behavior. It seems logical then that raising the age of eligibility for Medicare would cause people to work longer, precisely because they would need to continue working to pay the health care costs that Medicare no longer would cover.

So this strategy might work to save money in the short term, but its political feasibility seems highly dubious in the long term. Raising the age of eligibility is equivalent to reducing the level of Social Security and

Medicare benefits. Most voters presumably will be sophisticated enough to see what is happening. It is unlikely that they will tolerate this reduction in benefits.

Reducing Medicare Provider Payments

The current Clinton health reform proposal envisions substantial reductions in the projected growth in Medicare (and Medicaid) spending. Much of the Medicare "savings" is to be used to pay for new prescription drugs and long-term care benefits, with a little left over to subsidize coverage for people under 65 who work for small, low-wage firms. The implicit assumptions behind this proposal are that projected levels of Medicare spending contain substantial excess payments to providers and that cutting those payments will cause providers to provide the same for less.

As of this writing, neither of these assumptions seems to be especially plausible, and no obvious empirical evidence can be applied to them. Cutting Medicare payments and simultaneously capping private spending may avoid some of the worst aspects of "Medicaidizing" Medicare, but considerable resistance toward this method of financing new benefits is likely to come from the elderly lobby.

Means Testing

An alternative way to reduce Medicare benefits to some retirees is to link the level of benefits to income and wealth, paying less generous benefits to the higher income elderly. Another strategy that appears to be different (but is not) is to tax higher income elderly to reflect the value of their Medicare benefits. Either way, this represents a devaluation of Medicare benefits.

Means testing benefits will doubtless raise opposition from the usual elderly lobbies and from those who believe that maintenance of social insurance requires uniformity of benefits (but not taxes). The fear is that, by reducing the value of Medicare benefits to high-income elderly, those elderly may cease to support the program. Although well-to-do beneficiaries are a minority among the elderly, they can be more influential politically than the average older person, because they are more likely to vote and because they probably have the education and influence to make their views felt. The intrinsic fairness of limiting Medicare benefits for higher income elderly may be persuasive to some groups.

The next type of benefit limitation is a formal means testing of Medicare benefits. In this scenario, the size of out-of-pocket payments would be related to income, with low-income elderly receiving free care and high-income elderly facing deductibles and, perhaps, with coinsurance rates substantially greater than those under present law. In principle, this mechanism could eliminate the need for Medicaid coverage of elderly people for acute care, because it would lower or eliminate deductibles and coinsurance for very poor people.

Another strategy for reducing benefit payments to retirees is to increase the level of beneficiary costsharing, either by raising the deductible in either part of Medicare or by increasing the coinsurance rate. The latter seems unlikely, but there is a real possibility of increasing the size of the Part A or Part B deductible, especially if the increase could be confined to higher income beneficiaries. Such an increase not only would have a direct effect on reducing Medicare outlays, but it also would help contain overall costs by imposing a larger share of the full price of care on beneficiaries.

The main problem with this reform is that it will be seen, correctly, as a reduction in total benefits. Consequently, it is likely that the elderly would oppose such an obvious benefit-reduction strategy. One possible alternative would be to offset higher Medicare costsharing, at least in part, by increasing the size of the Social Security pension payment. Such a shift simply would not wash but, instead, would lead to reduced total expenses because the higher out-of-pocket payment would reduce moral hazard. Even this logical approach seems implausible, at least in the current political environment.

Adding Benefits to Medicare

Paradoxically, in the context of discussing health reform and in the face of Medicare's dire financial straights, some policymakers appear to be contemplating increases in the services that Medicare covers. The two most frequently discussed additional services are coverage of prescription drugs and coverage of long-term nursing home care.

Coverage of prescription drugs seems to have two motivations. On the one hand, there is a small set of elderly people who bear substantial out-of-pocket payment for prescription drugs because Medicare fails to cover them, and their families have no Medigap coverage to take up that slack. Of course, prescription drug coverage was included in the Medicare catastrophic law, which subsequently was repealed. It is speculated that one reason for the repeal was that a powerful minority of elderly already were covered for prescription drugs under Medigap policies provided by former employers, and these people were strongly opposed to any plan that required them to pay additional taxes and receive no additional benefits. A health reform plan to pay for additional Medicare benefits that would be financed by taxes imposed on the general population rather than on the Medicare population alone might avoid this objection. On the other hand, some politicians would seek a platform for criticizing drug company prices and product selection strategies. Without a major public insurance program that purchases these services, however, such criticism seems disembodied and not tied to any particular governmental program. If Medicare were a major buyer of prescription drugs, not only would it have a much more specific interest in controlling the price, it probably would also have the means to do so. The other possible extension of Medicare coverage would repeat an aspect of the catastrophic coverage act and would provide better coverage for hospital days in excess of the usual maximum. When hospital expenses mount to their highest levels, this gap in Medicare coverage appears to be a major deficiency.

More generally, what Medicare needs to do is to move its coverage from a late 1960s form, with emphasis on inpatient care and upper limits on coverage, to a 1990s form of major medical coverage that makes no distinction among types of medical expenses but does have catastrophic coverage. It is possible, although not guaranteed, that the value of such a rationalized Medicare benefits package might be great enough that beneficiaries would be willing to pay more than the cost of the additional benefits for the improved package. Some part of this excess payment could then be used to offset the deficit. Given present beneficiary attitudes, however, this is probably wishful thinking, unless there is a major push to sell an enhanced benefits package to middle and upper income elderly beneficiaries.

The final additional benefit that might possibly be added to Medicare is coverage for long-term nursing home care. Given the perilous state of Medicare financing, it would be impossible to support this additional benefit. The payroll tax rate required to pay for it would simply be out of the question in the near future, and the ability to finance it with general revenue taxation, given the current federal budget, seems limited at best.

Medicaid offers social insurance for nursing home care and provides universal coverage for such care, with a deductible approximately equal to the individual's wealth. For the majority of elderly who use this care and who have no dependents, such a policy may be socially optimal. It might be possible to add coverage for those few elderly who still have dependents, for whom drawing down of the beneficiary's wealth would seriously affect living standards; however, it seems unlikely that any long-term care benefits will be added to the program soon.

Overall Health Care Reform

The most current evaluation of health care reform does not look for the kind of piecemeal approaches to cost containment or rationalization of coverage that already have been discussed. Instead, it envisions a wholesale overhaul of the medical care finance, delivery, and production systems, with competitive managed care plans, largely in the form of health maintenance organizations (HMOs) as its centerpiece.

The first question is whether or not Medicare should be included in overall health care reform. The answer always turns on issues of practicality, not principle. Except for proposals that envision "Medicare for all," most strategies do not incorporate Medicare explicitly into their health care reform. In most cases, the view is that, eventually, the financing and delivery of care for people over age 65 will need to become an intrinsic part of a reform system, but the reasons are good for postponing full-scale integration until after health care reform is implemented for people under age 65.[3]

The reasons for postponing the integration of Medicare are based in part on the observation that universal coverage (98% or greater) has been achieved for the elderly, and that, fears about costshifting aside, the tools are in place for the government to cap or control its outlays for Parts A and B of Medicare as it wishes. The primary tool, of course, is governmental control over the annual update in both systems. There is still some leakage in terms of cost containment, primarily because hospital outpatient care is still partially paid on a cost-reimbursement basis, but the general conclusion is that Medicare already has achieved universal coverage and needs little additional structure to achieve cost containment.

Another practical reason for postponing the incorporation of Medicare is simply that the task of health reform for the under-65 population will be difficult enough without tackling a system that is not broken enough to require immediate fixing. The power and sensitivity of the elderly lobby suggest to many politicians already scared off by the Medicare catastrophic coverage debacle that Medicare reform is a fight that would best be postponed.

Despite the desire to leave Medicare out of the first round of health care reform, some aspects of reform will necessarily impinge on the Medicare program, especially the impact of Medicare expenditure limits on prices in the non-Medicare sector, and vice versa. To take a specific example, the short-run desire of policymakers who are distressed by the contribution that rising Medicare spending adds to the federal budget deficit, regardless of how much of that increase was caused by fairly recent additions to the benefits package, might be expected to take as the first line of attack the limiting (i.e., capping) or controlling of growth in federal outlays, without tampering with the private sector. Fundamentally, it would seem plausible to argue that the government should reform that part of health care for which it already has been responsible, that is, health care for the categorically eligible poor and the elderly, before it tackles the problems endemic to the rest of the population. It might be argued that the government should follow Voltaire's advice and clean up its own backyard before moving on to relandscape the rest of the world.

The main impediment to limiting initial health care reform to those areas in which the government already has a major responsibility is the fear that spillover from Medicare policy will invade the private sector. In particular, there is a strong belief that successful attempts by Medicare to hold down the unit prices that it pays for services or its total expenditures will inflate prices and costs for private sector patients. Most policymakers believe that costshifting indeed will occur, and that, therefore, they will be blamed by voters if Medicare costs are controlled. The implication is that, to control Medicare costs successfully, government needs to get its arms around the entire system.

The curious feature of this discussion is that strong reason exists to believe that costshifting may not be that important, and that the empirical evidence for its existence is not very strong. The theory behind this is well known, at least among health economists: if a health care provider sells in two markets, a Medicare market and a non-Medicare market, and if Medicare then reduces the price it pays, then the response of a provider who initially was maximizing profit should be to leave the private price unchanged or *reduce* it. The intuition is that, if the firm already had set the price to private sector patients that maximized its profits, then a reduced price from Medicare would not cause the private sector price (that already maximizes profits from existing levels of private sector business) to change. Moreover, if the lower price for Medicare patients causes the profit maximizing provider to replace them with private sector patients, then the vehicle for attracting more private patients is to reduce the price to them, either by reducing the price that people pay out-of-pocket or by offering a discount to managed care plans (to channel more private sector patients the provider's way).

The only scenario in which costshifting can occur under this logic is if the provider initially was not maximizing profits. The irony, then, is that costshifting, far from being the response of greedy providers to valiant attempts by the government to reduce the burden of health care costs on society, proves that providers had previously been generous to consumers in not taking the maximum payment available. At a minimum, this discussion would seem to imply that, if costshifting happens, it is much more likely to occur among not-for-profit hospitals—which, arguably, may not have been setting the profit maximizing price—than among physicians, who have less explicit reason to set a price below the level that maximizes their net incomes.

The most important practical observation on the issue of costshifting, if it indeed is a real phenomenon, is that steps obviously could be taken, short of wholesale health care reform, to prevent or inhibit it. For instance, Medicare could be forbidden to pay below-cost prices to health care providers; the Baucus Amendment places such a limit (although one difficult to interpret) on Medicaid. The other observation is that, as aggressive competition by health care plans spreads, it will become increasingly difficult for providers to respond to lower Medicare payments by costshifting. To be blunt, HMOs will not tolerate it.

But if costshifting is impossible, then that offers little reassurance that cutting Medicare expenditures can be done appropriately in isolation. If providers cannot costshift, they either will lose money and go out of business or they will have to cut some aspect of care, either quantity or, more likely, quality, to fit their costs within the limits of the revenues furnished for Medicare patients.

Exit of some hospitals and, perhaps, some physician specialists ought not be cause for concern; it is the real world manifestation of the belief that the bloated health care sector must be shrunk. If it is to shrink, then some suppliers must leave. A more serious dilemma for Medicare is that, if providers do choose to tailor what Medicare patients get against what Medicare pays, then a distinction may arise in the quality of care or access to care between what Medicare patients receive and what people insured in the private sector receive. Such a distinction is unsightly and unseemly as far as politicians are concerned, and they may wish to avoid the "Medicaidization" of Medicare by forbidding the private sector from furnishing a class of medicine higher than that which the government budget cares to allot for the Medicare program.

These observations suggest that it would be difficult to limit health care reform to Medicare alone. There is no doubt that the need to control Medicare expenditures is more pressing in light of the government's fiscal problem than the need to help Fortune 500 firms who cannot control their own health benefits or cover their non-poor uninsured. It would not be surprising then that control of Medicare would be the first, rather than the last, step to health care reform.

Now, change perspective and assume that health care reform for people under age 65 will come first. There are reasons then to believe that it may be difficult to leave Medicare out. Those reasons often have more to do with politics, however, than with economics. The most prominent argument for a spillover arises in connection with the standard benefits package given to people under age 65 in a reformed health care system. It has become accepted that a uniform benefits package needs to be offered to all persons, regardless of income or need. In addition, although this sentiment is not universal, some policymakers believe that the package should contain minimal to zero costsharing by patients, and, almost surely, not at the level of costsharing embodied in the current Medicare program.

On its face, this implies that the benefit package that citizens may be mandated to buy under health care reform will tend to look more generous than the current Medicare program. The mandated package surely will include some coverage for prescription drugs, which Medicare currently does not, and might even include coverage of long-term care for the non-elderly, if only because the cost of such coverage for younger people who are at a lower risk of needing chronic care is a relative bargain. Then the political dynamic forces consideration of the question, "Why, if drug and long-term care coverage are right for people under age 65, should they not be added to Medicare?" Moreover, as already noted, there is a strong, independent demand to add these coverages to the Medicare program, despite the virtual impossibility of financing them under any plausible modification of the current Medicare tax and transfer structure.

Attempts to reconcile Medicare and private sector health benefit packages under the rubric of health care reform could impact private retiree benefits, the most obvious being the fact that many group Medigap policies already cover prescription drugs. If such coverage were added to Medicare it no longer would be required or needed in the supplemental policy. As already noted, politicians will be sorely tempted to require those retirees who currently have insurance coverage for drugs to continue to pay for that coverage, or to have their employers continue to pay for it, rather than shift the cost to government. The possible elimination of serious costsharing in a generally mandated package might also spill over to Medicare, although the fiscal burden of having Medicaid pay for at least the deductibles and coinsurance would seem to impede any rapid shift.

The other aspect of health care reform that could have profound consequences on Medicare and, therefore, on private insurance benefits for retirees is the overall push to managed competition. Elaborate schemes in which employers (in firms below a certain size) are required to process their employees' insurance coverage through a local health insurance purchasing cooperative (HIPC) have been developed with the primary intent of inducing almost all Americans to purchase managed care or HMO-type coverage as health insurance, while, at the same time, taking away from the firm the decision about choice of plan and lodging it with the HIPC and, to some extent, with the individual worker in a multiple-choice, limited-options setting.

Although the availability of a managed care option for Medicare beneficiaries has been present for years, it has not been very popular. The key question here is whether health care reform that relies heavily on a managed competition structure will not force the elderly to obtain insurance in the same fashion. Changes could come on either (or both) of two fronts. First, the government could pick up and change its basic Medicare benefit, requiring that it take the form of choice among a set of managed care plans or options, possibly with a point of service option. The main impediment here is that, for more than twenty-five years, the government has run the Medicare insurance plan, and turning that responsibility over to private HMOs would create a substantial upheaval. But, surely, requirements and pressure will come about to coordinate the HMO option under Medicare with the "accountable health partnerships" that the HIPCs select for the under-65 population. In part, this coordination will result from the bureaucratic desire for tidiness in structural arrangements, and, in part, it will result from a need to permit those persons under age 65 who select and come to love a particular AHP to continue coverage with that plan when they become Medicare eligible. The other front concerns employer-provided health benefits for retirees. The logic here is that, if employers below a certain size are mandated to funnel health coverage for people under age 65 through the HIPC/AHP vehicle, should not the same mandate be extended to retirees? Almost surely the use of this new mechanism will be required for early retirees. Exactly how it might be coordinated with employer and employee plans for Medigap coverage is unclear at this point, but it is likely to be a topic of intense discussion.

Finally, the overall global budget, which is likely to be included in some form or another in health care reform, surely will impinge on retiree health benefits. At a minimum, those benefits will not escape the long arm of price and spending controls. To the extent that the budget limit program takes the form of regulated or administered unit prices for providers, something that states are apparently being encouraged to pursue, retiree health benefit programs will be faced with the need to consider that the benefits they purchase will be bought from providers who are operating under price controls. The immediate impact of price controls, in the ordinary circumstance, should be to lower unit prices. Over time, controls may produce other provider and patient actions, depending on the extent of permissiveness for things like balance billing and the skill of providers and buyers in avoiding laws that forbid them from charging or paying higher prices for medical services.

To the extent that budget controls take the form of limits on insurance premiums, which seems likely, some serious design issues may complicate supplementary retiree health policies. Those benefits provided through managed care plans almost surely will be controlled primarily through limitations on the premiums charged, rather than on unit prices.

Implications of Health Care Reform for Employer Plans

Many of the probable or possible consequences of changes in the Medicare program for private insurance for retirees have already been discussed. Those changes in Medicare that envision shifting more of the burden for retiree health care costs back to the private sector have obvious implications. Among the possible changes in Medicare, increasing the age of eligibility or means-testing Medicare would seem to have the most dramatic financial impact on private plans—either those plans provided by employers or those paid for by retirees. As a sweeping generalization, it seems reasonable to anticipate that future changes in Medicare will require that the private sector assume more of the responsibility for payment of retiree health care benefits, either to the employer, when the workers are still employed—which really means the workers pay in the form of lower cash wages—or to retirees with some command over income and wealth when they retire.

In addition to the obligation to pay, there is likely to be more federal control over the content and design of coverage for retiree benefits. The movement to managed competition, if it becomes reality, entails a wholesale reorganization of the way in which health care is provided and the places in which decisions about benefits and rationing rules are made. Particularly as a result of health care reform, employers and individual citizens are likely to find more government limitation on their ability to choose whether or not they want to purchase health benefits and what the form of those benefits is to be.

The specific consequences that changes in Medicare or that the results of health care reform will have on employer plans have already been discussed. Under some scenarios, employers will lose their role as managers of health benefits for current workers and retirees alike. Employers simply will become conduits for a portion of the insurance premium—the part taken from employees' total compensation before the paycheck is written out and transferred to a quasi-governmental organization such as a HIPC, which then will make most of the decisions that firm benefit managers traditionally made about health plan choice and levels of expenditure. Large firms still may be permitted, at least temporarily, to make some of their own choices to run or select health plans, but the support for this exemption is not likely to be permanent.

President Clinton has proposed that the governmental plan assume most of the burden of paying for early-retiree benefits, even for firms that had already agreed to do so, but the political prospects for this proposal are in question, largely because of its budgetary cost. The direction that the Clinton reforms have taken does, however, suggest that a strategy of requiring employers to bear more of the burden of retiree benefits appears less likely, at least for the moment. Paradoxically, those employers who never involved themselves in retiree health benefits before the reform will find themselves least affected, positively or negatively, by these crosscurrents.

Politics of Retiree Health Care

The speculative character of the foregoing discussion is inevitable because, at this point, the $900 billion question regarding the outcomes of overall health care reform is still an open one. No firm definition has been offered yet of what might be a proto-proposal for various political interests to draw a bead on their target. In particular, the political interests that purport to represent retirees have been unusually quiet, so that any attempt to predict political outcomes is a gamble. Even so, it seems worthwhile to speculate on which of the foregoing elements is likely to be combined in what form at what time in the future.

It might be easier to begin by listing the things that are least likely to happen. It seems unlikely, for instance, that Medicare's future financial problems will be solved by substantial increases in taxes paid by the non-elderly; that is, by increases in the payroll tax for Part A and general revenue financing for Part B. In addition to the facts that the elderly are less likely to be poor than the rest of the population, current political trends seem to be opposed to any substantial redistribution of costs from the non-elderly to the elderly. Under the defunct Medicare catastrophic coverage act, it was explicitly assumed that the elderly would have to finance any increase in their benefits themselves. This consensus still seems to be present and is likely to extend to increases in tax rates to maintain existing benefits in the face of growing prices or growing numbers of elderly. Today's younger people expect to grow old, but there is no necessary connection between their paying more for today's elderly and what they should expect to get when they retire. Indeed, the history of Social Security and Medicare is one in which each succeeding generation gets a smaller net surplus.

The brief and tragic history of the Medicare catastrophic coverage act also hints that it will be difficult to means test Medicare taxes or benefits in order to offer new benefits or stave off cuts. The political (as opposed to the ideological) opposition for means testing comes not from those devoted to idealized social insurance but, rather, from the political opposition of well-to-do elderly, which, so far, seems the most formidable part of the elderly lobby.

The key short-run political question is whether Medicare will be incorporated wholesale into health care reform (whatever form it takes), or whether the status quo (with some slight modifications) is likely to continue at least until the trust fund really is depleted. It is likely that some modified business-as-usual format will be the short-run strategy for Medicare.

For one thing, the job of health reform is going to be extraordinarily difficult, even if it is limited only to Medicaid and the private sector. Modifying Medicare to the same extent and to the same form as envisioned for the private sector more than doubles the work, because of the larger number of catastrophic and high-risk cases among the elderly and because of the elderly lobby. For another thing, addressing the question of Medicare reform means dealing with the dilemma of adding benefits to Medicare and, thereby, worsening federal fiscal prospects. The current macro-economic policy surely wants to avoid this. Also, the Medicare system is not so badly broken yet that it cannot continue to function, with caps or limits placed on the annual update or conversion factors in Part A inpatient care and Part B physician benefits.

The possibility of costshifting to the private sector and a "Medi–caidization" of Medicare in which access is reduced will cause problems, to be sure, but the drive to reduce the budget deficit will overshadow any substantive action here. There may be some cosmetic fix-ups – largely unenforceable requirements that providers continue to provide access to Medicare patients and not raise private sector prices; but the final outcome for Medicare, whatever happens to the rest of the health sector, is surely going to be a Medicare global budget.

Finally, it is possible that overall health care cost growth may slow down, with or without public global budgets, purely because economic forces finally kick in. Had it not been for the paralysis engendered by continuous discussion of health reform, employers and insurers might already have implemented more vigorous versions of devices and incentives to control new technology. There are some intriguing hints that, in some places, this already has been successful. Moreover, the economic system is not crazy; it would never permit the medical care share to rise high enough as to impoverish people. Someone or some institution would find a feasible and salable product to prevent this, especially if there is enough pressure on overall well-being. So far, this has not happened, but only because the average American is not yet miserable enough.

If Medicare were to be blended with the current strategy for health reform, as designed by the Clintons, what form would it take? To date, two aspects of that reform are apparent in the private sector that would shake up the Medicare program even more than it will change the private sector. First, employers are to be used as conduits for financing but with little or no role on benefit choice or monitoring. Second, individuals are to be permitted an opportunity to choose among various different health plans (although with a single basic benefit), and the plans are not to be government run. The current tax-financed, government-monopoly-operated Medicare plan does not look anything like this. The dissonance between current Medicare and health reform will be even more pronounced if reform emphasizes HMOs, something that is part of managed competition but, as of now, is being disavowed by the Gore wing of administration health policy.

There could be some cosmetic adaptation of Medicare to health reform, like restructuring the Medicare HMO option by allowing beneficiaries to purchase coverage from AHPs through HIPCs. The low rate of take-up for that option suggests, however, that there will be little impact. So, in the short-run, there is a good chance that immmediate changes in Medicare will be minor. But what of the long run (around the year 2000), *if* health care spending growth has not slowed by that point? In the next section, three broad, possible strategies are discussed.

Two scenarios seem unlikely. The first is that the rest of the health care system would be structured like Medicare—a government-run, tax-financed, indemnity insurance in a fee-for-service system but with administered prices and supplemental private insurance. Presently, little pressure has been brought to put the entire system in the government's hands. The second scenario is to turn over to employers (either voluntarily or by mandate) the responsibility of financing and organizing coverage for their workers after retirement as well as during the period of active work. Self-confident employers have volunteered from time to time to provide coverage to their retirees if Medicare would turn over to them what it would have spent; however, distrust of employer choices and motives, concern about the adverse labor market effects of linking insurance coverage too closely to employment at one firm, and demise of the lifetime career argue against this.

A more plausible option, first, is extension of the employer mandate/ HIPC/AHP/global budget model to post-retirement coverage. In this model, the employer is only a pipeline for funding insurance, with the key decisions made by a local quasi-public body such as an HIPC, followed by decisions among HIPC-approved plans made by individuals. The foundation for support of this approach rests largely on an economic misconception: the belief that if the employer is required to turn over funds to pay for coverage, it really is the boss who pays. Economic theory and empirical research both suggest that employees ultimately pay in the form of lower real wages. So, the success of this strategy, especially if its applicability to Medicare is delayed until after its implementation for the rest of the population, depends mainly on whether voters see through the "employer-mandate" subterfuge. It depends as well on the satisfaction with the choice of plans under managed competition.

The second scenario is the bureaucratic dream version of the first.

Create HIPCs, but have them just be local field offices of a Washington commissariat. Turn the employer mandate into a real tax, with offsets or subsidies to give it at least more progressivity than the head tax implied by a simple mandate. Make the AHPs alternative and barely distinguishable versions of government-run insurance nominally contracted out to nongovernmental firms but run as closely regulated public utilities, with controlled budgets, benefits, and prices. All important decisions are to be made politically. This scenario could happen, because it is the direction in which the political process naturally flows.

Indeed, it would not be too difficult to convert the employer mandate into a payroll tax, like the Medicare Part A tax, to reconcile benefits (e.g., by requiring that all providers be paid according to a Medicare reimbursement policy). Employers might still have a more active role to play if some supplemental coverage for the non-poor survives, but this role is likely to be small.

The third and, arguably, the most preferred scenario defines a set of minimum benefits for Americans of all ages; permits the minimum required benefit to take the form of catastrophic coverage for non-poor persons of all ages; provides closed-end, refundable tax credits for those who cannot afford to pay for minimum benefits; abolishes all other tax subsidies, including the tax subsidy to employer-paid premiums, whether for current workers or retirees; and lets citizens choose whether they wish to secure the required coverage as a tie-in with their employment (and thus get the cost advantage of group insurance), whether they want to buy it on their own, or whether they want to enhance their pensions to offer a defined contribution that could be used to buy group insurance after retirement. Existing Medicare coverage could be grandfathered for current retirees, but other arrangements might permit a switch to the incentive-neutral, free-choice setting. The overall objective, as Senator Daniel Moynihan recently expressed, is to avoid economic behavior that is affected by the tax code.

This last scenario would challenge employers to choose ways of structuring workers' health insurance, before and after retirement, in ways that succeed best in the competitive labor market. For some small firms, this may mean letting employees arrange things for themselves. For larger firms, the employer may be able to lend assistance in arranging group coverage and providing information about choices under that coverage. Because medical expenses, unlike other insured losses, are likely to remain a large but uncertain share of total spending for American families, it may continue to be good employment policy for employers to help with these costs.

This approach is not in the current political cards, although there is now some talk of providing individual tax credits as the most efficient and least distortive way to help the self-employed and employees of small firms. The best advice for employers probably is to prepare for a rational strategy under a rational plan such as the one just outlined.

Conclusion

Business as usual with regard to retiree benefits is not a viable long-term policy for Medicare, any more than it is for the private sector. No real crisis exists at the moment, however, and there is time for rational planning in the public sector and by private agents who must adapt to the public sector. Anticipating an increasingly constrained but not fundamentally altered Medicare program is probably the best short-run strategy. For the longer run, the great gamble of health reform is difficult to handicap. Within cautionary boundaries, planning for the best is probably the best planning.

References

Advisory Council on Social Security. *Income Security and Health Care: Economic Implications 1991-2020: An Expert Panel Report to the Advisory Council on Social Security.* Washington, DC: December, 1991; 72, 76.
Congressional Budget Office, Human Resources Cost Estimation Unit, Budget Analysis Division. *February Baseline.* 1993.

Notes

1. For purposes of discussion, the long term will be interpreted to mean the time from now until approximately the year 2030.

2. The dramatic jump in the physician update in fiscal year 1990 was part of the phase-in for the new Resource Base Relative Value Scale.

3. In contrast, most plans seek to incorporate coverage for all people into a reform strategy, either intergrating or abolishing the Medicaid program.

Commentary: Joseph R. Antos

Every discussion on the provision of health care benefits in retirement inevitably revolves around Medicare. Indeed, private health benefits for retirees consist of Medicare wrap-around policies designed to fill in the gaps now present in the government insurance program. Poised today on the brink of potentially sweeping reform of the health care system in the United States, now is a good time to reconsider the roles of Medicare and private insurance in providing for the health needs of 35 million elderly and disabled Americans.

Mark Pauly has written an interesting chapter that addresses major Medicare reform ideas in the context of broader health care reform. The range of these ideas is vast, and the issues are far from settled. Rather than discuss all the issues, this commentary will focus briefly on a few of the major themes in Pauly's chapter.

Why Reform Now?

The history of health care reform in this country is long. The vision of comprehensive health reform reaches as far back as 1945, when President Harry Truman recommended a compulsory national health insurance system similar to Medicare (but available to everyone). Although numerous proposals for health care reform have been offered over the years by the federal government and other groups, those proposals almost always have failed to lead to action. Why is *now* the time to undertake reform?

People who lack health insurance are certainly not a new phenomenon in this country. As long as health insurance has existed, there have been uninsured people. Certainly, the proportion of the population without insurance coverage has increased somewhat over the past decade. It cannot be argued, however, that correcting our health insurance prob-

The author would like to thank Marian Gornick and James Lubitz for their helpful suggestions. He also drew upon the work of Edgar A. Peden, who also deserves thanks. The views expressed here are solely those of the author and do not represent the position of the Health Care Financing Administration.

lem became more important only when the number of uninsured reached 39 million than when that number was 30 million (Levitt, Olin, and Letsch 1992).[1]

Rising costs in health care represent an old problem, as Table 6.1A illustrates. Measured as a percent of gross domestic product (GDP), national health care expenditures rose by 3.4 percent annually from 1960 to 1970. This compares to an annual growth rate of 2.9 percent in the 1980s (Letsch, Lazenby, Levit, and Cowan 1992). There is little question that the problems facing our health care system have been present for decades.

TABLE 6.1A Trends in National Health Expenditures[a]

Year	Expenditures (% of GDP)	Annual Rate of Increase [b]
1960	5.3%	–
1970	7.4	3.4%
1980	9.2	2.2
1990	12.2	2.9

[a] *Source:* Letsch SW, Lazenby HC, Levit KR, Cowan CA. National Health Expenditures, 1991. *Health Care Financing Review,* 1992; 14:(3); see Table 5.

[b] The annual rate of increase of national health expenditures (as a share of GDP) is calculated as the compound rate over each decade (i.e., 1960-1970, 1970-1980, 1980-1990).

What has changed recently is that the middle class has become more aware of the bitter realities of the American health care system. Insurers have taken steps to segment the health insurance market and to select good risks. Changing jobs or losing a job often means loss of health insurance coverage. For many workers, especially those employed in small firms, major illness can be a double-barreled tragedy. The illness itself may be physically and emotionally draining and can result in substantially higher premiums or even loss of insurance coverage for the entire small group. Competitive pressures on employers, along with recent accounting changes, have forced everyone to realize that health benefits are enormously expensive, and that retiree health benefits are substantially underfunded. Increasingly, people believe that they are not getting good value for their health expenditure dollars.

Accompanying these facts is the sobering realization by "baby boomers" that they have begun to reach the age of health vulnerability. Concerns about the health care system are no longer some abstract consideration but have become increasingly personal. Moreover, the baby-boom generation is now in a position to do something about this dilemma. If the problems are to be resolved soon, baby boomers must search for—and implement—the solutions.

The magnitude of the health care financing problems that face the

American public is illustrated in Table 6.2A. The projected increase in national health expenditures from just over $900 billion in 1993 to almost $16 *trillion* in 2030 suggests the need for policy actions that will slow the cost spiral (Burner, Waldo, and McKusick 1992).

TABLE 6.2A National Health Expenditure Projectons[a]

Item	1993	2000	2030
National Health Expenditures			
Total ($ billions)	$903.3	$1739.8	$15,969.6
Per capita amount	$3380	$6148	$47,891
Percent of GDP	14.4%	18.1%	32.0%

[a]*Source:* Burner ST, Waldo DR, McKusick DR. National Health Expenditures Projections Through 2030. *Health Care Financing Review.* 1992; 14:(1); see Table 7.

As disturbing as these statistics are, it is not well known that these official projections assume a moderation in the rate of increase in national health expenditures in the out-years. For example, for 1993 the annual increase in health expenditures is estimated to be 10.2 percent. By 2030, that rate of increase in expenditures is assumed to drop to 7.4 percent. Thus, these estimates *assume* that actions will be taken in the future to dampen the health care cost spiral.

One final comment on these projections is in order. Economists frequently observe that there is no necessary limit to the share of GDP that can be devoted to any category of expenditure, such as health care. From the current vantage point, spending 32 percent of GDP on health care in 2030 seems implausible to most people. This is no more implausible, however, than the current 14.4 percent share of GDP would have appeared to analysts in 1960, when national health expenditures consumed 5.3 percent of GDP.

Nonetheless, a practical limit to health care expenditures is fast approaching. Spending continues to rise rapidly, and complaints about inadequate insurance coverage and problems with the service delivery system are increasing just as rapidly. This is a clear indication that the country would welcome sweeping health care reform.

What About Medicare?

After decades of debate, sweeping health care reform appears to be on the horizon in the United States. In Chapter Six, Mark Pauly considers whether Medicare will be a part of that reform, and what program changes are now being analyzed by the White House and others. It is safe to say that Medicare is part of the overall health care problem in this country.

It is far less clear how Medicare will be made part of a proposed solution, at least in the near term.

Medicare's Board of Trustees recently reported that Medicare's Hospital Insurance (HI) Trust Fund is likely to be exhausted in 1999 unless policy changes are made. Over the next 25 years, the HI trust fund deficit will amount to $1.4 trillion (in present value terms).[2] The fact that insolvency is only almost here, coupled with the magnitude of the deficit, illustrates the fiscal momentum behind Medicare's underfunding. To be effective, policy actions must be taken early enough to slow that momentum. Current estimates suggest that time may be running out to enact reasonable and necessary reforms to avert substantial financial dislocation in the Medicare program.[3]

Many changes could be made to the Medicare program to place it on a sounder financial footing and to improve the beneficiary's access to quality care. Before considering some of these policies, it is useful to reexamine the role of Medicare within the larger system. In short, must there be a separate Medicare program to provide insurance coverage for the elderly and disabled?

In 1965, the answer to this question was "Yes." The elderly, as a group, had relatively low incomes and could not obtain private health insurance. Medicare was enacted to ensure access to health insurance for people most at risk for medical expenses.

In 1993, the answer is not so obvious. Income and asset status of the elderly have improved since 1965. The insurability of the elderly is no longer in doubt as long as insurers can structure insurance appropriately and charge a fair premium. No longer must the elderly be confined to their own risk pool, subject to rules very different from those that affect the non-elderly. With the proper system of premiums and subsidies to the low-income elderly, this population could be integrated into general health insurance risk pools. Such integration could reduce, but would not eliminate, the intergenerational wealth transfer to the elderly that has been characteristic of the current Medicare program. The balance between need for medical services and ability to pay almost certainly will require that younger generations subsidize the elderly. That subsidy, however, need not continue to go to *all* elderly regardless of medical need or income insufficiency.

Substantial technical challenges are involved with establishing the structure of premiums and subsidies. Nonetheless, one goal of health reform is to create an insurance system that provides seamless coverage. A person's ability to obtain insurance coverage should not be affected adversely by a job change or by a coworker's illness. Similarly, no logical reason exists for shifting the over-65 group to a different insurance system characterized by different operating rules and different financial consequences.

Corrections should be made to the problems and inequities that face young and old alike.

Achieving comparable insurance treatment for persons in objectively comparable circumstances (with regard to income and health status, for example) could be accomplished through various different reforms, from a national insurance system to a highly decentralized system. In 1965, the Medicare program was established with the goal of improving the circumstances facing the elderly, who were clearly disadvantaged. Whether or not a separate Medicare program will be retained in any future reforms remains to be seen, but the guiding principle should be to seek equitable treatment for all.

Some Specific Medicare Policy Proposals

Mark Pauly describes a variety of proposals that have been, or could be, considered to improve the financial viability of the Medicare program. Unfortunately, there are only two ways to accomplish this goal: raise revenues or lower program expenditures.[4] Neither approach will be universally welcomed, no matter what specific proposals may be adopted. Regrettably, as Pauly's chapter suggests, there really are no new ideas. There are, however, a fair number of bad, old ideas, specifically, those proposals that (inadvertently) create incentives for overutilization of medical services, reduce incentives for efficient production, or lead in other ways to inappropriate increases in health expenditures. Also to be avoided, if possible, are proposals that lead to inappropriate decreases in health expenditures and those that would work in theory but cannot be implemented successfully. Obviously, finding the subset of good proposals is not a simple undertaking.

It is impractical here to parse out the advantages and disadvantages of the many proposals that Pauly discusses. Instead, let the focus fall on one issue: the consequences of reducing beneficiary coinsurance on the utilization of services.

Some proposals would have the effect of reducing beneficiary coinsurance, thus eliminating a significant barrier to care for low-income individuals. Such a proposal also could reduce the financial disincentives for using medical services among the non-poor, who may already overuse services. Another approach, mentioned by Pauly, would tie reductions in Medicare benefits to a requirement that employers or individuals purchase supplementary private insurance to replace the lost Medicare coverage. This would shift the cost of care toward other payers in the system and away from Medicare. Such a proposal could have the perverse result of increasing total expenditures if it reduced high-income beneficiaries' awareness of the full cost of health care.

A recent analysis[5] shows the importance of beneficiary coinsurance on the level and trend of health care utilization. If the coinsurance rate (as measured by the percent of national health expenditures that constitutes out-of-pocket spending) is lowered by 5 percentage points, then national health expenditures would increase in the first year by 2.2 percent. The expenditure trend would also increase, so that, in 10 years, national health expenditures would have risen by 11.7 percent. Ultimately, expenditures increase by 14.6 percent.

Medicare's history of expenditure growth and this analysis of aggregate expenditure growth suggest strongly the need for beneficiaries to maintain a fiscally healthy understanding that health care choices directly impact their other consumption choices. Although the beneficiary ultimately pays for health coverage, the "tragedy of the commons" is that the cost of one individual's overuse is not fully borne by that same individual. Insurance spreads the risks, and, therefore, the costs and, therefore, the responsibility for socially inappropriate choices. Systems must be devised that improve decisionmaking by beneficiaries, providers, insurers, and employers if health care costs are ever to come under control.

Various short-run steps could be taken to make Medicare a more rational and appropriate insurance program for the elderly and disabled. The artificial distinction between Parts A and B of Medicare could be abolished and replaced with a simpler deductible and coinsurance structure that would apply to all Medicare services. Establishing limits on the total annual and lifetime liability that faces Medicare beneficiaries remains a worthwhile idea, despite the political history of the Catastrophic Coverage Act. To be sure, some obvious gaps are apparent in Medicare coverage that also could be filled, like payment for outpatient drugs. The need for supplementary coverage, which is known to drive up costs, would diminish if limits were established on beneficiary liability and if some outpatient drugs were covered under the Medicare program. Given the potentially strong demand for new services, however, broadening of the Medicare program must proceed with caution. Facilitating the transition from employment-based insurance to the retiree health insurance system also makes sense if a separate system is retained for the elderly. No good reason can be found for why employees should not be able to remain with the provider of choice after retirement.

Conclusion

America's health care system is in crisis. Part of that crisis is the inequitable distribution of health resources among different groups in the population. Mark Pauly sees no real crisis in retiree health care at the moment, however, and feels that there is time enough for rational planning regarding any future reform of the retiree health system.

By some standards, there may not be a real crisis for retiree health now. But the inevitable big fight that will be waged over reform will revolve around redistribution of resources, and, in this battle, the resources dedicated toward retiree benefits cannot be overlooked. Even if retiree health benefits are not explicitly modified by health care reform, any reform that occurs necessarily will change the environment in which those benefit programs operate. Implicitly or explicitly, the retiree health system will undergo a transformation along with the rest of the country.

References

Burner ST, Waldo DR, McKusick DR. National Health Expenditures Projections Through 2030. *Health Care Financing Review*, 1992; 14:1.
Letsch SW, Lazenby HC, Levit KR, Cowan CA. National Health Expenditures, 1991. *Health Care Financing Review*, 1992; 14:3.
Levit KR, Olin GL, Letsch SW. Americans' Health Insurance Coverage, 1980-91. *Health Care Financing Review*, 1992; 14:3; 33.

Notes

1. In 1980, 30.5 million Americans were uninsured. Throughout the 1980s, the number rose, finally reaching 39.6 million in 1991. (See Levit, Olin, and Letsch 1992.)

2. This compares to projected 1993 expenditures of $91.2 billion.

3. Note the analogy between the Medicare Trustees Report and the corporation balance sheet under Financial Accounting Statement 106 (FAS 106). FAS 106 requires that firms treat the present value of future outlays for retiree health coverage as a liability, thus highlighting the private financing problem. The Medicare Trustees Report has been reporting in a similar way for the Medicare program. Nonetheless, political pressure to resolve the Medicare financing problem has not been intense. It is not clear whether FAS 106 will serve as a more effective catalyst for meaningful reforms.

4. Note that lowering program expenditures does not necessarily mean reducing benefits. If more efficient ways of providing those benefits can be found, the benefit level can be maintained.

5. This observation is based on the unpublished work of Edgar A. Peden who performed a time-series analysis of national health expenditure data for the years 1960 to 1991.

Chapter 7
Managed Competition and the Elderly: An Analysis of Potential Benefits and Pitfalls

William R. Greer and Alan L. Hillman

With the enactment of Medicare nearly 30 years ago, health policymakers sought to reduce the financial burden of health insurance for the elderly and provide universal access to everyone over 65 years old. Today, issues of cost and access are propelling the rest of the nation into a health care reform as sweeping as the one that reshaped health care for the elderly in 1965. Ironically, the rest of the nation may end up leading Medicare to a resolution of issues that have plagued the program since its inception— the continued high cost of health care for the elderly and, consequently, continued barriers to full health coverage.

More than any other single health care program, Medicare has fueled the continued rise in American health care costs. Since 1970, government expenditures on health care, of which Medicare consumes the major share, have risen faster than inflation, faster than private expenditures, and faster than state and local health care expenditures (OECD 1992). Of the average annual 5.5 percent increase in health care costs over the past 20 years, about 3 percent can be attributed to an increase in the volume of health care services consumed disproportionately by the Medicare population. The remaining 1.5 percent rise in health care costs can be attributed to increased costs over and above inflation.

One factor that has contributed to the overall increase in health care costs and, specifically, to the increase in Medicare spending is the steady rise in the proportion of the population 65 years old and over. This group represented 8 percent of the population in 1960 but now represents 12 percent. By some estimates, these people require four times as much health care as the rest of the population, which, when coupled with their growing numbers, have been estimated to increase health spending almost three quarters of a percent per year since 1967 (Washawsky 1991). Perhaps most discouraging, however, is that for such a large federal investment in fulfilling Medicare's commitment to provide universal health care to the elderly, the program still pays for less than half of the medical expenses of its beneficiaries (OECD 1992).

President Clinton and the members of his task force on health care reform have identified cost and access as two of the principal problems that reform should address. The President also has indicated that the reform most likely will implement a system of health care insurance purchasing called *managed competition*, and the public expenditure for health care will most likely be limited by a global budget.

Any health care system reform will have to address the increasing share of health care costs generated by the growing elderly population in this country, and managed competition, under a global budget in particular, could well address some of the shortcomings of Medicare. At the same time, it could open new gaps in the health care coverage for the elderly, for example, by limiting expenditures at the extremes of life. It has the potential to pose a threat to a segment of the population that lives on a fixed income and consumes an increasing share of health care services.

It would be in the best interests of the elderly to consider the impact of managed competition and then to help shape health care reform to redress the shortcomings of Medicare while avoiding the potential pitfalls of a new system. The sections of this chapter that follow examine important themes relevant to reform:

- *Shortcomings of Medicare.* High copayments, inadequate coverage of preventive health care, lack of long-term care coverage, and no prescription drug reimbursement have long been seen as unresolved problems.
- *Managed Competition under a Global Budget.* Key architects of the president's task force on health care reform have described this system of insurance purchasing, its philosophical grounding in managed care, its structure, and its cost-containment potential under a national budget. Where does Medicare fit in?
- *Redressing Medicare's Shortfall.* Certain inherent elements of managed competition may resolve issues that have plagued Medicare since its inception, many of them lifted directly from managed care, others from the benefit of a national health insurance system.
- *Potential Pitfalls.* A system reliant on cost-effective, outcomes-based medicine may be less willing to fund high-cost medicine near the end of life than to fund preventive programs. Reimbursement adjustment may be inadequate (or simply inaccurate), leading providers to attempt to discourage elderly subscribers.

Although allusions are made here to contributions from an extensive geriatric literature, social science literature, and examinations of Medicare's social health maintenance organization (HMO) and Medicare competition demonstration projects, this chapter is not intended to be a comprehensive review of these areas (see Newcomer, Harrington, and Friedlob 1990). And although it would seem that the long-term care controversy has critical bearing on any discussion of health care reform, space is not adequate here to discuss this issue in depth. Instead, this chapter addresses how the acute and chronic (nonlong-term) care needs of the elderly will fare under managed competition and what specific aspects of the reform proposal bear on Americans aged 65 and over.

Shortcomings of Medicare

At Medicare's enactment, 38 percent of the elderly who were no longer working had private health insurance, and spending for medical care consumed a major portion of the elderly's income. Medicare is credited with addressing most of those needs through its Part A coverage (for short-term hospital care, postacute skilled nursing facilities, and home health services) and Part B coverage (a voluntary supplementary program that covers physician charges and ambulatory care).

Despite multiple revisions and amendments to Medicare since1965, substantial gaps still exist in the program. Specifically, it lacks provisions to cover the cost of prescription drugs, physician charges in excess of the amount Medicare defines as reasonable, hospital stays over 150 days, and most long-term care services (Rowland 1991).

In attempts to address initial shortcomings, the federal government expanded hospital coverage in 1967, established coverage for intermediate care facilities and skilled nursing facilities in 1972, and established rural health clinics in 1977. (Table 7.1 lists major revisions since 1965.)

Financial Burden

Since Medicare's creation those persons over age 65 who could, bought supplemental health insurance called "Medigap." It is estimated that 72 percent of the elderly Medicare beneficiaries own such policies. In 1989 the mean annual premium was $718 and the market for such policies was estimated to be approaching $20 billion (Rice and Thomas 1992). Another 8 percent of Medicare recipients who cannot afford to buy their own Medigap policies receive Medicaid assistance to pay premiums, deductibles, and other portions of costsharing.

An examination of the costs of health care shared by the elderly demonstrates the need for such Medigap policies, as well as the continued

TABLE 7.1 Health Legislation and the Elderly: 1965-1989[a]

Year	Legislation	Provisions
1965	Social Security Amendments of 1965	Established Medicare and Medicaid.
1967	Social Security Amendments of 1967	Expanded hospital coverage and durable medical equipment.
1970	Public Health Service Amendment of 1970	Authorized grants and contracts for research on provision of home health services.
1972	Social Security Amendments of 1972	Added disabled and ESRD for Medicare; increased premiums and deductibles; established Medicaid ICFs; Medicare ECF converted to SNFs.
1977	Rural Health Clinics Act	Medicare coverage of rural health clinics.
1980	Social Security Disability Amendment of 1980	Voluntary certification of Medicare; supplementary health insurance policies.
1982	Tax Equity and Fiscal Responsibility Act 1982	Medicare hospice benefit.
1986	Omnibus Budget Reconciliation Act of 1986	Medicaid option to poverty level for full coverage or buy-in 1987.
1987	Omnibus Budget Reconciliation Act of 1987	Nursing home reform.
1988	Medicare Catastrophic Coverage Act of 1988	Expanded Medicare benefits; Medicaid buy-in, spousal impoverishment.
1989	Omnibus Budget Reconciliation Act of 1989	Medicare mental health benefits; pap smears.
1989	Medicare Catastrophic Coverage Repeal	Repeals all except Medicaid provisions.

[a]*Source:* Rowland D. Financing Health Care for Elderly Americans. *In:* Ginzberg E, ed. *Health Services Research: Key to Health Policy.* Cambridge: Harvard University Press, 1991.

financial burden of health care. In 1993 patients are required to pay

- $676 as an initial deductible for hospital stays;
- Daily copayments of $169 for hospital stays in excess of 60 days, but not in excess of 90 days, and $338 for 60 "lifetime reserve" days for stays in excess of 90 days;
- A $100 annual deductible on physician and related "recognized" charges;
- 20 percent coinsurance on additional physician and related charges deemed "reasonable" by Medicare.

Catastrophic Coverage

In 1988 the Medicare Catastrophic Coverage Act was passed, representing the most significant expansion in Medicare's scope and the first major restructuring of benefits since the enactment. It placed a ceiling on out-of-pocket spending for costsharing, eliminated the restriction on days covered under hospice care, and added coverage for outpatient prescription drugs, respite care, and mammography screening. Although it was repealed in 1989, in part because of resentment among the elderly over its financing, which would have been shouldered entirely by Medicare beneficiaries, the Catastrophic Coverage Act filled longstanding gaps in Medicare coverage.

Prescription Drugs

Analyses of out-of-pocket expenses among the elderly before and after the enactment of Medicare showed decreasing protection from out-of-pocket liability. A major share of these costs were prescription drugs, which account for 10 percent of health care spending (7 percent outpatient and 3 percent inpatient use) (Rosenblum 1985). The Medicare population uses a disproportionate percentage of the prescription drugs sold in the United States. The lack of a comprehensive prescription drug benefit, therefore, is a significant hardship for this population.

Preventive Health Services

The repealed Catastrophic Coverage Act included coverage for mammography screening, which had been shown to be cost effective. Mammography screening was reinstated as part of 1990 legislation and remains a reimbursable expense. However, Medicare still specifically excludes coverage for preventive health services such as routine physical examinations (although many recipients receive such examinations when visiting physicians with more specific complaints), most immunizations (special exception was made for pneumonia vaccines in 1980), screening examinations, and health education and counseling.

Long-Term Care

The Medicaid program is the major public source of funding for long-term care, although, of the estimated $62 billion spent on nursing home care for elderly in 1992, nearly 60 percent was paid by elderly patients and their families (Cohen et al. 1992; Waldo et al. 1989).

Adverse Selection

The Medigap market offers insurers an opportunity to "cherry pick," that is, to tailor policies to discourage particularly risky groups of potential subscribers (Enthoven 1993). Of course, whether this or any other short-comings in the Medicare program will be addressed by health care reform in the form of managed competition will depend on Congress's reaction to the Clinton administration's proposal. Recall that the Catastrophic Coverage Act was an attempt to redress at least some of the short-comings; but, no renewed effort has been made to pass a new version of the act in the four years since its repeal.

Managed Competition Under a Global Budget

To understand how some of the current proposals in health care reform can redress some of Medicare's shortcomings, and, in contrast, how they potentially may create new gaps in health care for the elderly, this section reviews managed competition as it has been described by the principal architects of President Clinton's health care reform effort.

The concept of managed competition grew out of the experience of managed care, and, specifically, the experience of early prepaid group practice health care plans, although it differs significantly from such plans now (Enthoven 1993). These health care plans contracted with employers to provide comprehensive health care services in exchange for a pre-arranged per capita charge, thereby shifting the financial risk from the employer to the health care plan. The plans had an economic incentive to deliver cost-conscious medicine and, in this way, departed from the cost-unconscious, fee-for-service plans. In fee-for-service, consumers are insulated from costs because insurers agree to pay all reasonable charges and physicians have cost-increasing incentives to deliver more care, not less. Prepaid plans, in contrast to fee-for-service plans, competed with one another based on their ability to deliver care of adequate quality at lower costs. Although managed competition focuses on managed care, the two are not synonymous.

Managed Care

Managed care describes a health care delivery system such as a health maintenance organization (HMO) in which a third party influences the doctor-patient interaction to a greater or lesser degree. An HMO's administration, for example, may specify what physicians a patient can use, what specialists may be consulted, or whether an admission is covered or not. The old style, traditional fee-for-service payment system, in which an insurance company pays all or a portion of services billed after treatment, is not managed care. However, managed care organizations comprise a broad range of health care delivery systems. They include indemnity style entities in which the physicians are paid by fee-for-service but are subject to some level of managerial oversight. For example, they may be required to use a restricted panel of specialists or certain hospitals. In fact, HMOs also may pay their physicians fee for service, rather than a capitated rate.

Managed Competition

Managed competition is a health care purchasing system in which groups of patients purchase health care services from accountable health care plans, and these may include managed care organizations as well as traditional fee-for-service insurance companies. The "competition" takes place between these plans, and they vie to attract individuals from these pools of patients. The patient groups have administrative representatives, formerly called health insurance purchasing cooperatives (HIPCs) and now called health care alliances (HCAs), that determine which providers may compete for the patients in the pool. These administrative representatives probably will be required to accept a range of providers, including an old style, fee-for-service insurance company, although they will be encouraged to emphasize managed care organizations. Large employers and current Medicare intermediaries also may act as administrative representatives.

Health Alliances

The role of the health alliances has not been publicly defined, and, within working groups in Washington, the definition is the subject of controversy. If the flow of money spent on health care is followed closely, then the role of the health alliance becomes clearer.

Money will be pooled from several sources. These sources may include employers and employees who contribute a portion of the payroll, HCFA for current Medicare and Medicaid recipients, and additional sur-taxes such as the so-called "sin taxes" on cigarettes and alcohol, an energy tax, and a new tax on employer-paid health benefits that exceed a certain basic level (currently, all employer health benefits are tax sheltered.) That pool of money will then be used by health alliances to purchase health care services from a selected panel of accountable health care plans for everyone in the population. Some employers may be allowed to bypass the pool of funds, however, and purchase health care services directly from their own panel of health care plans for their own employees, in effect serving as their employees' health care alliance. Medicare, simi-larly, may also serve as an independent health alliance for the current enrollees, purchasing services from a panel of health care plans for the elderly. Allowing small employees, individuals, and the uninsured to be represented by health alliances will give these groups increased purchas-ing power and, as a result, market forces may provide them with lower cost health care. Large employers and current Medicare intermediaries may also be administrative representatives.

The health alliances may be regional entities. States may oversee these regional buying groups, although they also may be allowed exemptions from the national system if they develop their own system for providing their populations with universal access. A National Health Board prob-ably will be established to set criteria for a minimum health benefit pack-age that each state in turn will be required to meet. The National Health Board may serve other important functions in the larger organizational structure as well, such as collecting and interpreting data on health out-comes or monitoring the distribution of comparative information among subscribers.

The accountable health care plans will be paid a capitated annual fee, that is, an age- and sex-adjusted fixed amount of money to provide a com-prehensive benefit package to each patient. Their revenue would rise or fall based on the number of subscribers they attract and the efficiency with which they deliver health care. Competition for subscribers would be managed by the health alliance with a system of rules and incentives to protect subscribers from free market failures such as *risk selection*, which is the practice used by health insurance companies to refuse insurance to patients who are likely to incur high costs (often patients with pre-exist-ing conditions, chronic illnesses, or the elderly). Similarly, *experience rat-ing* (charging higher premiums to people with pre-existing conditions) would be replaced by *community rating*. The health alliances would man-age the enrollment process in which all subscribers have an annual op-portunity to change plans. The alliance may be directly responsible for providing the information necessary for subscribers to choose between plans based on their cost, what benefits they may offer above the basic package (for these added benefits, subscribers would pay a premium), and their quality. The plans themselves may choose to charge copayments or deductibles to influence patients to do their part in reducing costs.

Global Budget

What differentiates managed competition as discussed by key members of President Clinton's task force on health care reform from earlier notions of "managed competition" is an additional cost-containment strategy called global budgeting. Many other nations, for instance the United Kingdom, Germany, Canada, and the Netherlands, use different forms of *global budgeting* or expenditure targets to check increases in health care costs. In all likelihood, President Clinton will propose such a global budget to contain health care costs, although some advocates of managed competition believe that this will not be necessary once market forces exert their effect on a more mature system.

Top-down budgeting holds particularly important implications for the elderly. Such a budget limit may require that the marginal benefit of a given medical expenditure be weighed against its cost. Less value, therefore, may be placed on therapies that benefit patients with shorter life expectancies, which raises the specter of a system in which a potentially lifesaving therapy such as dialysis for end-stage renal disease will be denied to patients based on age. This is an informal, although accepted, practice in other countries with limits on health care expenditures. Such rationing of health care could be brought about either by the imposition of a budget limit, such as a global budget, or by the kind of market competition inherent in managed competition. For example, market competition may lead certain health care plans to decrease costs by reducing the availability of an expensive medical therapy, like coronary artery bypass grafting to patients over a specified age. Thus, although these plans may not be directly subject to a national global budget, they have their own budget limits imposed on them by the need to remain financially solvent.

Medicare Reform

To date, little specific information has been released about the role of Medicare and the treatment of health care coverage for the elderly. Some of President Clinton's health care advisors feel that, initially, Medicare beneficiaries could elect to maintain their same health care coverage under a Medicare program that acts as a kind of national health alliance, but that, as more Medicaid enrollees elect to join other plans within their regional health alliances, traditional Medicare eventually will wither away (Starr and Zelman 1993).

Other members of the task force argue that Medicare should be maintained in its present form. Such a solution is politically expedient, and surveys of Medicare recipients show that most participants prefer to have their own health care plan and are concerned that their interests would be discounted if health care is folded into a larger national pool. Proposing to shift the 31 million elderly Americans from Medicare into a disparate group of health alliances could be disruptive to the health care system, and it might impede the acceptance and passage of the entire program (Kronick 1993). Whether Medicare is significantly restructured or not, the impact of any reform on the rest of the health care system still will affect Medicare beneficiaries.

Redressing Medicare's Shortfall

The most significant impact of managed competition on the elderly may come with a pervasive shift in the philosophy of medical care delivery in America. This anticipated shift goes from a system of medicine that believes that more is better to one of managed care that rewards more efficient care. Drugs, devices, and procedures, although usually beneficial or at least not harmful, nevertheless carry with them statistically significant risks of adverse outcomes that may outweigh a marginal benefit. Surgical treatment of prostate cancer, for example, may lead to impotence and incontinence. Prostate cancer is usually slow growing, however, and a man over 65 years old is more likely to die of other causes than the prostate cancer itself. In this case, the risks of impotence and incontinence, although relatively small, probably outweigh the benefit.

The traditional system of medical care in this country is embodied in the fee-for-service system. Each additional procedure performed by the physician increases the physician's income. The patient is largely insulated from cost—except for deductibles and copayments—by an insurance policy. Such a system has been called cost-increasing, cost-unconscious medicine and may lead to overtreatment. Such overtreatment not only fuels the rise in health care costs but also may actually lead to a poorer quality of health care in certain situations.

The movement toward more cost-conscious, cost-effective medicine is embodied in managed care systems such as the HMO, the preferred provider organization (PPO), the independent practitioner association (IPA), and the point of service (POS) plan. In an HMO, for example, the physician (or group to which the physician belongs) is often paid a fixed fee to provide comprehensive care for an individual for a fixed period. A portion of this fixed fee is allocated to pay for hospital care, diagnostic procedures, and treatments, in addition to routine health care. The incentive, therefore, is to deliver less rather than more care.

More recent innovations in managed care systems have made the financial arrangements between physicians and the managed care organizations more complex. In the IPA model, for example, physicians practice in their own offices with their own management style and see patients outside the HMO. They have a less direct relationship with the HMO than more traditional HMO arrangements in which physicians practice together and see only HMO members. The financial outcome and the allegiance of the physician to the IPA is less direct than to a traditional staff-model HMO. Some IPAs have sought to achieve a better "buy in" by physicians in the culture of the HMO by creating two- and three-tier HMOs (Hillman, Welch, and Pauly 1992). Two-tier HMOs contract directly with physicians, paying them outright and offering financial incentives through bonuses. They also withhold accounts and other mechanisms to contain costs through reducing hospital, specialist, or other service use. Three-tier HMOs differ in that they contract with an intermediary organization—a middle tier—that in turn contracts with physicians. Examples of such intermediaries are hospital medical staffs, physician groups, and physicians in geographic areas that receive capitation payment from the contracting HMO but then are free to negotiate different contractual arrangements and incentives with individual physicians.

Traditional two-tier systems, in which HMOs contract directly with physicians and often pay them by capitation, put the financial risk of treatment more directly on the individual physician, whereas the managerial control of the patient (for example, the extent of utilization management and other nonfinancial constraints) often remains with the HMO. Such arrangements may produce physician resentment, however, because the control (but not the financial risk) remains remote and adversarial. In a three-tier system, the financial risk of under- or overtreatment can be retained by the middle tier and removed from the individual physician. For example, a middle-tier contracting organization may choose to replace financial incentives with other influences on individual physicians, such as utilization management, intense information feedback, or some other change in the culture in which the physician practices. In this way physicians have more flexibility to manage their own behavior, independent of financial concerns. Decisionmaking is removed from remote third parties.

Such a three-tier arrangement simulates the proximity and peer group influences that occur in non-IPA HMOs and, although not yet fully evaluated in scientific studies, holds promise for improving competition's ability to change constructively the medical practice styles of physicians in different types of managed care organizations so that more participants in a system of managed competition practice more cost-conscious, more cost-efficient medicine. Managed competition is a system of financing, but its potential for cost savings lies in its ability to change the style of medical practice and structures of management, to promote cost-conscious, high quality medical decisionmaking (Starr and Zelman 1993).

Although regional health alliances may be required to offer a fee-for-service option and Medicare recipients may be allowed to continue the relationship with their current physicians, substantial inducements also may be offered to attract them into managed care plans, because these often offer more comprehensive benefits at a lower price.

Case Management

Medicare patients are sicker and their care is more complicated than average patients. They often are prescribed a wide array of drugs for multiple medical problems, and these medications must be monitored and adjusted frequently as the patient's condition changes. These factors argue strongly for case management, a technique often used by managed care organizations to provide uniform, coordinated care by assigning patients to one responsible case manager or primary care physician. Managed care organizations also use such case managers as gatekeepers, to reduce the number of patient self-referrals to specialists, another contributor to the high cost of medical care. The primary care physician evaluates the patient's need for a specialist before making a referral. Then the primary care physician takes responsibility for orchestrating the patient's health care. Primary care physicians refer patients to specialists when needed, confer with specialists, and prevent redundant or counterproductive therapies and medications. Such coordination would be especially useful for the elderly, because they often see multiple specialists: for example, a rheumatologist for arthritis, a dermatologist for skin cancer, a cardiologist for congestive heart failure, and a pulmonologist for chronic obstructive pulmonary disease.

Medicare's Managed Care Competition

Most elderly Americans prefer the old style, fee-for-service system. Acceptance of managed care among all ages varies by region, with greatest enrollment in the West and limited enrollment in the Northeast. Medicare formally encouraged enrollment of Medicare recipients in managed care plans in 1982 with the passage of the Tax Equity and Fiscal Responsibility Act. And in 1983, HCFA initiated the National Medicare Competition demonstration in which managed care plans were recruited to provide comprehensive care to Medicare recipients. By 1992, the demonstration project had recruited 100 HMOs and had enrolled one million Medicare recipients (Retchin et al. 1992). Few Medicare recipients joined for several reasons. Many did not want to lose the opportunity to chose their own physician, and they wanted to hold on to longstanding relationships with physicians whom they trusted and who knew their complicated medical histories. Medicare recipients also feared that they might not get the care they wanted because the managed care organization might deny benefits it deemed unnecessary. In addition, HMOs did not join the demonstration projects as rapidly as expected because most of their experience was with a healthier population, and they either had difficulty or believed they would have difficulty in delivering comprehensive care to a sicker population for a fixed fee.

Several studies addressed the concerns of the elderly as well as those of the HMOs. For example, comparison of Medicare recipients treated in HMOs with Medicare recipients treated in traditional plans showed no significant differences in functional status and no significant differences in medical visits, suggesting comparable quality and access to care (Retchin et al. 1992). Another comparison of participants in the HMO demonstration project with others in traditional forms of care showed no significant differences in utilization with two exceptions: the HMO patients made more frequent visits to community health clinics and had longer stays in hospitals for medical procedures, suggesting that they may have received a higher level of care (Wan 1989).

Most studies on managed care plans have involved the non-elderly. Some have postulated that retired enrollees of HMOs will demonstrate different usage patterns because of greater need and more free time (Thomas and Kelman 1990). An examination of this issue showed no statistically significant effect of retirement on the use of health services, suggesting that the costsavings of managed care plans applied equally well to the elderly as to the non-elderly (Soghikian et al. 1991).

Financial Burden

The level of financial burden that would be borne by Medicare recipients depends on the level of benefits guaranteed by the standard basic benefit package. President Clinton is considering multiple levels of benefits, with the most generous being increased coverage for those persons 65 and older, whereas the least generous would reduce the benefit now available through Medicare. Details of the various funding mechanisms, which will determine whether the new health plan will cost Medicare recipients more or less than currently, are still unclear. Greater reliance on payroll taxes, for example, would benefit the elderly because they no longer pay such taxes. Greater reliance on energy taxes or on a sin tax would affect the elderly to the same extent that they would affect other segments of the population.

The choice of funding mechanisms and the composition of the basic benefit package will determine whether the elderly will find themselves paying higher or lower copayments and deductibles than currently. For those who chose to join managed care organizations, however, their out-of-pocket contribution might be less because these organizations typically offer more comprehensive benefits at a fixed price (Bates and Brown 1988). Fee-for-service plans generally use higher copayments and deductibles as mechanisms to reduce patient use of services. A fee-for-service plan offered under managed competition could potentially continue to use such negative financial incentives. Managed care plans, however, use different financial incentives to reduce costs, and such plans could be offered to Medicare recipients more widely.

Prescription Drugs

The costs of prescription drugs have risen faster than inflation and the volume of prescription drug use by the Medicare population (the major user of pharmaceuticals) has also risen, both contributing to the increasing proportion of health care expenditures for prescription drugs. These rising costs have led to recent calls for governmentally imposed price controls. Such controls, however, pose a challenge for managed competition, which will likely be asked to balance the need to rein in drug prices with the need to allow pharmaceutical companies sufficient profits to sustain adequate research and development programs. American pharmaceutical companies are world leaders in new drug development. Aggressive price regulation risks the slowing or even stalling of such innovation. Although the elderly could benefit from lower priced drugs, this should be weighed against the potential harmful effect of such costsavings from price controls on the potential future benefit of drug development. Appropriate profits that allow adequate spending on research and development without reducing access to drugs are necessary.

The potential of managed competition to address the lack of comprehensive Medicare prescription drug plans lies with the focus on managed care. If the Medicare population joins more comprehensive health plans, such as HMOs, they would be more likely to receive prescription plans as part of the standard coverage. In one survey of HMOs that accept Medicare recipients, the majority offered unlimited coverage with a copayment of from $2 to $5 on each monthly supply of a drug (Bates and Brown 1988). Like many specific issues in managed competition, the composition of the standard basic benefit package will determine whether prescription drugs will be a standard benefit or one offered at a higher price by some plans (Berthgold 1993).

Preventive and Routine Health Care

Some gerontologists believe that managed care systems, with their reliance on primary care physicians as gatekeepers to the system and as case managers, will offer the elderly more coordinated care (Parker and Secord, 1988). Such plans routinely cover regular physical examinations, screening examinations, health education and counseling, and immunizations. It is in the financial interest of these systems to offer primary care, for example, by catching an illness early, when it is simpler (and cheaper) to treat.

Medicare currently does not pay for vision and hearing deficits, but the majority of HMOs do cover vision and hearing examinations: two thirds place no limit or copayment on auditory evaluations, and one third do not restrict vision benefits. Coverage for glasses or hearing aids has occurred less frequently. Almost half the HMOs surveyed covered some dental benefits, and a few paid for dentures (Bates and Brown 1988).

Long-Term Care

Although it is unclear whether the basic benefit package will cover long-term care for the elderly, economic analyses, health policymakers, and advocates for the elderly have supported the establishment of a formal program. Although managed care programs are more likely to pay for skilled nursing facilities, they apply the same limits on length of stay that traditional Medicare providers use. The basic benefit package will address the level of long-term care offered.

Although many of the shortcomings in today's Medicare system have yet to be addressed specifically by President Clinton's health care reform proposal, a shift in the philosophy of medical care delivery toward cost-conscious, comprehensive care plans seems likely to redress the financial burden and economic barriers to care found in Medicare. The experience of the elderly in such managed care systems, although theoretically beneficial, has yet to be tested adequately. Moreover, it is unclear whether the elderly will be willing to give up a system that they know well for plans that traditionally have appealed most to younger people.

Potential Pitfalls

Health care reform may conflict with the interests of the elderly simply because of the increasing share of national health care expenditures devoted to this segment of the population. Any effort to reduce expenditures, therefore, could potentially limit health care services for those aged 65 and over, or increase the elderly's financial burden.

Global Budget and Market Competition

Two distinct cost-containment strategies have been promoted by the current health care reform proposal, and each has the potential to reduce Medicare benefits or increase the financial contribution expected from Medicare recipients. One strategy relies on market competition. That is, the accountable health plans must compete with one another for patients and the fixed annual fees these patients bring. Faced with a fixed fee for each patient, these plans will seek to deliver care as efficiently as possible. Even after adjusting the capitation paid to the AHP for age, gender, and possibly, comorbidities, there still may be an incentive to seek out low-cost patients, (for example, employed young adults), and to avoid high-cost patients (those with chronic disease and the elderly). Similarly, the plans will seek to reduce costs by delivering less care per patient, which carries the risk of undertreatment. Both cost-reducing strategies may put the elderly at risk.

The second cost-containment strategy, the global budget, was added to the reform plan to ensure that overall expenditures on health care would stop rising immediately. Some health care economists believe it will take from five to ten years before the competitive marketplace exerts its cost-reducing effects. It is unclear now who will be responsible for setting, imposing, monitoring, and enforcing a global budget. Such an expenditure limit could be enforced at the national health board level, at the state or regional levels, at the health alliance level, at the accountable health plan level, at the bedside by the physician.

The reason that these cost-containment strategies—the global budget and market competition—have potential pitfalls for the elderly is that older Americans incur a disproportionate share of health care budget expenditures. The biggest utilizers in the system are at highest risk.

A small proportion of medical care users account for disproportionate costs (Freeborn et al. 1990). In 1990, for example, HCFA reported that 18.8 percent of those eligible for Medicare incurred 80 percent of Medicare's total payments, and that 45 percent accounted for only 2.2 percent of total Medicare payments (Iglehart 1972). A high proportion of medical care expenditures takes place at the extremes of life. Despite broader discussion of putting limits on such treatments, a recent study showed that, since 1976 among Medicare recipients, no significant change has occurred in the proportion of Medicare expenditures accounted for by persons in their last year of life. The share has remained about 27 to 30 percent of such expenditures (Lubitz and Riley 1993). Could this high concentration of expenditures be distributed more evenly throughout the population or, for that matter, throughout life?

The exigencies of meeting a fixed budget may force health policymakers to answer yes to this question and begin to require that clinicians make judgments about directions in treatment based on more than clinical evidence. To some degree, these considerations already have surfaced in the clinical literature. In evaluating aortic valve replacement in an 87-year-old patient, the author of a recent case study in the New England Journal of Medicine asked at what age a patient was "too old" to be treated. The answer would have to await a national consensus, the author suggested (Thibault 1993).

Such a discussion marks a departure from the practice of medicine in the past but may indicate what would happen under a fixed health care budget, as well as under the influence of the competitive market place. One example of rationing made explicit is the Oregon program for Medicaid health care rationing. In Oregon, policymakers created a list of health care services, which they ranked by perceived benefit and relative merit, and then funded as many as the state's Medicaid budget would allow. The proposal planned to leave unfunded those services whose cost/benefit ratio placed them lower on the list. Depending on how significant a factor the ranking system considers patient age and potential life-years gained from treatment, the elderly could find that services now routinely funded could be reduced. Less explicit rationing takes place in Great Britain, as well as in other countries that have national health services, and age restrictions are accepted for procedures like dialysis and open heart surgery.

Living Wills

A similar discussion arises when advanced directives or living wills are considered. In a cost-conscious health care system, those patients who elect to have all medical treatment, even when the cost exceeds the marginal benefit, could reasonably be asked to pay more for these higher cost services. If a patient is willing to pay for such treatment, then it may be allowed, as long as the cost is not subsidized by the public system. The ethical challenge to society arises when those who are unable to pay for more aggressive treatment are denied it.

Case-Mix Adjustors

Managed competition carries an inherent risk of discrimination against enrollees who incur high health care costs (Hillman et al. 1993). In managed competition, accountable health plans will be paid per enrollee, not per service rendered. Therefore, as discussed previously, managed health plans have the incentive to seek those enrollees who cost the least and to avoid high-risk groups such as the aged, the chronically ill, and people with acquired immunodeficiency syndrome (AIDS).

In managed competition, several mechanisms have been proposed to prevent such risk selection and to ensure equity. These include universal coverage in which all plans will be required to accept any enrollee who chooses them; subsidized access to a basic plan; a standard comprehensive basic benefits package; continuous coverage; and community rating.

Community rating, however, is problematic. Plans naturally would seek to avoid more costly patients, because they alone could jeopardize the economic viability of a plan. The RAND Health Insurance Experience showed that the most expensive 1 percent of patients accounted for 28 percent of the plan's costs (Manning et al. 1984).   Some people have proposed that community rating be modified to allow for "age rating" if it is felt that pure community rating would require excessive subsidies of the old by the young (Enthoven 1933).

The problem with such rating systems is that they depend on case-mix adjustors, formulas used to predict the medical costs of different groups. Experience with such equations, however, is disconcerting. None has been shown to predict costs accurately, even when comparing seemingly equivalent conditions.   Two patients with HIV, for example, can have widely different clinical courses and costs. No case-mix adjustors have been shown to predict these differences accurately.

Administrative Complexities

Managed competition poses complex administrative problems that fail to lend themselves to ready solutions. The current Medicare system, with overlapping Medicare coverage and supplemental coverage, requires patients, physicians, and hospital billing departments to fill out multiple forms to receive reimbursement. In 1991, 75 percent of Medicare recipients had supplemental private insurance. About 37 percent purchased the supplementary insurance on their own, employer-sponsored coverage accounted for 33 percent, and five percent had both forms of supplementary coverage (Chulis et al. 1993). It is unclear whether health care reform will reduce or exacerbate such complexity. Employers still may find themselves paying for some supplementary benefit, and Medicare recipients may find themselves faced with a more complex decision of what such supplementary coverage should be used for—certain surgical procedures not deemed cost effective, for example, or the choice of long-term care facilities. The composition of the basic benefit package may clarify some of these issues.

Quality of Care

A potential pitfall in a cost-effective health care delivery system is lower quality care. Americans and American physicians have long embraced the notion that another laboratory test, the addition of a second or third drug, or yet one more imaging procedure represented better medical care. It is a notion that managed care organizations have sought to dispel. Studies in regional variations in medical treatment have shown wide disparities with no apparent differences in outcomes. But the belief seems to remain that *more care* represents *better care.* A risk of a competitive health care plan is a reduction in the intensity of care, perhaps even undertreatment. Studies of managed care organizations that are faced with the kind of financial incentives likely to affect health care alliances have shown that they practice a different style of medicine, one in which patients are admitted to hospitals and referred to specialists less often (Luft 1978). Although no adverse outcomes have been found in evaluations of such care, no clear benefit has been found either; but reductions in the quality of care, although not yet detected, may occur. Incentives to undertreat may be greater under managed competition, creating greater risks for undertreatment. High-cost patients, including the elderly, would logically be at higher risk of undertreatment. Members of President Clinton's task force have sought to create a system of rules and incentives to safeguard quality in managed competition (Hillman et al. 1993). Yet, it is important to repeat that the traditional "more is better care" can be potentially harmful to patients as well. No matter what the final outcome of health care reform may be, it seems clear that the elderly, with their high costs and fixed incomes, are at risk of receiving less than optimal health care or are in line to pay an increased share of the costs for that care.

Conclusion

The flaws in the current Medicare system, inadequate coverage and a prohibitive financial burden of copayments, may well be corrected under a new health care plan. Managed competition under a global budget offers to change the philosophy of medical decisionmaking, creating a cost-conscious system with a comprehensive benefit package, coordinated care, and reduced financial burden. However, inherent in this particular program is a philosophy dedicated to a balanced health care budget with benefit.

The elderly population is at risk because those persons over aged 65 are responsible for the largest and most rapidly growing portion of the public health care budget. After all aspects of President Clinton's health care reform are revealed to the public, it is highly likely that the elderly will again try to tailor the standard benefit package to meet their needs. The elderly will need to demonstrate, however, that the benefits of such expenditures are worth the costs.

References

Bates EW, Brown BS. Geriatric Care Needs and HMO Technology: A Theoretical Analysis and Initial Findings From the National Medicare Competition Evaluation. *Medical Care.* 1988; 26(5): 488-498.

Bergthold LA. Benefit Design Choices Under Managed Competition. *Health Affairs.* 1993; supplement: 99-109.

Chulis GS, Eppig FP, Hogan MO, Waldo DR, Arnett RH III. Health Insurance and the Elderly. *Health Affairs.* 1993 Spring: 111-118.

Cohen MA, Kumar N, Wallack SS. Who Buys Long-Term Care Insurance? *Health Affairs.* 1992; 11(1): 208-223.

Enthoven AC. The History and Principles of Managed Competition. *Health Affairs* 1993; Supplement:24-48.

Freeborn DK, Pope CR, Mullooly JP, McFarland BH. Consistently High Users of Medical Care Among the Elderly. *Medical Care.* 1990; 28(6): 527-540.

Hillman AL, Greer WR, Goldfarb N. Safeguarding Quality in Managed Competition. *Health Affairs* 1993; Supplement: 110-122.

Hillman AL, Welch WP, Pauly MV. Contractual Arrangements Between HMOs and Primary Care Physicians: Three Tiered HMOs and Risk Pools. *Medical Care.* 1992; 30(2): 136-148.

Iglehart JK. Health Policy Report: The American Health Care System - Medicare. *New England Journal of Medicine.* 1992; 327 (20): 1467-1472.

Kronick R. Where Should the Buck Stop: Federal and State Responsibilities in Health Care Financing Reform. *Health Affairs.* 1993; Supplement: 87-98.

Lubitz JD, Riley GF. Clinical Problem-Solving: Too Old for What? *New England Journal of Medicine* 1993; 328(15):1092-1096

Luft HS. How do HMOs Achieve Their "Savings"? Rhetoric and Evidence. *New England Journal of Medicine.* 1978; 298:1336-1343.

Manning WG, Liebowitz A, Goldberg GA, Rogers WH, Newhouse JP. A Controlled Trial of the Effect of a Prepaid Group Practice on Use of Services. *New England Journal of Medicine.* 1984; 310: 1505-1510.

Newcomer R, Harrington C, Frieblob A. Social Health Maintenance Organizations: Assessing Their Initial Experience. *Health Services Research* 1990; 25(3):425-454.

Organization for Economic Co-Operation and Development. Health Policy Studies No. 1. *U.S. Health Care at the Crossroads.* Paris: 1992.

Parker M, Secord LJ. Private Geriatric Case Management: Current Trends and Future Directions. *Quality Review Bulletin.* 1988; July: 209-214.

Retchin SM, Clement DG, Rossiter LF, Brown B, Brown R, Nelson L. How the Eldrly Fare in HMOs: Outcomes from the Medicare Competition Demonstrations. *Health Services Research* 1992; 27(5):651-660.

Rice T, Thomas K. Evaluating the New Medigap Standardization Regulations. *Health Affairs* 1992; Spring 11(1):194-207.

Rosenblum R. Medicare Revisited: A Look Through the Past to the Future. *Journal of Health Politics, Policy and Law.* 1985; 9(4): 669-681.

Rowland D. Financing Health Care for Elderly Americans. *In:* Ginzberg E, ed. *Health Services Research: Key to Health Policy.* Cambridge, MA: Harvard University Press; 1991.

Soghikian K, Midanik LT, Polen MR, Ransom LJ. The Effect of Retirement on Health Services Utilization: The Kaiser Permanente Retirement Study. *Journal of Gerontology* 1991; 46(6):S358-360.

Starr P, Zelman WA. A Bridge to Compromise: Competition Under A Budget. *Health Affairs* 1993; Supplement 12: 7-23.

Thibault GE. Clinical Problem-Solving: Too Old for What? *New England Journal of Medicine.* 1993; 328(13): 946-950.

Waldo D, Sonnefeld ST, McKusick DR, Arnett RH III. Health Care Expenditures by Age Group, 1977 and 1987. *Health Care Financing Review* 1989; 10(4):111-120.

Wan TTH. The Effect of Managed Care on Health Services Use by Dually Eligible Elders. *Medical Care* 1989; 27(11):983-1001.

Warshawsky MJ. Factors Contributing to Rapid Growth in National Expenditures on Health Care. Board of Governors of the Federal Reserve System. Finance and Economics Discussion Series No. 182. Washington, DC; December 1991.

Commentary: John Rother

In Chapter Seven of this book, William Greer and Alan Hillman caution that "the elderly population is at risk because those people over age 65 are responsible for the largest and most rapidly growing portion of the public health care budget." Although their analysis is presented in the context of "managed competition," it could be inferred from this reasoning that the nation's aged population should be wary of any approach to health care reform. The elderly do use more medical services than those under age 65 and, because the nation has chosen to provide health insurance to its aged citizens through a federal program, federal health expenditures for this group are greater than for any other. That said, however, it is important to keep in mind that the single largest contributor to the deficit has come from increases in *system-wide* health care costs that persist despite significant reductions in Medicare. Between 1984 and 1990, an estimated $82 billion was saved from Medicare Part A. The Omnibus Budget Reconciliation Act 1990 (OBRA) cut Medicare by an additional $43 billion from fiscal year FY 1991 to FY 1995. Because providers were able to shift costs, these reductions have not altered total health care spending trends dramatically. Medicare accounts for about 16 percent of total health care expenditures in the United States (CBO 1993).

Medicare Shortfalls

Greer and Hillman correctly note that the current Medicare program has numerous shortcomings. Although Medicare is highly valued by the nation's older population—the program enrolls virtually all (95 percent) of the aged population—it is significant that Medicare still covers only about half of beneficiaries' health bills. As a consequence, more than three fourths of beneficiaries are covered by insurance that supplements Medicare. It is estimated that, in 1991, elders spent more than twice as much (after adjusting for inflation) on out-of-pocket health care costs as they did *before* the establishment of the Medicare program (Lewin/ICF for Families USA 1992). The nation's elders spend more out-of-pocket than any other age group for premiums, deductibles, and coinsurance, as well as for liabilities for noncovered services, such as outpatient prescription drugs. In marked contrast to employer-sponsored insurance, where most plans have out-of-pocket caps of $1000 to $2000 for individual coverage (Sullivan et al. 1992), Medicare has no upper ceiling on beneficiary out-of-pocket liabilities.

Medicare's lack of coverage for most long-term care services represents a major shortcoming, particularly because of the high costs for such care and the absence of adequate and affordable alternatives to public coverage. Although Medicaid covers long-term services—it covers about 46 percent of all nursing home care costs (or about 12.5 percent of total Medicaid expenditures)—elders must impoverish themselves by "spending down" to the federal poverty level to qualify for this aid. Furthermore, Medicaid has an institutional bias that favors nursing home care at the expense of home and community-based care, which most older people prefer.

Long-Term Care and Reform

The inclusion of long-term care coverage in a reformed system is critically important to public support and is especially important to older Americans. A recent poll conducted for the American Association of Retired Persons (AARP) indicated that the inclusion of long-term care raised the overall level of support for health care reform among respondents from 46 percent to 83 percent (ICR Survey Research Group 1993). The array of complex financing and delivery issues makes the task of crafting an acceptable long-term care benefit uniquely challenging. Certain elements, however, are essential: a long-term care system should be based on a social insurance model, and it should provide care for all who need it. Ultimately, the program should become a part of Medicare to promote and facilitate better care management. It should be financed broadly and include meaningful cost-containment provisions. Although most policymakers recognize that a full-blown benefit will have to be phased-in over time, older Americans will be looking for a meaningful downpayment toward comprehensive long-term care coverage. In the long run, a federal long-term care program will provide an ideal opportunity to develop mechanisms that provide a genuine continuum of care by integrating acute and long-term care.

Although the specifics are still uncertain, President Clinton's health reform proposal appears to incorporate several features from earlier managed competition proposals. The plan should provide a reasonably comprehensive benefit package and probably will encourage enrollment in managed care organizations through various incentives to employers and consumers alike; most likely, multiple health insurance options will be available through large purchasing coalitions or corporations known as health alliances. Medicare beneficiaries also will be given options and incentives to enroll in the new managed care plans. The intent of health care reform is to reorder priorities and restructure financing *and* health delivery. If successful, beneficiaries and all others will be affected by a shift in philosophy, from "more is better" to "less can be good too."

Because of its current shortcomings, Medicare needs to be part of comprehensive health care reform. At the same time, the effects of integrating Medicare into a managed competition strategy must be understood fully. Indeed, the emphasis on managed care delivery systems could be beneficial to Medicare beneficiaries. Traditional managed care organizations, such as health maintenance organizations (HMOs), typically provide a more comprehensive range of benefits than Medicare, including outpatient prescription drugs and preventive services; however, current Medicare experience with managed care organizations, particularly nontraditional models, is very limited. As of May 1993, only 1,644,411 Medicare beneficiaries, or about 5 percent of the total Medicare population, were enrolled under 96 Medicare Tax Equity and Fiscal Responsibility Act (TEFRA) risk contracts in the health care financial administration's (HCFA's) coordinated care program. Medicare's experience with preferred provider organizations (PPOs) has just begun under the Medicare Select program in which 15 states are participating in a demonstration of this model. An evaluation of Medicare Select will be conducted to determine patient satisfaction, quality, program savings, and so forth. Neither beneficiaries nor HCFA has experience with other models that exist in the private sector.

Greer and Hillman have enumerated the reasons why the Medicare HMO risk program has failed to thrive. Added to their list are the deficiencies of the reimbursement methodology. It is noteworthy that only 17.5 percent of HMOs participate as risk contractors in the Medicare program. HMO reimbursement is based on the average adjusted per capita cost (AAPCC) and thus is pegged to the fee-for-service system. County-based, the AAPCC methodology results in wide variation across the country. Correction of the AAPCC methodology is necessary to encourage reasonable HMO participation levels in the Medicare program and to ensure that Medicare payments are set at appropriate levels.[1]

Clearly, managed care is not for everyone. Even if Medicare beneficiaries were more familiar with it, the emphasis on this delivery system could be problematic for those beneficiaries who prefer not to join one of these plans, particularly if benefits favored by beneficiaries, such as outpatient prescription drugs or long-term care, are used as enrollment incentives. President Clinton's plan retains a fee-for-service option, as must the Medicare program. In addition to the underlying importance of choice, Greer and Hillman note some of the pitfalls that Medicare beneficiaries could encounter under a managed competition-like strategy; these point to how important effective quality assurance and consumer representation will be on the health alliance governing bodies that arise out of the reformed system. The authors warn that under a global budget, plans may have incentives to avoid enrolling older, higher cost patients. In addition, plans may attempt to reduce costs by undertreating enrollees. Until risk adjusters become more sophisticated and more accurate, these very real possibilities might pose problems for Medicare beneficiaries. With stringent requirements and timely appeal procedures to ensure appropriate responses to consumer grievances, with vigilant external review of the quality of care provided, and with rigorous enforcement, any adverse potential of underserving should be avoidable.

Greer and Hillman also suggest that the elderly may suffer under managed competition because plans will interpret cost-containment strategies as license to ration, reasoning that, in a budgeted system, "the elderly could find services reduced that now are routinely funded." Here again, managed competition, or any other reform strategy, need not limit expenditures inappropriately at the end of life. The need to safeguard against this possibility certainly exists. Widely accepted misconceptions abound that rapidly rising health care costs can be attributed to the cost of treatment during the last year of life and that heroic measures account for a substantial share of Medicare expenditures. On the contrary, the share of Medicare payments for care provided at the end of life has been stable since 1976 (Lubitz and Riley 1993). In addition, the intensity of treatment actually declines with age and functional ability. In 1987, had all medical care been withheld from every Medicare beneficiary in the last year of life, then total savings would have been about $22.7 billion out of approximately one half trillion dollars spent on health care in that year (Jahnigen and Bienstock 1991). Talk of fiscally necessary rationing is therefore premature. With effective cost containment, the United States has the resources to ensure access to acute and long-term care services for all individuals, without compromising the quality of care.

Conclusion

Ultimately, the scope and content of health care reform is a reflection of national priorities. Although it is expected that the needs of older persons will be recognized, there is more theology than hard evidence regarding the advantages of managed competition for this population. Although the potential to combine a better designed program with broader health reforms is great, the integration of Medicare and managed competition should only proceed with extreme care as unavoidable trial and error help make the health care system more responsive to consumer needs and make it more fiscally sustainable.

References

Congressional Budget Office. *Projections of National Health Expenditures*, 1993 Update. Washington DC: CBO, 1993.

Families USA Foundation. *The Health Cost Squeeze on Older Americans.* Washington DC: Families USA, 1992.

Group Health Association of America. *1993 National Directory of HMOs.* Washington, DC: GHAA, 1993: 9.

ICR Survey Research Group. Long-Term Care Public Opinion Survey. Conducted for the American Association of Retired Persons (AARP). Washington, DC: 1993. Photocopy.

Jahnigen DW, Binstock RH. Economic and Clinical Realities: Health Care for Elderly People. In: *Too Old for Health Care: Controversies in Medicine, Law, Economics and Ethics.* Baltimore: Johns Hopkins University Press, 1991; 29-30.

Lubitz J, Riley G. Trends in Medicare Payments in the Last Year of Life. *New England Journal of Medicine.* 1993; 328:1092-1096.

Marion Merrell Dow. *Managed Care Digest—PPO Edition.* Kansas City, MO: 1992; 3.

Sullivan C, Miller M, Feldman R, David B. Data Watch: Employer-Sponsored Health Insurance in 1991. *Health Affairs*, Winter 1992; 176.

Notes

1. In contrast to Medicare's limited exposure to managed care, 41.4 million people nationwide are enrolled in HMOs, and an additional 85 million are eligible to participate in PPOs (GHAA 1993; Marion Merrell Dow 1992). Over half of all workers covered by employer-sponsored coverage are enrolled in managed care plans. Conventional indemnity insurance accounts for only about eight percent of employer-sponsored plans (Sullivan et al. 1992). The trend, even in nonmanaged care plans, is to apply utilization management techniques such as preadmission certification or concurrent review; 92 percent of employees covered under employer-sponsored programs are in plans that have some form of utilization management (Sullivan et al. 1992).

Commentary: Peggy M. Connerton and J. Peter Nixon

William Greer and Alan Hillman examine many deficiencies in the Medicare program, such as high copayments, inadequate coverage of preventive health care, and the lack of coverage for long-term care and prescription drugs. They argue that one way to extend coverage and still reduce costs for Medicare recipients is to encourage care through health maintenance organizations (HMOs) and other managed care institutions. Not only would this lower costs for recipients, but it also would save the federal government money, especially if the system could be constructed so that managed care providers would compete with one another for Medicare clients under a regulatory framework known as *managed competition.*

In drafting the recently released Health Security Act, the Clinton administration was heavily influenced by advocates of managed competition. Medicare is retained as a separate program, although states would have the option of integrating Medicare beneficiaries into the Health Alliances that will serve the majority of the under-65 population. They would only be allowed to do this if they could guarantee that the federal government's costs would not increase and that Medicare beneficiaries would have access to the same or better coverage as standard Medicare benefits. The Clinton plan would also provide Medicare beneficiaries with a new prescription drug benefit.

Although eventual incorporation of the Medicare program into the reformed system should remain the goal, the Clinton administration's caution is well warranted. By contrast, Greer and Hillman appear too confident that managed competition can contain Medicare's growing costs without affecting significantly the quality of care received by program beneficiaries.

Boiled down to its essentials, the argument from Greer and Hillman is based on four propositions. The first is that moving Medicare recipients into prepaid health plans (such as HMOs) will reduce the program's costs through more aggressive case management and lower utilization. The second is that competition between plans will help reduce costs still further. The third is that a switch to prepaid plans would not affect adversely the quality of care that Medicare beneficiaries receive. The final assumption is there are no significant barriers to incorporating the Medicare population into a new national system.

The argument set forth in this commentary is that none of these propositions is entirely true. In the next few pages, each issue will be addressed in greater depth.

Can Managed Care Cut Medicare Costs?

In theory, prepaid health plans like HMOs are expected to have lower costs than traditional fee-for-service plans, because the provider faces financial incentives to provide less care rather than more. The opposite is true for fee-for-service medicine, where the more services that the providers deliver, the more they benefit.

In practice, however, managed care has been somewhat disappointing. Although the average cost per employee in 1991 for HMOs was almost 15 percent less than the average cost per employee for indemnity plans, HMO premiums increased almost as fast as the premiums for indemnity plans (9.8 percent versus 11 percent) (Iglehart 1992). HMOs have benefitted from their ability to reduce hospital admissions and shorten lengths of stay, but they have been unable to alter the long-term rate of increase in health care costs.

More specific data on the potential impact of managed care on Medicare costs are available from the Health Care Financing Administration's (HCFA's) National Medicare Competition Demonstration, which recruited HMOs to provide care to Medicare recipients. Numerous evaluations of the demonstration were prepared by Mathematica Policy Research, Inc., showing mixed results that suggest that the use of prepaid plans may not reduce program costs as much as was previously believed.

HMOs seem to be able to reduce the number of services used by Medicare clients. For example, HMO patients in hospitals had lengths of stay that were 17 percent lower than patients in the traditional fee-for-service plan, although HMOs did not affect the rate of admission to hospitals (Hill et al. 1992). Substantial reductions in utilization of mostly discretionary tests and procedures were found among HMO patients, compared to those in fee-for-service settings. Reductions also occurred in the amount of rehabilitative care provided by HMOs, both in and out of the hospital.

Despite reduced utilization, HMOs did not reduce Medicare's program costs. HCFA paid 5.7 percent *more* for enrollees in HMOs than would have been spent on them under a fee-for-service plan. The principal reason was favorable selection, with HMOs recruiting, on average, healthier Medicare recipients than traditional plans. Because these beneficiaries used fewer services, it would have been cheaper for the federal government to reimburse providers on a fee-for-service basis (Hill et al. 1992).

Will Competition Reduce Costs?

Many advocates of managed competition are not deterred by the lack of success that prepaid health plans have had in bringing costs under control. They argue that because prepaid plans compete with less efficient fee-for-service plans, they are able to "shadow price" (i.e., price their plans just under the level of the fee-for-service plans). Because many employers offer only one or two prepaid plans in addition to their fee-for-service plan, competition between plans is severely attenuated.

By contrast, under a pure managed competition approach, all plans are prepaid, and the traditional tax exemption granted employees for employer contributions to health insurance is limited to the cost of the lowest priced plan available. If subscribers opted for more expensive plans, then they would have to pay taxes on the difference in cost between their plan and the lowest cost plan. Advocates of managed competition argue that this system would increase the competitive pressures on all plans, leading to cost reductions. Greer and Hillman argue that such a system could be used to reduce the costs of the Medicare program.

Although this seems attractive in theory, there are a number of reasons why it would probably not function as effectively as Greer and Hillman believe. Medicare recipients are even less likely than the non-elderly population to behave like the consumers of classical economic theory, carefully comparing price and quality information across many different plans. The majority of Medicare recipients are known to value long-term relationships with one or more physicians and are probably unwilling to switch plans except under exceptional circumstances.

The other principal problem is medical technology, which is one of the single most important factors in explaining the rapid rise in medical costs. Although the move toward managed care can ameliorate some of the pressures to use new technologies, primarily by removing the physician's financial incentive to "do more," it cannot eliminate them. In fact, the highly competitive market envisioned under managed competition could exacerbate the problem if each health plan acquires these technologies to recruit plan participants or new physicians. This has happened with hospitals in large metropolitan areas. For example, the hospitals in the Minneapolis-St.Paul area have five bone marrow programs, 13 open-heart surgery centers, and 23 magnetic resonance imaging centers (one more than exists in all of Canada) (Kent 1992).

One of the best working models of managed competition is the California Public Employees Retirement System (CalPERS), which administers a health program with 25 plans that compete for the business of nearly one million state and local government workers, family members, and retirees. CalPERS announced at the beginning of 1993 that the premiums for its basic health plans would rise an average of 1.5 percent, compared to 10 to 12 percent nationally. Stanford Professor Alain Enthoven, father of the managed competition concept, argues that "this is powerful evidence that managed competition works."

The truth is somewhat more prosaic. Throughout the 1980s, CalPERS experienced higher premium increases than employers nationally. Only in the last two rounds of premium negotiations, for plan years 1992-93 and 1993-94, were costs held well below national trends. The reason is that, in response to California's fiscal crisis, the state froze contributions to the program and used its clout as a multiemployer purchasing cooperative to negotiate aggressively any premium increases charged by CalPERS plans (SEIU 1993).

Can Prepaid Plans Maintain High Quality Care for Medicare Patients?

A major risk inherent in moving Medicare beneficiaries into prepaid plans is that the very incentives designed to eliminate the provision of unnecessary care may result in the denial of needed care. The debate over whether prepaid plans provide lower quality care has raged for years without being settled definitively. The weight of the evidence suggests that HMOs have been successful in reducing utilization without having a negative impact on patient outcomes.

Although Greer and Hillman argue that a switch to prepaid plans would not result in lower quality care for Medicare recipients, the evidence from HCFA's HMO demonstrations is more equivocal. It is true, for example, that comparisons of the inpatient care received by HMO and fee-for-service clients for two conditions, stroke and colon cancer surgery, showed no differences, on the one hand, in death or readmissions (Retchin et al. 1992). On the other hand, one third of Medicare recipients enrolled in HMOs disenrolled within the first two years. More than two thirds of those who disenrolled returned to the fee-for-service sector, suggesting dissatisfaction with some aspects of the care they received (Langwell et al. 1992).

Does the Medicare Population Face Special Barriers?

Although incorporation of the Medicare population into prepaid plans as part of a unified national health care system is attractive for many reasons, it is important to appreciate the difficulties involved. If done improperly, the incorporation of Medicare beneficiaries could destabilize the new system or lead to a political backlash that would make the furor over catastrophic health insurance look mild by comparison.

The root of the problem is that Medicare beneficiaries have significantly different needs than younger, healthier individuals, who historically have gravitated to prepaid plans. As one ages, health becomes more valuable relative to other goods, because the probability of a severe illness increases. The development of an established relationship with a physician who is aware of a person's medical history becomes much more important, as does access to specialized services. HMOs try to limit the use of specialist care, and, in some cases, they may not even have an ongoing relationship with certain types of specialist providers. For these reasons, the elderly tend to favor plans that give them greater choice of providers, and they resist changing health care plans, even as the plans become more expensive.

The experience of retirees in the CalPERS system illustrates this phenomenon. PERS-CARE, the principal fee-for-service plan in the CalPERS system,[1] serves a disproportionate number of retirees, rural employees, and the less healthy. As of January 1993, the average age difference between CalPERS HMO and PERS-CARE enrollees had climbed to eight years (51 for a PERS-CARE member and 43 for an HMO member), which represents one-and-one-half times the age difference just 10 years ago (SEIU 1993).

The tendency of retirees to cluster in plans that give them greater choice of provider drives up the price of those plans, causing younger and healthier individuals to leave, which drives up the price even higher.[2] The gap between the family premium for PERS-CARE and the average HMO now exceeds $100 a month for a one-person plan, $160 a month for a two-person plan, and $210 a month for a family plan (SEIU 1993).

The potential of Medicare recipients to destabilize a prepaid health plan could well lead to discrimination against them, either in enrollment or in treatment. Although it is likely that any Medicare reform legislation will require plans to enroll anyone who applies, the history of antidiscrimination legislation suggests some discriminatory practices can escape the definition of the law. A more significant problem is likely to be discrimination in treatment, where the elderly are denied access to clearly beneficial care that is extremely costly. A 1991 study of California HMOs by the Medicare Advocacy Project concluded that "Medicare beneficiaries are extremely vulnerable to misleading marketing by HMOs," and that those who enroll in HMOs "have few meaningful appeal rights" if they disagree with a physician about seeing a specialist (Perry 1993).

The incentive to discriminate can be reduced by risk-adjusting the capitation rates that the federal government would pay to prepaid plans. As Greer and Hillman point out, however, risk adjustment is not an exact science, and many insurance carriers believe it cannot be done. It will probably also be necessary to develop enforcement mechanisms for the antidiscrimination provisions if there is a future attempt to incorporate the Medicare population into a reformed system.

Prepaid plans are likely to complain bitterly, however, if antidiscrimination provisions are used to prevent them from denying costly forms of care that appear to yield little benefit to Medicare patients. This raises the extremely complicated issue of how to "ration" health care. Greer and Hillman are correct to point out that whether costs are controlled through a global budget or by competitive pressure, any finite limit on expenditures implies that at some point care must be denied. The advantage of the current Medicare system is that it is subject to some degree of democratic accountability. Moving Medicare beneficiaries into prepaid health plans attenuates that accountability. Given that the United States lacks a national system of practice guidelines and quality standards for health care, the risk is that the idiosyncratic choices of the insurance industry about when and how to deny care will affect the elderly disproportionately because, as Willie Sutton replied when asked why he robbed banks, "that is where the money is."

Conclusion

The problems with the Medicare program that Greer and Hillman outline are real ones, and they have performed a valuable service by reviewing them. Undoubtedly, reform of the Medicare system should be linked to reform of the whole health care system. For years, the private sector has been allowed to insure the young, the healthy, and the financially secure, whereas the public sector has been left with the job of insuring the elderly, the sick, and the poor. Although costs have risen for the private and public sectors alike, the burden of public sector programs has been especially heavy of late, and threatens to bankrupt federal, state, and local governments. Folding all private and public insurees into one purchasing system would allow risk and cost to be spread more widely over a larger pool, easing the burden on taxpayers.

Unfortunately, having outlined the problems with Medicare, Greer and Hillman do not advance the debate significantly as to what the solutions should be. They are unable to move beyond the vague, if appealing phraseology of "managed competition under a global budget." Implementing such a proposal for the Medicare population faces a number of obstacles that advocates of managed competition have not thought through seriously. These advocates, who range from Professor Alain Enthoven to the

New York Times editorial page, continue to believe, despite mounting evidence to the contrary, that market forces alone are capable of controlling rapidly rising health care costs.

This is not to say that Medicare recipients should not take advantage of new kinds of delivery systems, or that market forces should not be used to improve certain aspects of plan management. Caution must be exercised to ensure that organized delivery systems include institutional mechanisms to guarantee that Medicare beneficiaries and the entire health care system are not affected adversely. Some proposals along these lines include the requirement that prepaid plans for Medicare beneficiaries have "point-of-service" options so that the elderly can receive care from providers outside the system without incurring severe financial losses. Another idea would be to establish "centers of excellence" for certain capital-intensive surgical procedures so that competitive pressures do not lead plans or hospitals to intensify the technological "arms race." It is extremely important for public authorities to collect and disseminate to consumers information about the quality of the health plans from which they may choose. Quality should be defined broadly to encompass not only medical outcomes but also customer satisfaction.

Finally, and in this Greer and Hillman are correct, Medicare and the entire health care system must be brought under the discipline of a global budget. Only a global budget can protect families, employers, and governments from the staggering burden of health care costs.

References

Hill J, Brown R, Chu D, Bergeron J. *The Impact of the Medicare Risk Program on the Use of Services and Cost to Medicare.* Princeton, NJ: Mathematica Policy Research, Inc., 1992.

Iglehart JK. The American Health Care System–Managed Care. *New England Journal of Medicine.* 1992; 327(10): 742-747.

Kent C. Hospital Wars: Is Peace In Sight? *Medicine and Health* 1992; 46(41):2-3.

Langwell K, Sterns S, Nelson S, Bergeron J, Schopler L, Donahey R. *Disenrollment Experience in the TEFRA HMO/CMP Program, 1985 to 1988.* Washington, DC: Mathematica Policy Research, Inc., 1989.

Perry NJ. A Report Card on HMOs. *Fortune.* June 28, 1993; 110-114.

Retchin SM, Brown R, Cohen R, Clement DG, Stegall M, Abujaber B. *The Quality of Care in TEFRA HMOs/CMPs.* Richmond, VA: Medical College of Virginia; 1992.

Service Employees International Union. *The CalPERS Experience and Managed Competition.* Washington, DC: SEIU Department of Public Policy; 1993.

Notes

1. PERS-CARE is a Preferred Provider Organization (PPO), a modified fee-for-service plan that offers reduced costsharing if plan members use certain designated providers.

2. This trend explains the difficulty that PERS-CARE has had in controlling premium increases, which have averaged 13.9 percent a year over the last five years (SEIU 1993).

Chapter 8
Resolving the Conflict Between Cultural Values and Limited Resources in Providing Health Services to the Elderly

Sylvester J. Schieber

Mounting costs of health care in the United States have stimulated an increasing interest in the allocation of health care services. The discussion about the allocation of health care resources has proceeded down two distinctive paths. One focuses on the macroallocation of resources to the health care sector of our economy. This path generally concludes with the idea that the sustained high growth of the health care sector relative to other sectors in the economy must be curtailed. This conclusion implies that the aggregate flow of resources to the health sector should be stabilized or even diminished, which, in turn, implies that some health services currently available for delivery may be not be available to everyone in the future who might benefit from them.

The other path focuses on the microallocation of resources in the health sector and the ethical issues raised when a wealthy society limits the resources used to sustain individual lives. Microallocation of health care resources is often construed, sometimes pejoratively, as rationing. This path often concludes with the idea that imposing rationing on the health sector is unacceptable. Proponents argue that the emphasis should be on making the existing system of delivery more efficient by simplifying administration and eliminating ineffective services to free added resources for the delivery of necessary care. If these resources are then insufficient to meet overall needs, then the next step is to free resources currently committed to national defense or other governmental activities, to en-

The comments and opinions expressed in this chapter are solely those of the author and do not necessarily represent the opinions of The Wyatt Company or any of its associates.

sure that resources are adequate to provide medical services for everyone who needs them.

Although the debate on whether to ration health care has only recently unfolded, practical realities already have resulted in the relatively widespread rationing of health care services in the United States. Today, between 35 and 40 million people in the United States do not have health insurance, and, without insurance, they do not have the same access to health services as those who are insured. The government has tried to fill this gap through the Medicaid program, but as many as half the poor Americans do not qualify for Medicaid. To address the limits in coverage under Medicaid, the State of Oregon has proposed an explicit limitation on services given under its Medicaid program, to broaden coverage to all the poor. The Clinton administration has approved implementation of this proposal.

The prospect of any sort of rationing in health services is particularly important to the elderly for many reasons. As a group, the elderly tend to suffer from more chronic illnesses, which are generally incurable, than other groups. Many chronic illnesses, like rheumatoid arthritis and diabetes, can be managed effectively over long periods, but doing so requires an ongoing level of expenditures. Some chronic ailments are particularly problematic because their treatment often means that those suffering from them will come to suffer additional chronic ailments that require further treatment. Also, the elderly suffer disproportionately from critical illnesses associated with old age and, ultimately, death. As a result, they consume disproportionately greater amounts of health service resources.

Advances in medical science and the underlying demographics of the American society portend that, in the future, the elderly will need even more health services than now. The general level of resources that will be available to provide medical services to the elderly and the allocation of those resources cannot be ignored. Before investigating why Americans feel that all medical services should be available to everyone and before investigating whether this philosophy should be curtailed, it is important to assess the nature of the resource limitations giving rise to the debate over health care rationing.

Are Resources Really Limited?

The United States spends more of its national economic output on health care than any other major developed country. Not only do we spend more on health care than other countries, there is a growing sense that Americans are now limiting consumption of other goods and services because of their spending for health care. Figure 8.1 shows the level of

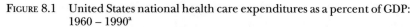

FIGURE 8.1   United States national health care expenditures as a percent of GDP: 1960 – 1990[a]

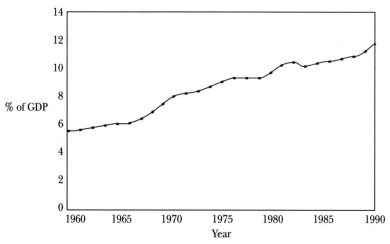

[a] *Source:* Health Care Financing Administration. Office of the Actuary. Data from the Office of National Health Statistics.

national health care spending as a percent of gross domestic product (GDP) for the period 1960 to 1991. Certainly, the figure indicates that the United States has been dedicating an ever growing segment of its GDP to delivering health services. Other segments of the economy grow and shrink over time, however, without raising the same concerns that health care expenditures have elicited recently.

An International Perspective on Health Care Spending

George Schieber, Jean-Pierre Poullier, and Leslie M. Greenwald have compared the economic performance of the health systems in the 24 countries who are members of the Organization for Economic Cooperation and Development (OECD). They found that in 1990 the 24 countries spent an average of 7.6 percent of their GDP on health care, compared with the United States expenditure of 12.1 percent. They also found that the United States had experienced the largest absolute growth in health care expenditures between 1980 and 1990, growing 2.9 percentage points, compared with 0.6 percentage points across the OECD (Schieber et al. 1992).

In an earlier analysis, the same authors had documented a relationship across nations between national income and spending on health. Richer countries tend to spend more on health care than poorer countries (Schieber et al. 1991). In their more recent analysis, the authors estimate three regressions to show the relationship between GDP and health spending across the 24 countries for 1980, 1985, and 1990. These results indicate that between 83 and 87 percent of the variation in per capita health spending across the various nations can be explained by variations in levels of per capita income. When applying this model of the 24 countries to the United States, Schieber et al. found that actual per capita expenditures exceeded expected expenditures by $150 in 1980, $350 in 1985, and $700 in 1990 (Schieber et al. 1991). In other words, the United States has been spending relatively more on health care than other major developed nations in relation to American income levels, and the extent to which this has been happening is steadily increasing.

Joseph Newhouse has taken the data developed by Schieber, Poullier, and Greenwald for the seven largest industrial countries in the OECD, looking at the real growth in per capita health spending over the period 1960 to 1990, and he develops somewhat different conclusions (Newhouse 1993). His results are shown in Table 8.1, where he concludes that in inflation-adjusted terms, the rate of increase in health care spending in the United States is not so different from the rate of increase in other major industrial countries. The most significant numbers in Table 8.1 are those in parentheses. They indicate the difference in the rate of growth in GDP and health spending for each of the periods. On this basis, during the 1960s, the United States was in roughly a median position of growth in health care expenditures relative to its overall economic growth. During the 1970s, except for Canada, United States' health care expenditures grew less rapidly than in the other comparison countries. In the United States, however, relative growth in health expenditures compared against GDP outstripped all other countries during the 1980s. Although Newhouse did not show the difference in the health and GDP growth rates over the 30-year period (1960 to 1990), he indicates that the United States' rate was the median for the countries shown. Over the 30 years, the difference in the two rates for the United States was 4.6 percent, compared with 7.7 percent for Japan, 5.7 percent for Italy, 5.2 percent for France, 4.4 percent for Canada, 4.2 percent for Germany, and 3.5 percent for the United Kingdom.

The conclusions drawn by Schieber et al. and Newhouse might seem inconsistent. The former conclude that the United States is spending a constantly increasing share of its resources on health care compared with the other six countries in the group. Newhouse's analysis suggests that the United States growth in the share of resources devoted to health care is in the middle of the other countries. The reason both conclusions are right relates to the underlying base of expenditures devoted to health care in the various countries. Table 8.2 shows the share of GDP devoted to health care for selected years in each of the seven countries in

TABLE 8.1   Real Per Capita Growth Rates in Health Spending and Difference Between Growth Rates in Health Care and GDP for Seven Countries: 1960-1990[a]

	1960-1990	1960-1970	1970-1980	1980-1990
	Annual Growth in Health Spending Per Capita[b]			
Canada	4.7%	6.1% (2.8)	3.7% (0.5)	4.3% (2.5)
France	5.5	7.8 (3.5)	5.3 (3.0)	3.3 (1.7)
Germany	4.4	5.6 (2.2)	6.3 (3.9)	1.4 (-0.4)
Italy	6.1	8.9 (4.1)	6.2 (3.4)	3.4 (1.3)
Japan	8.2	14.0 (5.1)	7.1 (4.2)	3.7 (0.1)
United Kingdom	3.7	3.7 (1.5)	4.4 (2.9)	3.1 (0.8)
United States	4.8	6.0 (3.6)	4.2 (2.5)	4.4 (2.9)

[a]*Source:* Newhouse JP. An Iconoclastic View of Health Cost Containment. *Health Affairs* 1993. Supplement; 163. Calculated from Schieber GJ et al. U.S. Health Expenditure Performance: An International Comparison and Data Update. *Health Care Financing Review.* Summer 1992; 1-88. Gross domestic product (GDP) deflator for country used to deflate.
[b]Difference between health and GDP growth rates, in percentage points, is shown in parentheses.

Newhouse's analysis. The reason why the aggregate shift of resources to the health care sector is widening relative to the other countries is that the United States started with a larger base of health spending.

TABLE 8.2   Share of Gross Domestic Product Devoted to Health Services in Selected Countries for Selected Years[a]

	1960	1970	1980	1990
Canada	5.5%	7.1%	7.4%	9.3%
France	4.2	5.8	7.6	8.8
Germany	4.8	5.9	8.7	8.1
Italy	3.6	5.2	6.9	7.7
Japan	2.9	4.4	6.4	6.5
United Kingdom	3.9	4.5	5.8	6.2
United States	5.3	7.4	9.2	12.1

[a]*Source:* Calculated from Schieber GJ, et al. U.S. Health Expenditure Performance: An International Comparison and Data Update. *Health Care Financing Review.* Summer 1992; 1-88.

Even though the United States may have had lower rates of growth in the shifting of resources for some periods relative to other countries, more money was devoted to health care services to begin with. Therefore, when the lower growth rate is applied to the bigger base, the United States continues to redeploy relatively more resources into health care services than other countries. For example, the difference in Japan's health expenditure growth rate and their GDP growth rate exceeded that of the United States (2.9 versus 2.8) over the period 1960 to 1990. Japan, however, was spending only 2.9 percent of its GDP on health services in 1960 compared to 5.3 percent in the United States. By 1990, Japan was spending 6.5 percent of GDP on health compared with 12.1 percent in the United States. Although their rate of redeployment was greater over the period, the Japanese redeployed 3.6 percent of their GDP to health care, compared to 6.8 percent of the GDP in the United States.

Whether analysts focus on the rate at which resources are being redeployed into health care or on the relative magnitude of resources devoted to health care, the international comparisons lead many to conclude that too much of the GDP is devoted to this sector of the American economy. There is no absolute measure, however, that certifies that the American level of expenditures on health care is too high, or that other levels of spending in other countries are just right. If those paying for health care are willing to bear the burden of higher expenditures or more rapid redeployment of resources to health care, then no pressure should be exerted to limit the allocation of these resources.

Third-Party Payers

During 1992, 19 percent of the health services delivered in the United States were financed by direct consumer payments. Most of the remaining services were financed through government transfer programs for needy individuals, social insurance programs to cover the disabled and aged, and private insurance, most of which is paid through employer-sponsored health benefit programs. Various federal government programs accounted for 32 percent of the purchases of health care services. State and local government programs accounted for 14 percent. Private insurance paid for 31 percent of the services delivered. Other private financing, including philanthropy and special grants, accounted for 4 percent (Burner et al. 1992). The major payers for health services delivery have become significant forces in the movement to limit financing for health services.

The Federal Government As Health Services Purchaser

The federal government is the largest single purchaser of health services in the United States. The two health care programs on which it spends the most money are Medicare and Medicaid. In addition, it sponsors many smaller programs aimed at special groups. For example, the Veterans Benefits program provides health services to military veterans, along with other services. The Department of Defense sponsors CHAMPUS to provide health benefits to current military personnel and their dependents. In addition, the federal government subsidizes the purchase of health insurance by its civilian employees. It also is a major funding source for much of the health research in the country. The relative level of federal government expenditures under five major groupings of programs is shown in Table 8.3. Although the government is concerned about all of these programs, the relative size of Medicare and Medicaid and their growth patterns over the years make them the focal point of most policy discussions related to the federal government as a payer for health services.

The Medicare program was established in 1965 under the auspices of the Social Security Act. At that time, Medicare extended health insurance coverage to individuals over age 65 who were eligible to receive Social Security benefits. Medicare consists of two separate programs: Part A is the Hospital Insurance (HI) program, and Part B is the Supplementary Medical Insurance (SMI) program. In 1973, Medicare coverage also was extended to disabled individuals who were entitled to Social Security or railroad retirement cash benefits. At the same time, coverage was extended to individuals who suffered from end-stage renal disease (ESRD). Medicare is funded through the payroll tax system.

TABLE 8.3   National Health Expenditures by the Federal Government as a Share of GDP for Calendar Years 1960-1990[a]

Share of Gross Domestic Product	Medicare	Medicaid/ Public Assistance	Veterans Administration and Defense Department	Research	Other
1960	0.0	0.0	0.3	0.1	0.1
1965	0.0	0.1	0.3	0.2	0.1
1970	0.8	0.3	0.4	0.2	0.2
1975	1.0	0.5	0.4	0.2	0.2
1980	1.4	0.5	0.4	0.2	0.2
1985	1.8	0.6	0.4	0.2	0.1
1990	2.0	0.8	0.4	0.2	0.2

[a]*Source:* Health Care Financing Administration. Office of the Actuary. Data from the Office of National Health Statistics.

Medicaid was also established in 1965 to provide health benefits to low-income families and individuals. Medicaid is a joint venture between the federal and state governments. The federal government provides funding to the states for Medicaid based on a formula that relates each state's average per capita income to the national average. The federal government also establishes guidelines under which the states establish program provisions and then administer them.

When Medicare and Medicaid legislation was being considered, there was grave concern in the medical profession that the government would intervene in the doctor-patient relationship and also would establish a system of administered prices for services delivered under the programs. To ameliorate these concerns, the original legislation had specific language that prevented intervention in the doctor-patient relationship and provided that charges for health services delivered under the programs would be reimbursed on the basis of "reasonable and customary" charges for similar services.

The federal cost of Medicare and Medicaid exceeded original expectations. Beginning in the early 1980s, numerous modifications were introduced to bring costs under control. The steady rise in the federal government's cost of its health benefits programs has pushed it into an increasingly aggressive posture of limited budgets and administered prices. Limiting federal health care expenditures when the elderly population is growing and the need for subsidized health services is expanding in the low-income population suggests that something has to give. Some policy analysts believe that aspects of the federal budget other than health care should be limited (Etzioni 1991). They argue that cutbacks should be made on defense spending, space exploration, or other things that have far less merit than providing health services to those who need them.

TABLE 8.4   Federal Budget Expenditures, Revenues, and Deficits as a Percent of GDP For Fiscal Years 1979 and 1990 [a, b]

	1979	1990
Expenditures	20.7%	21.9%
Social Security	4.3	4.6
General Operating Budget	16.4	17.3
Health Care[c]	1.7	2.7
Net Interest	1.8	3.4
Subtotal	3.4	6.1
All Other	13.0	11.2
Defense	4.8	5.5
Civilian	8.2	5.8
Revenues	19.1	18.9
Social Security	4.0	5.2
General Operating Budget	15.1	13.7
Surplus or Deficit	-1.7	-3.0

[a]*Source:* Schultze CL. Paying the Bills. In: Aaron H, Schultze CL, eds. *Setting Domestic Priorities, What Can Government Do?* Washington, DC: The Brookings Institution. 1992; 298.
[b]For 1990, the expenditures and deficits exclude the deposit insurance outlays associated with the savings and loan bailout because of their special and temporary nature.
[c]Excludes administrative costs and the inflow of Part B Medicare premiums, both of which are included in the "all other" civilian category.

Charles Schultze's analysis, as presented in Table 8.4, suggests that some of these other limitations already may have been made. He picks 1979 as the baseline year for his analysis because it was the last nonrecessionary year before Ronald Reagan became President. The 1979 budget reflects the federal government's broad spending priorities before President Reagan's election, without the abnormalities that recessions introduce into government spending. Schultze picks 1990 as the year that best represents the nonrecessionary spending priorities of the federal government toward the end of the Reagan-Bush era. His analysis indicates that, during President Reagan's and President Bush's tenure, there was a decline in most government operations relative to the size of the economy. Social Security increased a small amount, but that was primarily because of growth in the elderly population. Interest expenditures increased, but that was related to the overreliance on deficit financing of government operations during the period. Defense expenditures increased, but President Reagan had made that a central tenant on which he campaigned and was elected. By 1990, defense expenditures accounted for 15 percent more of domestic output than in 1979. Expenditures on discretionary spending on other civilian programs, not including Social Security or major health care programs, had declined by nearly 30 percent over the period, but health care expenditures had expanded by nearly 60 percent.

TABLE 8.5   Projected Federal Budget Expenditures, Revenues, and Deficits as a Percent of GDP for Selected Fiscal Years[a, b]

	1992	1997	2002
Expenditures	23.8%	23.0%	24.3%
Social Security	4.9	4.8	4.9
Health Care[c]	3.4	4.5	6.1
Net Interest	3.4	3.7	4.2
Subtotal	6.8	8.2	10.3
All Other	12.1	10.0	9.1
Revenues	18.6	19.0	19.0
Surplus or Deficit	-5.2	-4.0	5.3

[a]*Source:* Derived by the author from Congressional Budget Office, *The Economic and Budget Outlook.* Washington, DC: Congress of the United States. August, 1992; 39.
[b]The expenditures and deficits exclude the deposit insurance and Desert Storm outlays because of their special and temporary nature.
[c]Includes only Medicare and Medicaid.

With the collapse of the Soviet empire, priorities in federal spending are again under political review. During President Bush's tenure, expenditures on military operations began to be curtailed. There was also a growing concern among public policymakers over the magnitude and persistence of the federal deficits incurred in the Reagan-Bush era. Much of the rhetoric surrounding the 1992 presidential campaign focused on the overall level of federal deficit spending and the priorities for future spending on government programs. During the summer of 1992, in the midst of the national campaign, the Congressional Budget Office (CBO) released their annual analyses on the economic and federal budget outlook (CBO 1979). In their report, the CBO projected government operations 10 years into the future, under the assumption that current policies would remain in place over the decade. A summary of their projections is presented in Table 8.5. These projections suggest that to continue existing federal policies for Medicare and Medicaid would increase federal government expenditures for health care by 2.7 percent of GDP over the period, an expansion of nearly 80 percent above current levels.

When President Clinton assumed office in January 1993 he was confronted with the intransigent federal deficit. At the same time, he was trying to develop policies to deliver on one of his major campaign promises: access to adequate health care services for everyone. It quickly became clear that curtailing the growth in federal health care expenditures was crucial to dealing with the government's deficit problem. Table 8.6 shows the effect of bringing Medicare expenditure growth in line with projected growth in Social Security cash benefits and Medicaid in line with expected growth in GDP.

TABLE 8.6   Projected Federal Budget Deficits as a Percent of GDP, Assuming Control of Federal Health Costs for Selected Fiscal Years[a]

	1992	1997	2002
Deficit under current policy assumptions	-5.2%	-4.0%	-5.3%
Savings if Medicare growth constrained to growth rate in Social Security	0.0	0.7	1.6
Savings if Medicaid growth constrained to growth rate of domestic output	0.0	0.5	1.1
Savings in interest payments if health costs constrained as assumed[b]	0.0	0.1	0.5
Deficit under assumed control of federal health expenditures	-5.2	-2.7	-2.0

[a]*Source:* Derived by the author from Congressional Budget Office, *The Economic and Budget Outlook* Washington, DC: August, 1992; 39.
[b]An assumed 4.0 percent rate of interest was used to derive the estimated savings in interest payments.

Over time, Social Security benefits increase as the number of retirees grow and as benefits get larger. Each succeeding cohort of Social Security beneficiaries receives higher real benefits than prior cohorts because of general growth in wages. From Table 8.5, it is clear that the CBO projection suggests that Social Security benefits will grow at the same rate as the national economy over the next 10 years. In other words, assuming that Medicare benefits would be constrained at the same rate as Social Security benefits, then some real increase in Medicare expenditures would be permissible.

If the growth of Medicare and Medicaid expenditures can be slowed, it would reduce future federal deficit financing at the margin needed to reduce future interest payments. In developing Table 8.6, a 4 percent annual interest rate was used to calculate the interest savings if Medicare expenditure growth could be held to the Social Security rate growth and if Medicaid could be held to the rate of growth in GDP. Compared to current policy projections, the reduction in each year's reduced program outlays was assumed to accrue evenly during the year. So, the reduction in program outlays nets only a 2 percent savings in the year in which it occurs; but the reductions in deficit financing are cumulative, and a billion dollars saved last year is a billion less in debt now and for future years. Because the United States is projected to remain in deficit financing for the immediate future, a billion dollars borrowed in one year grows in each subsequent year as more money is borrowed to pay the interest. When the savings from each year are added to a cumulative total, the interest savings become significant, growing to a total of 0.5 percent of GDP by 2002.

Indeed, Table 8.6 suggests that bringing Medicare and Medicaid expenditure growth under control is potentially the most effective means of reducing federal deficit financing in the future. It can be argued that more resources should be redeployed from national defense expenditures to meet health care needs, but the practical matter is that defense spending already is being cut significantly to the point that some policymakers are concerned about going too far.

Each American can look to a host of other activities funded by the federal government and point to some things that could be dispensed with happily, but spending on most of these activities was reduced significantly during the Reagan-Bush administrations, and many government programs are in line for further reductions in the future. While the federal government is undertaking its budget trimming exercise, opinion polls show that the public is not willing to limit the types of health services generally available. Americans say they want to have more new technologies and provide more services for the elderly (Gallup 1992). This philosophy must be reconciled, however, with a 10-to-15 year record of political unwillingness to collect the taxes needed to fund such public commitments, along with everything else.

State Governments As Health Services Purchasers

State and local governments also are large purchasers of health services through various programs, the largest being Medicaid, which finances health care for some 27 million low-income people. In addition to Medicaid, states also fund the delivery of health services through workers' compensation, vocational rehabilitation, and temporary disability programs. They are responsible for general public health programs, as well as prenatal health and programs aimed at young children. In many communities, public hospitals and clinics are funded to provide health services for the lower income populations. Table 8.7 shows the level of expenditures as a percent of GDP through these various state and local programs for selected years between 1960 and 1990.

As stated earlier, Medicaid is funded jointly by the federal, state, and local governments, with the federal contribution being determined by a formula based on the per capita income in each state. John Iglehart calculates that between 1980 and 1988, the cost of the states' share of Medicaid expenditures grew at a compound rate of 9.3 percent. Between 1988 and 1992, the costs grew at a rate of 21.1 percent. Iglehart points out that this rapid, uncontrollable cost of Medicaid, carrying with it a matching obligation on the part of the federal government, is crowding out federal grants-in-aid aimed at supporting cash welfare payments, school-lunch and nutrition programs, subsidized housing, highways, and education (Iglehart 1993).

TABLE 8.7   National Health Expenditures by State and Local Governments as a Share of GDP for Calendar Years 1960-1990[a]

Share of Gross Domestic Product	Medicaid/ Public Assistance	Workers' Comp./ Voc. Rehab/ Short-Term Disability	Public/ Maternal/ Child Health	State and Local Hospital plus School Health	Other
1960	0.1	0.1	0.1	0.4	0.1
1965	0.1	0.1	0.1	0.4	0.1
1970	0.3	0.1	0.1	0.3	0.1
1975	0.4	0.2	0.1	0.3	0.1
1980	0.5	0.2	0.2	0.2	0.1
1985	0.5	0.2	0.3	0.2	0.1
1990	0.7	0.3	0.3	0.3	0.1

[a] *Source:* Health Care Financing Administration. Office of the Actuary. Data from the Office of National Health Statistics.

Many factors are behind the rapid increases in expenditures on Medicaid benefits. First, Medicaid is subject to most of the same inflationary pressures that plague the health sector in general. Second, Congress recently has mandated a variety of expanded services aimed at pregnant women and infants. It also established more stringent quality-of-care standards for nursing homes (Pallarito 1991). Lately, many of the cases that qualify for Medicaid benefits are extremely expensive. Today, more than 50 percent of the long-term care provided in the United States is funded through Medicaid (Gallant 1992). In California, nearly half of all AIDS patients and the majority of children with AIDS are treated under Medi-Cal, its Medicaid program. California also reports a growing population of children born to drug-addicted mothers under Medi-Cal. The annual costs of treating a single infant can run to several hundred thousand dollars per year (Rosenblatt 1993). Another reason that Medicaid costs have risen over the last few years is the recession in the American economy, which has resulted in higher levels of unemployment and increased numbers of unemployed workers who now meet the need criteria for eligibility.

For many states, deficit financing of government operations is prohibited by their constitutions. Thus, rapid increases in costs in any major segment of state budgets can cause immediate, significant fiscal problems. The states responded to their Medicaid cost increases in several ways. Some of them imposed rate freezes on benefits provided under their programs. In many instances, however, hospitals sued the states because they were paying unreasonably low rates under the program. The right of the providers to bring these cases was confirmed by the United States Supreme Court in *Wilder v. Virginia Hospital Association*, which set precedent. Several states then were forced to provide higher rates through court rulings (Rosenblatt 1993).

In response to their budgetary problems, some states pursued creative financing schemes to support the state-level Medicaid expenditures and to qualify for larger federal matching contributions. One scheme had the states impose provider taxes on doctors and hospitals that were treating Medicaid patients. These taxes then were added to the bills for services provided under the program, thus raising the overall cost of services provided and, in turn, leading to an increase in the federal contribution. Pennsylvania was one state in which the hospitals had brought suit against the state because it was paying inadequate rates for acute care provided under the program. The federal court ordered a substantial increase in the rates to be paid by the state, thereby increasing the Medicaid budget by $340 million. To deal with the resulting budget shortfall, 170 hospitals that were treating Medicaid patients formed a foundation and borrowed $365 million from a bank. They then donated this money to the state treasury to fund Medicaid benefits, generating enough matching money from the federal government to pay the higher rates without having to raise anyone's taxes. The hospitals were reimbursed immediately for their original donations (Morgan 1993).

In response to these creative funding devices, Congress passed the Medicaid Voluntary Contribution and Provider-Specific Tax Amendments of 1991, sharply curtailing the use of such funding approaches. The states increasingly find themselves in an untenable situation relative to Medicaid. They are caught between soaring costs, budget limits on spending, declining federal contributions, and federal mandates to expand eligibility. In many cases, less than half the poverty population of a state is eligible for benefits, and the provision of benefits is based more on categorical eligibility than on medical need. Providers are increasingly reluctant to give services under the program, and they are restive about the reimbursement received when they participate. The result is that some states are looking for alternative ways to provide services to their needy populations.

The most widely heralded effort is Oregon's plan to expand Medicaid and private insurance coverage to many citizens who currently do not have any insurance. Because the state already has limited resources, it has proposed that coverage be dropped for some medical procedures that had been covered previously, albeit for a narrower population. Jean Thorne has listed many reasons why Oregon is moving away from the traditional Medicaid program. These include the fact that, in Oregon, the current system provides benefits to a working poor woman if she is pregnant but not before she conceives the child; benefits are provided to a poor five-year-old, but not to an eight-year-old sibling; poor men and women without children are excluded; coverage for a poor woman is discontinued when her children complete school; and the system requires open-ended treatment to those who meet the categorical criteria but denies the most basic benefits to those who do not (Thorne 1992). Although Oregon has received approval from the federal government to implement this plan, it has not yet made the necessary funding provisions, and it is possible that the plan may never be put into effect.

Recently, Governor Ned McWherter of Tennessee announced that he would ask the Clinton administration to allow his state to withdraw from Medicaid. Tennessee's Medicaid expenditures went from just under $1 billion in 1987 to $2.8 billion in 1993. Tennessee provides benefits to more of its population than required under the federal rules. Medicaid now covers 20 percent of the total population in the state. The program covers the cost of half the state's births and half the expenses incurred in catastrophic illness cases.

Tennessee was one of the states that had used the creative financing techniques outlawed by Congress in 1991. To make up for the budgetary shortfall that arose because those financing opportunities were no longer available, Governor McWherter unsuccessfully attempted to get the state's first income tax passed in 1992. He then pushed successfully for a 6.75 percent tax on the revenue of the state's 152 acute care hospitals. This measure fell apart, however, when the state announced that the 1994 budget would still be $764 million short of the $3.4 billion needed to continue the existing Medicaid program. When state officials indicated they would make this up by cutting payments to hospitals, the hospitals turned on the prior legislation and got the tax repealed. The loss of the revenue from the tax, along with its matching federal contributions, translates into a budgetary shortfall of nearly $1 billion for Tennessee Medicaid. In response to the Medicaid funding shortfall, Governor McWherter has proposed and the federal government has approved that the existing system be replaced with a managed care program, where those eligible would be turned over to an HMO. The state and federal governments would set rates, quality standards, and eligibility requirements under the plan (Morgan 1993).

It is easy to think of Medicaid as a program oriented primarily at low-income families with small children. In 1990, nearly 68 percent of all Medicaid recipients were children or eligible adults in Aid for Families of Dependent Children (AFDC) families. But the Medicaid participants in AFDC families received only 27 percent of the benefits provided under the program. By comparison, the elderly comprised 13 percent of the recipient population but received 33 percent of the benefits. The remainder of the recipients, 19 percent, were blind or permanently and totally disabled individuals who, in the aggregate, received 39 percent of the benefits paid by Medicaid in 1990 (Social Security Administration 1991). The Medicaid program was envisioned originally as a general poverty program, but because it is the only source of public money for long-term care in nursing homes, the spending on care for the aged and disabled has crowded out the spending for young, poor families. Together the low-income elderly and disabled populations depend almost entirely on these programs and are allotted the majority of resources under them. The prospect that money is going to be readily available to resolve the budgetary and distributional concerns now facing the states appears slim. The states therefore are being forced to limit the availability of resources to fund the health services that have fallen to their responsibility. The allocation decisions implied here cannot be avoided.

Employers as Health Services Purchasers

Employer-sponsored health benefit programs constitute the second largest purchaser of health care services in the United States, larger even than the state governments. Tabulations of the March 1992 *Current Population Survey* (CPS) indicate that 60 percent of the American population benefits from employer-provided health insurance. Among the non-elderly, 64 percent of the population enjoys such coverage. Among those over age 65 (eligible for Medicare), only 33 percent have employer-sponsored health insurance. Although employers have played a predominant role in the provision of health care insurance since the end of World War II, the inflation that has occurred in the costs is now straining that commitment. Table 8.8 shows the level of health care expenditures made by employers and other private payers for selected years between 1960 and 1990.

Like other major payers for health care benefits, employers are paying more for the benefits provided under their health plans, going from 0.8 percent of GDP in 1965 to 3.1 percent in 1990. And the expenditure levels shown in Table 8.8 do not reflect the full increases in the cost of benefits for those employers who actually provide them. The reason is that as the cost of employer-provided health benefits has risen, the extent of employer-provided health insurance coverage has fallen. The rising total cost is being distributed then across a smaller base of companies every year.

TABLE 8.8   National Health Expenditures by Private Payers as a Share of GDP for Calendar Years 1960-1990[a]

Share of Gross Domestic Product	Consumer Payments/ Out-of-Pocket Payments	Employer- Paid Benefits	Private Insurance	Other
1960	2.6	NA	NA	0.2
1965	2.7	0.8	0.6	0.3
1970	2.5	1.2	0.5	0.4
1975	2.4	1.5	0.6	0.4
1980	2.2	2.1	0.6	0.4
1985	2.3	2.6	0.7	0.5
1990	2.5	3.1	0.9	0.6

[a] *Source:* Health Care Financing Administration. Office of the Actuary. Data from the Office of National Health Statistics.

Table 8.9 shows the declining levels of employer-sponsored health benefits coverage by industry for selected years. Between 1980 and 1991, health insurance coverage declined in virtually every industry, except among the self-employed. A 1990 survey of senior level executives in 1800 large firms in the United States found that rising health care costs were the most important human-resource issues facing their companies (Wyatt Company 1990). Employers look at their health benefits programs as an expense of doing business. Recently, some employers have been facing increases in health benefits as high as 50 to 60 percent per year. In response to the escalating costs, employers have moved to shift more of those costs directly to their employees, by requiring higher employee contributions for coverage and higher out-of-pocket payments for expenses covered under these plans. Wyatt Company surveys indicate that employee premiums for single and family coverage under comprehensive indemnity plans increased 40 percent between 1987 and 1992. For the typical family plan, the employee's share of the total premium in 1987 was just under $500 per year but had risen to nearly $1000 per year in 1992. The average deductible under a family plan had risen from $265 to $460 over the same period. Despite the increases in the employee cost of participating in employer-sponsored health benefit plans, employers' shares of total plan costs rose from 77 to 85 percent for single coverage between 1987 and 1992 and from 69 percent to 80 percent for family coverage over the period.

TABLE 8.9   Percent of Workers with Employer-Sponsored Health Insurance Coverage by Industry and Selected Years[a]

	1980	1985	1990	1991
Agriculture, forestry, and fisheries	24.7	22.7	21.9	20.8
Mining	85.0	78.3	79.3	79.5
Construction	55.2	50.0	47.1	44.8
Manufacturing	80.7	79.8	75.2	74.8
Transportation, communications, and public utilities	81.3	77.6	74.4	73.4
Wholesale trade	71.5	69.8	64.2	65.6
Retail trade	38.6	36.7	33.6	32.1
Finance, insurance, and real estate	67.5	69.2	64.8	65.3
Business and personal services	34.9	35.4	38.3	36.9
Professional services	54.2	57.4	54.3	54.1
Government	69.1	71.1	69.6	66.6
Self-employed, unincorporated	16.2	15.7	18.5	17.7
All industries	57.3	56.2	53.4	52.3

[a]*Source:* Levit KR, Olin GL, Letsch SW. Americans' Health Insurance Coverage, 1980-91. *Health Care Financing Review.* 1992: *14(1); 38.*

At the end of 1990, the Financial Accounting Standards Board (FASB) adopted Financial Accounting Standard 106 (FAS 106), entitled *Employers' Accounting for Postretirement Benefits Other Than Pensions.* FAS 106 requires employers to account for post-retirement life and health benefits on an accrual basis similar to that required for pension plans. The standard dictates cost and attribution methods and requires recognition of liabilities on an employer's balance sheet as well as expenses on an employer's income statement. Although FAS 106 introduced some symmetry between the accounting for the accrual of pensions and retiree health liabilities, tax law treats the two benefits very differently—it allows tax-effective funding of pension obligations as they accrue but does not provide similar funding opportunities for retiree health benefits. The net result of FAS 106 on the one side and tax law on the other is that any employer who sponsors a retiree health benefit is faced with the prospect of creating a sizeable unfunded liability on its balance sheet. For most employers, the standard becomes effective for fiscal years that began after December 15, 1992.

Some employers are concerned that the retiree health liabilities implied by FAS 106 could threaten their economic viability in the capital markets. Some economists argue that investors in the capital markets already had looked through the veil of accounting rules and considered retiree health liabilities when assessing the value of companies (Reinhardt 1989). Although the economists may be correct theoretically in their assessment of the capital markets, it is the employers who can vote with their feet in this case. Since the promulgation of FAS 106, many companies have moved to limit their retiree health liabilities. Some have implemented vesting schedules to curtail sharply the benefits provided to short-term workers. Other companies have shifted their plans from a promise of a defined benefit to the promise to pay a certain amount of the worker's health care insurance premium at retirement. These defined contribution benefits also tend to vary with length of service with the employer. Finally, some employers have eliminated their retiree health plans altogether.

Uwe Reinhardt argues that employers are not adversely affected by health benefits cost increases, at least not those related to active employees (Reinhardt 1989). He contends that health benefits costs are part of the wage bill, and, that as health costs have increased, escalation of other elements of the wage bill have been retarded. Although Reinhardt might be correct in theory, 1800 executives of large companies do not agree completely. Table 8.10 shows their responses to the question, "How does your company try to cover increases in the costs of employer-sponsored health benefit plans?" A substantial majority, 64 percent, believe that some sharing exists for the burden of health benefits cost increases. Among the respondents, 73 percent believe that at least some health cost increases are passed on to consumers in the form of higher prices; 71 percent believe that health cost increases retard profits; and less than half, 49 percent, agree that health cost increases reduce other forms of compensation.

How employers perceive their relative role in bearing the costs of benefit plans is important in the context of whether they should be dedicating ever increasing resources to the provision of health services for workers and retirees. If employers think that health cost increases are borne by the workers, it is likely they also feel that the workers will let them know the limit on the health benefit share of total compensation. If employers think that health cost increases are passed on in the form of higher prices, however, then their ability to support these benefits indefinitely will depend on competitiveness within the markets in which they operate. Those companies that operate in strong, internationally competitive markets will be at a particular disadvantage because health costs and health inflation rates are so much higher in the United States than in other countries. If employers think that health cost increases are financed at the expense of reduced profits, then their ability to support these benefits indefinitely will depend on profit levels and management's fiduciary obligations to owners.

TABLE 8.10 Methods of Covering Cost Increases in Employer-Sponsored Health Benefits Programs[a]

	Percent
Benefits cost increases are passed along to consumers as price increases	14.9
Benefits cost increases reduce profits alone	9.8
Benefits cost increases hold down other forms of compensation to workers	11.2
Combination of lower profits and higher prices	26.3
Combination of lower profits and lower wages	6.0
Combination of higher prices and lower wages	2.7
Combination of all three	29.1

[a]*Source:* Wyatt Company. Employer-Sponsored Health Benefits Programs: A Chronic Affliction or a Growing Malignancy? *Management USA Leading a Changing Work Force.* Washington, DC: Wyatt Company. 1990; 12.

Each perception, whether right or wrong, suggests that some real practical limits will determine what can be pumped into the delivery of health benefits by private sector employers. The declines in the provision of health benefits across almost all sectors of the economy, as documented in Table 8.9, suggest that those limits already are being reached in many firms.

The Perspective of Individual Consumers

Table 8.8 shows that the level of individual consumer out-of-pocket expenditures has remained relatively stable over the period 1960 to 1990. Undoubtedly, some consumers could spend more on health care services than they do now. The elements of society who engender the concern—those people who do not receive adequate medical services in the current environment—tend to be those people in the lower income ranges who already have extremely limited resources to redeploy for their health care needs. Certainly, they do not have enough to meet the high costs of treating many of the chronic and acute illnesses that threaten them today.

Use of Current Resources

If no additional resources are readily available to redeploy to the health care sector in the American economy, then another alternative to rationing might be the more efficient reallocation of already available resources. Indeed, Arthur Caplan argues that moral ethicists who are asked to provide rationing criteria should not be willing to develop these criteria until the inefficiencies and fat in the system have been wrung out (Caplan 1992). Three areas of reorganization or reform are often cited as potential sources of significant savings. These include the unwieldy and overly expensive administration of the system, the prevalence and size of malpractice awards and the defensive medicine practiced to avoid them, and the incentive structure that encourages unnecessary services or services at unreasonable prices.

Reducing Administrative Costs

Joseph Califano, former Secretary of the Department of Health and Human Services, estimates that the administrative costs associated with the American health system are close to $200 billion annually (Califano 1993). At that level, administrative costs would account for 20 to 25 percent of current health expenditures and would offer a likely target for considerable savings. The private health insurance system that operates in the United States is thought to be particularly expensive because of all the variation in plans' claims filing and review processes. If a consistent package of health benefits were to be offered to everyone, and if a consistent claims process were implemented at the same time, theoretically, much of the current inefficiency could be eliminated.

In June 1991, the General Accounting Office (GAO) released an analysis of the costs and effects of moving to a Canadian-style, single-payer health delivery system in the United States. The study asserted that a universal system like the Canadian one, administered by a nonprofit agency, would reduce costs because it no longer would be necessary to determine coverage, eligibility for benefits, or risk status. It also would eliminate marketing costs. For providers, it would mean lower billing and clerical costs. The GAO study estimated that if the United States could lower its insurance overhead to the Ontario level, $34 billion could be saved. Under the Ontario system, American physicians would be able to reduce expenses related to billing, saving an added $15 billion. Similarly, if hospitals could reduce billing expenses down to the Ontario levels, this would cut expenses by $18 billion. The GAO posited that these total savings of $67 billion could be diverted to added health care benefits for those people who currently get unsatisfactory services (GAO 1991).

In December 1991, the CBO released an analysis of two alternative approaches to delivering health care in the United States. Under both scenarios, this study assumed that health insurance would be extended to everyone now uninsured and that health providers would be reimbursed on the basis of Medicare's payment rates. Under one approach, the current diversity of private and public payers would be retained in an all-payer system. In the other approach, the current system would be replaced with a single-payer system. The CBO estimated changes in administrative costs under these proposals that would range from an increase of $4.4 billion to a decrease of $17.5 billion under the all-payer system, depending on underlying assumptions. It is estimated that administrative cost savings would range from $18.2 billion to $58.3 billion under the single-payer system (CBO 1991). The early discussions among members of the Clinton administration about health care reform suggested that they intended to recommend something that would resemble the CBO all-payer system more than a single-payer system. This approach will produce the least administrative savings.

In testimony during March 1993, Robert Reischauer, Director of the CBO, estimated that potential administrative savings gained by a single-payer system would be around $30 billion to $35 billion. He went on to suggest, however, that some of the perceived administrative waste that exists in the current system actually may be reducing current health care costs. Copayments and deductibles add to plan complexity but make consumers more sensitive to the prices involved in their consumption decisions. Utilization review makes administration more expensive but reduces the provision of unnecessary care (Reischauer 1993).

The Health Care Financing Administration (HCFA) has estimated that the combined administrative cost of public financiers of health care, philanthropic organizations, and private health insurers amounts to only 5.8 percent of national health expenditures (Levit et al. 1991). The HCFA

estimate does not include providers' expenses incurred in the maintenance of records and filing of claims, so there might be some additional
savings there. Although health care reform **may** reduce administration
expenses, it cannot possibly eliminate them. Any new system still will
require the collection of contributions from various segments of the population and payments to providers for people covered or benefits provided.
Providers still will have to collect and maintain information on the people
whom they cover and on the patients whom they treat. Some proposals
for health reform have included recommendations that providers will
collect and disseminate more extensive information on treatments and
outcomes than they already do now, possibly creating a whole new set of
administrative information requirements. The potential savings in this
area appear to be insufficient to cover the costs of the added benefits that
would be provided if health insurance is provided to everyone in the
United States.

One aspect of these potential savings that often is ignored is that much
of the administrative expense that potentially can be saved is related to
relatively labor-intensive activities involved in health plan administration.
If the CBO estimate of potential savings ($30 billion to $35 billion) could
be realized, then that expense level represents a significant number of
jobs lost in insurance companies and provider organizations. The elimination of jobs that tend to be clerical and data-processing will not free a
large group of people who can be redeployed easily to provide health
care services to those not currently getting adequate care. Diverting an
extra $30 billion or more to the direct delivery of care is going to put
added inflationary pressures on a delivery system already operating in a
highly inflationary environment.

Restraining Malpractice Awards and Defensive Medicine

One area often cited as contributing to the expensive nature of health
services in the United States is the cost of malpractice insurance and the
related defensive medicine that doctors provide because of their concerns about malpractice claims. Paul Weiler et al. (1993) have found that
the average cost of malpractice liability insurance for a doctor in New
York State in 1949 was $360 per year in 1990 dollars. By 1965, the cost of
such insurance had risen to $1000 per year. Ten years later, it was up to
$7500 per year. By the end of the 1980s, they found that reasonably full
insurance coverage cost an average of $40,000 per year. Although mal-
practice insurance is more expensive in New York than in many states, a
number of large states have similar rates. Even where rates are lower,
there still is a concern about the size of malpractice awards and their
effects on the practice of medicine.

In 1990, medical malpractice premiums in the United States cost medical providers $4 billion—0.6 percent of national health expenditures for that year (Insurance Information Institute 1993). Frank Sloan, Randal Bovbjerg, and Penny Githens (1991) have undertaken a detailed review of the medical malpractice market. They conclude that it is reasonably competitive, that coverage is generally available, that some insurers have relatively low premium-to-surplus ratios, and that profits are not excessive. They found little wrong with the operations of malpractice insurers as insurers. They did note that only about half of the premium dollar paid for medical malpractice goes to claimants. They concluded that the industry would make a greater contribution to the welfare of society if it were able to devote less energy to managing claims and litigation and more to managing injuries and rehabilitation.

Weiler et al. (1993) undertook a detailed survey and statistical analysis of the incidence and outcomes of medical malpractice injuries in New York State. Their study was designed to determine the incidence of injury resulting from medical intervention, the extent to which such injuries could have been avoided, the kinds of losses incurred, how much was covered by insurance, and the role that potential litigation plays in reducing such injuries. They performed an in-depth appraisal of the medical records for a sample of 31,000 patients hospitalized in the state during 1984.

The definition of a medical injury in the Weiler study was "any disability caused by medical management that prolonged the hospital stay by at least one day or persisted beyond the patient's release from the hospital" (Weiler et al. 1993). They estimated that about 4 percent of hospital admissions involved an injury, and about one quarter of those resulted from negligence on the part of the provider. Although many injuries were minor, 14 percent of the injured died. Applied to the American population, the authors conclude that 150,000 persons die per year from medical treatment.

In terms of the tort system's effectiveness at providing retribution to those injured in the medical delivery process, Weiler et al. found that

> On an aggregate basis, one malpractice claim was filed by a New York patient for every 7.5 patients who suffered a negligent injury (that is, a real tort). Because approximately one in two tort claims is ultimately paid, this means that the legal system is actually paying just one malpractice claim for every 15 torts inflicted in hospitals. And even when the focus is on only the most "valuable" tort claims—that is, serious injuries to patients under 70 years of age—the ratio was one claim paid for every three negligent injuries. (p. 137)

Weiler et al. conclude that no litigation surplus exists but that a litigation deficit is evident because so many people who are being injured do not get any retribution from the system.

Because medical malpractice insurance premiums are such a small part of total health care costs in the United States, malpractice reform could save only a small amount directly and might actually increase total system costs if wider access to retribution is provided to those injured while receiving services. Some analysts argue that it is not the direct cost of malpractice insurance that places the largest burden on the health delivery system but the unnecessary use of tests and procedures to avoid suits. The National Medical Liability Reform Coalition, a collection of various groups that includes the American Medical Association (AMA), estimates that malpractice reform could eliminate $35.8 billion in defensive medicine over five years (Riley 1993).

Evidence that threats of malpractice affect the nature and level of health services is often anecdotal. One study that sought to document the relationship between malpractice claims and child birth by cesarean delivery found that such deliveries correlated positively with physicians' malpractice premiums, with the number of claims against doctors per 100 doctors at the hospital level, and with the number of claims against hospitals per 1000 discharges (Localio et al. 1973). In 1970, the rate of cesarean deliveries was 5.5 per hundred total deliveries in the United States. By 1980, the rate of cesarean deliveries had jumped to 16.5 per hundred deliveries. By the mid-1980s, roughly one quarter of babies born were delivered in this fashion (United States Bureau of the Census 1992). Stephen Myers and Norbert Gleicher have estimated that the number of necessary cesarean births in this country should be 11.1 percent of total births (Myers and Gleicher 1988).

It was found that in New York State hospitals during 1984 cesarean delivery rates varied outside the range of expectations across hospitals and across doctors who practiced within individual hospitals (Localio et al. 1993). One underlying problem with the persistently high cesarean delivery rates in the 1980s appeared to be that the medical system did not provide enough control over doctors or obstetrical departments in regard to this form of child delivery (Gleicher 1984). But Myers and Gleicher reported on a project at Mount Sinai Medical Center in Chicago to reduce the cesarean-section rate at that hospital from 17.5 percent in 1985 to 12.5 percent in 1986, to 11.5 percent in 1987. The reductions occurred for private and teaching physicians alike. On the basis of their analysis, the authors concluded that the number of cesarean sections could be reduced by up to 450,000 per year nationally without detriment to mothers or offspring. Of particular interest in the context of malpractice liability as a motivator for delivery by cesarean section, Myers and Gleicher observed that the change in practice pattern had little effect on liability insurance rates (Myers and Gleicher 1988).

Concerns about liability insurance undoubtedly have resulted in the expanded provision of certain medical tests and procedures at an added cost to the system. If the cost of malpractice insurance and most of the cost of defensive medicine could be eliminated, as estimated by the National Medical Liability Reform Coalition, the savings would be less than 1 percent of the cost on an annual basis. Furthermore, the major studies on malpractice insurance that were cited earlier do not come down on the side of eliminating compensation for individuals injured in the delivery of health services but, rather, on the elimination or drastic reduction of the share of malpractice expense currently skimmed off by people involved in the legal process. If a more egalitarian process were developed for compensating everyone injured through the delivery of health services, then the cost of malpractice could increase significantly.

Economic Motivations That Affect Medical Service Delivery

Myers and Gleicher indicated that neither the hospital nor the doctors involved in reducing the rate of cesarean delivery at Mount Sinai Medical Center had any financial incentives to do so. In fact, the authors estimated that, at the time of their study, vaginal deliveries netted the hospital $3000 less than cesarean section deliveries. They also estimated that the doctor's fees for a vaginal delivery usually were $250 to $500 less than for cesarean sections (Myers and Gleicher 1988). Although the example of Mount Sinai indicates that the health delivery system can put the best interests of patients ahead of its own, the economic motivation of providers plays a major role in explaining the delivery patterns of many services provided today.

Alan Hillman asserts that "Society subscribes to the technologic imperative; patients and doctors generally both prefer arrangements that encourage the use of health care technology" (Hillman A 1990). If this is true, then the various means by which doctors are compensated for their services can affect the extent to which they are rewarded for delivering more, relative to less, technologically advanced medicine. Doctors typically are paid in one of three broad fashions: a fee for the services provided; a salary from an organization of which they are a member or an employee; or capitation payment based on the number of people assigned to them and for whom they must provide medical services.

In the fee-for-service arrangement, the doctor typically can realize a higher income by providing more services. Financially, at least, this payment mechanism would encourage the use of more expensive treatments, even though the treatment may be beyond what is required in some instances.

Doctors who work for a direct salary or who are paid on a flat dollar basis for each person who is eligible to receive services (i.e., a capitated basis) will not receive any higher compensation by prescribing more expensive treatments than necessary and often are affected adversely if they overtreat patients. Many HMOs withhold a portion of the salary or capitation payments until expenses related to referrals and hospitalizations have been settled. If a group of doctors exceeds its allotted budget for referrals or hospitalizations, some or all of the withholdings are lost. In some cases, the individual doctor may be subject to the penalty solely on the basis of assigned cases. Some HMOs even impose penalties over and above the basic withholding in cases of excess referrals and hospitalizations. Coming in under budget often means a bonus on top of payment of the withheld amounts. Finally, it is fairly common that doctors compensated on a capitated basis must pay for outpatient laboratory tests out of their own pocket. Needless to say, this discourages use of outside laboratory referrals.

Financial Incentives and Physician Behavior

Many studies have been done on how these various incentives affect physician behavior in providing health care services. For example, Alan Hillman, Mark Pauly, and Joseph Kerstein analyzed a national survey of HMOs, focusing on financial incentives, resource utilization, and financial performance. After controlling for case mix, they found that financial incentives affected not only the overall financial performance of the HMOs but also the ways in which resources are used. They found that capitation and salary compensation of primary care physicians resulted in fewer days of hospitalization compared with those proscribed by fee-for-service physicians. They also found that for-profit HMOs had lower hospitalization rates than not-for-profit HMOs. Cases in which the doctor was penalized beyond basic withholding for excessive hospital costs resulted in fewer visits per enrollee, but a higher percentage of the patients visited their HMOs more frequently. This suggests that heavy penalties on doctors establish an atmosphere that discourages visits to the clinic, but, that when a truly sick person gets into treatment, the HMO tends to provide services through multiple clinic visits rather than through hospitalization (Hillman et al. 1989).

One study by Sheldon Greenfield et al. analyzed 20,000 patients who visited their doctors during 1986. Resource utilization was measured across four specialties and five systems of care. The specialties were family practice, general internal medicine, cardiology, and endocrinology. The systems of care were HMO, multi-specialty group fee-for-service, single specialty fee-for-service, solo practice, and single-specialty group-prepaid. After controlling for patient mix, the authors found that the solo practice and the single-specialty fee-for-service systems had hospitalization rates 41 percent higher than the HMOs, and that the patients of the solo practices or single-specialty fee-for-service practices were taking 12 percent more drugs. HMO patients visited their doctors 8 percent more times per year. Payment method also affected utilization. Prepaid patients had lower rates of hospitalization and higher office visit rates than fee-for-service patients (Greenfield et al. 1992).

Another study by David Hemenway et al. analyzed the treatment patterns of 15 doctors who worked for Health Stop, a chain of ambulatory care centers, between 1984 and 1986. Health Stop had 20 centers in the Boston area during this period. Most were staffed by two full-time physicians who each worked shifts of roughly 40 hours per week. Until mid-1985, the physicians were paid $28 per hour. In mid-1985, the payment scheme was changed so that each doctor received the higher of a flat wage, which ranged from $28 to $32 per hour, depending on age and experience, or 24 percent of the first $24,000 in gross monthly charges and 15 percent of charges above that amount. The authors of this study compared the services provided and charges generated by 15 physicians during two periods: November 1984 through January 1985 and November 1985 through January 1986. They found that 13 of the 15 doctors ordered more laboratory tests per visit under the revised payment scheme. The average for the group increased 23 percent. In the latter period, the number of office visits per month rose by 12 percent, average charges increased by 15 percent, and total charges per month rose by 28 percent. Six physicians generated enough revenue for the volume-incentive package to take effect every month. Seven of them never received more than their base salary, even though most of them increased the intensity of service delivery (Hemenway et al. 1990).

Self-Referral and Physician Behavior

Another set of studies focused on physician ownership of health service facilities and their referral patterns of patients to those facilities compared with physicians without an ownership position in such delivery units. Recently, it has become common for physicians to enter into joint ventures that include buying or building various physical rehabilitation facilities, testing laboratories, radiation therapy centers, and imaging facilities. The concern about these joint ventures is that the doctors who own such facilities have a potential conflict of interest when they refer their patients to those facilities for services.

Jean Mitchell and Elton Scott have evaluated the effects of physician ownership of free-standing physical therapy and rehabilitation facilities on utilization. They found that visits per patient were 39 to 45 percent higher in joint-venture facilities than in those not owned by a group of physicians. Gross and net revenues in the joint-venture facilities were 30 to 40 percent higher. The two types of facilities tend to be staffed differently, with licensed physical therapists and licensed therapist assistants spending about 60 percent more time per visit treating patients in facilities not owned through joint physician partnership. Although the joint-venture operations tended to hire fewer licensed therapists, operating income and mark-up were significantly higher. The joint-venture operations generate more of their revenues from patients who have insurance policies that cover services provided than nonjoint-venture operations (Mitchell and Scott, October 1992).

In June 1988, Congress mandated that the Office of the Inspector General (OIG) at the Department of Health and Human Services (HHS) conduct a study on physician ownership and compensation from health care facilities to which they make referrals. The resulting report to Congress found that at least 25 percent of independent clinical laboratories and 27 percent of physiological laboratories are owned partially or wholly by referring physicians. Patients of the referring physicians who had ownership in independent clinical laboratories received 45 percent more total laboratory services and 34 percent more services directly from the independent clinical laboratories than all Medicare patients in general. Patients of physicians who had an ownership share in independent physiological laboratories received 13 percent more physiological testing than all Medicare patients in general (Kusserow 1989).

Bruce Hillman et al. used a large private insurance claims database to analyze the use of diagnostic imaging by more than 6400 physicians in 65,500 episodes of care. Their analysis focused on all patients who suffered from acute upper respiratory symptoms, pregnancy, or low back pain, and on men who had difficulty in urinating. They found that self-referring physicians ordered imaging examinations 4.0 to 4.5 times more often than physicians who referred patients to facilities in which they had no interest. Not only did the self-referring physicians have more tests done, but they also generated higher average costs for each imaging examination for chest radiography, obstetrical ultrasonography, and lumbar spine radiography. In combination, the higher frequency of examinations and the higher cost per examination resulted in imaging charges per episode that were 4.4 to 7.5 times higher for self-referring physicians (Hillman B et al. 1992).

In a separate study that used similar methodologies, Hillman et al. focused on diagnostic imaging in a Medicare population. In this analysis, they looked at differences in imaging use and charges for 10 clinical presentations. Across the 10 treatment categories they found that self-referral resulted in 1.7 to 7.7 times more imaging examinations, and that charges were 1.6 to 6.2 times higher for self-referring physicians (Hillman B et al. 1992).

Jean Mitchell and Jonathan Sunshine considered the effects of joint-venture ownership in radiation therapy facilities. They compared the operations of joint-venture facilities and nonjoint-venture facilities in Florida against comparable facilities elsewhere in the United States. They found that joint-venture facilities completely avoid inner city and rural areas. Where they do offer services, joint-venture operations provide relatively more services to individuals who have well paying insurance coverage. The frequency and cost of treatments in joint-venture operations were 40 to 60 percent higher in Florida than in the rest of the country. The differences in frequency and cost of treatment could not be explained by differences in hospital-provided radiation therapy or cancer rates in Florida. Although radiation physicists in the joint-venture clinics provided more treatment and charged more, they also spent 18 percent less time with each patient over the course of treatment than radiation physicists who worked in freestanding clinics. Finally, mortality rates were not reduced in the Florida joint-venture facilities relative to the others with which they had been compared (Mitchell and Sunshine 1992).

Because doctors who own a share in these various facilities apparently behave so differently from those who do not, the prevalence of ownership could be an important determinant in the overall costs generated in various categories of services. Kusserow, in the OIG report cited earlier, estimated that 12 percent of the physicians who bill Medicare had ownership interests in facilities to which they made referrals (Kusserow 1989). Jean Mitchell and Elton Scott cite a 1990 AMA study that estimates that about 8 percent of respondents on a survey of 4000 doctors indicated an ownership interest in a facility to which they referred patients (Mitchell and Scott Nov. 1992).

Mitchell and Scott also undertook a detailed study of physician ownership in Florida that was more intensive than prior studies (for example, see Mitchell and Sunshine 1992). They based their analysis on a mailed questionnaire with a subsequent vigorous call-back effort to nonrespondents and an effort to correct any information that was incomplete or inconsistent. They ultimately received completed questionnaires from 82.4 percent of a potential 2669 facilities. They found that more than three fourths of the ambulatory facilities and more than 90 percent of the diagnostic imaging centers were owned by referring physicians. By comparison, 5 percent of the acute care hospitals and 12 percent of nursing homes had physician owners. They estimated that at least

40 percent of the physicians involved in direct patient care in Florida are joint-venture owners in facilities to which they refer patients but in which they do not practice (Mitchell and Scott 1992).

Focusing on the structure of ownership for medical facilities and the incentives inherent in the way doctors are compensated would appear to have significant potential for freeing resources that could be redeployed to provide health services to those not receiving them now. This probably would be more fruitful than expecting large windfall gains from administrative simplification of the health delivery system or from malpractice reform. All avenues available to improve the efficiency of the American health system should be pursued as far as feasible. In the long term, however, the prospect of limitations on the general availability of some health services that become unaffordable must be faced, and everyone who might want these services may not enjoy free access.

The Philosophy of Limits

Ten years ago, Roger Evans undertook a detailed analysis of evolving health care technology and the implications for resource allocation and rationing decisions. In a two-part presentation of his analysis published in the *Journal of the American Medical Association,* he suggested that few clinicians had been faced with resource allocation or rationing decisions. Indeed, he observed that many would argue such behavior represents a "conflict of interest and is contrary to the Hippocratic oath" (Evans 1983). Putting the resource allocation issue in the framework of the Hippocratic oath provides an interesting perspective on the relative roles of various players in the provision of health care.

In 1965, when Congress was considering the amendments to the Social Security Act that eventually established Medicare and Medicaid, there was grave concern about the government's intrusion into the doctor-patient relationship. The final legislation that established Medicare was explicit—the government would not exercise "any supervision or control over the practice of medicine or the manner in which medical services are provided, or over the selection, tenure, or compensation of any officer or employee of any institution, agency, or person providing health services" (Social Security Amendments, Section 1801).

As noted earlier, to fulfill its commitment, the government gave license to doctors to carry out their Hippocratic oath and to bill the benefits provided under Medicare back to the government on the basis of "reasonable and customary" charges. Following the practice of Blue Cross, hospitals were to be reimbursed on the basis of the cost of providing services. Many employer-provided health insurance programs soon followed suit in paying for services provided on the basis of cost, or providing services for the reasonable and customary charges. To a large extent, the whole of society was co-opted into taking the Hippocratic oath implicitly in that everyone seemed willing to write the checks that paid for services provided by doctors carrying out their explicit oaths. It is now clear that the costs of some services are unaffordable under that arrangement. The federal government has been attempting to limit its expenses under Medicare and Medicaid for more than 10 years. State budgets are at the point of breaking under Medicaid. Employers are scrambling to get away from the financial burden of benefit programs.

If the federal and state governments and employers can begin to set effective limits on the aggregate amount of resources made available to the health sector, and if elimination of inefficiencies is not adequate to meet everyone's health care "needs," then microallocation decisions will still need to be made. This creates a direct conflict with what some people believe to be a "widely accepted social norm that any expenditure is justified in preserving an individual life" (Blank 1988). Unlimited services cannot be provided to all consumers at the micro level and be paid for under limited budgets at the macro level. Any discussion that concerns limitation of health services in any fashion has to incorporate the elderly, because they consume a disproportionate amount of the total services provided in relation to their relative numbers in the population.

Arthur Caplan has observed that "It is far easier to begin a moral discussion about the allocation of scarce resources, such as kidney dialysis units, than to ask health practitioners and patients to live with the fact that society has decided not to fund a sufficient number of machines to treat all who are in need" (Caplan 1992). It appears that Caplan draws a distinction between the concepts of macroallocation and microallocation of resources that were discussed briefly at the outset of this chapter. In the context of macroallocation, global budgets can be prescribed and grand allocation formulas can be devised to distribute resources on detailed, risk-related bases without looking a single patient in the eye. Because Caplan is the Director of Biomedical Ethics and a professor in the departments of philosophy and surgery at the University of Minnesota, he undoubtedly sees many of the difficult, real-life choices that doctors often face in allocating facilities, time, and other resources among individual patients.

Larry Churchill argues that philosophical medical ethics has been too focused on the micro-oriented problems of dealing with individual treatment situations and has largely ignored the macro issues of justice. If the focus truly is on the individual, then to pour fantastic amounts of resources into saving a single life is a justifiable goal, without considering the costs levied against society in pursuit of that goal. Part of the problem is that basic human impulses manufacture susceptibilities to malady.

If a drowning person calls for help, there is a natural "urge to rescue." In identifying with another person, humans tend to feel a moral obligation to help in distress. Ironically, that same moral obligation need not apply if the individual who wants help is part of a larger, amorphous mass that collectively and perhaps continually needs aid (Churchill 1987). Churchill offers an example of this conflicting sense of moral responsibility when he points to former President Ronald Reagan's appeal to the public for a liver to save a little girl from Accokeek, Maryland whom he had seen on television. President Reagan then sent an Air Force jet to fly her and her parents to Pittsburgh for a transplant operation at the same time that he was cutting back basic programs for low-income mothers and children. Unlike the transplant patient, these people were not individually recognizable to the President. Churchill believes that in sorting out moral obligations concepts of community welfare must be kept in mind. He argues that religious doctrines of stewardship prohibit the allocation of resources to extend one life at the great cost of others. Great sums should not be spent to extend a life at the margin if others in society are deprived of decent, basic health care (Churchill 1987).

Daniel Callahan contends that Americans have come to see a longer life as a basic right. The health care system has assumed a role of conqueror over disease and extender of life, but at a great cost. Callahan says that in many cities, it is the hospital that is the newest and most technologically equipped building with the schools among the oldest, forced to get by with technologically outdated equipment. As this system has developed, we have lost sight of our finite characteristics, subject to aging, decline, and death. Like Churchill, Callahan also argues that the focus of the health delivery system must shift from the individual to the community. The basic principles behind this system should include a guaranteed minimal level of health care for everyone and firm limits on individual demands for medical cures. In cases in which curative medicine no longer can resolve maladies, according to Callahan, "caring medicine," which includes social, psychological, and palliative support for the afflicted, should prevail (Callahan 1990).

Arthur Caplan also feels that the implementation of limits (i.e., rationing) on the delivery of health services represents a special subset of allocation issues from a moral perspective. He offers the paradigm of a lifeboat. Rationing is needed when everyone on the lifeboat wants the food and water that is insufficient to sustain the whole group. He argues that the following conditions are prerequisites for rationing: a shortage of life-supporting, life-sustaining resources; everyone wants whatever resources are available; resources cannot be replenished; there are not enough resources to supply everyone; and the amount of resources is too small to sustain everyone. In applying the lifeboat metaphor to medical services, Caplan concludes that "rationing" ought to be limited to cases where life-saving resources are truly scarce (e.g., supply of donor organs for transplantation); where existing resources cannot be subdivided further or stretched; where it is clear that these resources can save lives; and where people want access to the resources. Unless these conditions are met, Caplan concludes that rationing cannot be morally justified (Caplan 1992).

Paul Menzel has attempted to sort out the moral issues of allocation among competing groups. He addresses the vital question of how to develop principles and rules for directing limited resources to the young as opposed to the elderly, to the severely ill as opposed to the not so severely ill, toward illnesses that strike large numbers of people as opposed to those that strike only few people. Menzel concludes that society's primary priority is not to focus strictly on life extension. In a situation where young people who need services must compete with the elderly for the same services, it is not fair to count only the lives saved in allocating resources; it is better to count years of life saved. Improving the quality of older lives puts stronger claims on resources than mere life extension. In analyzing the issues and surveying the work of other philosophers on issues related to severity and numbers, Menzel unearths some competing, morally fundamental principles that leave the dilemma of how to allocate limited resources unresolved (Menzel 1983). In practical terms, however, the budget dilemmas discussed earlier are forcing attention onto the moral dilemmas. If these moral dilemmas cannot be eliminated, then ways must be found to live with them and deal with them on an ongoing basis.

The International Experience

Earlier analysis showed that the American experience with spending on health care had been somewhat different than that of most major developed countries in the world. Not only do Americans spend more on health care, but the rate of increase in these expenditures has exceeded that of most other countries in the last 30 years. Despite a relatively high rate of spending on health care, 89 percent of the general public in the United States feels that the system needs fundamental change or needs to be revamped completely. By comparison, 43 percent of Canadians, 48 percent of Germans, 52 percent of French, 51 percent of Netherlanders, and 53 percent of Japanese feel the same way about their respective systems (Blendon et al. 1990).

One aspect of the general satisfaction with health systems relates to the accessibility of care. Most major developed countries have constructed health care systems that give access to everyone. In recent discussions on health care reform in the United States, considerable time has been spent in figuring out how to provide universal access to a comprehensive package of benefits. Colleen Grogan points out that in other countries, policymakers have spent little or no time on deciding what goes into the universally available package of comprehensive benefits. In other countries, it is clear, however, that "comprehensive benefits does not mean unlimited care" (Grogan 1992). Although other governments do not define a specific package of benefits, they do control expenditures by limiting the consumption of certain medical services.

In some instances, they do this by designating specific groups as being ineligible for certain treatments. Henry Aaron and William Schwartz point out, that, until the early 1980s, most people in Great Britain over the ages of 55 or 60 who had chronic kidney failure were not offered hemodialysis. When costs for dialysis came down, the treatment was offered more frequently to the older population. Another way that other countries limit expenditures is simply to not provide certain services, or to limit their availability drastically. Again, Great Britain is a good example in that many tertiary-care university hospitals have no computed tomography scanner (Aaron and Schwartz 1990). In this case, the government can set limits on the procedures offered by fiat or by budget controls at the provider level.

The Canadian health care system is made up of 12 separate provincial or territorial plans financed largely through general revenues. Physicians' charges are fixed through a negotiated fee process, and hospitals operate on overall global budgets. Consumers can choose their own physicians who are in private practice and who are paid on the basis of services provided. The doctors do not bill patients but are paid by the public health plans. Most of Canada's hospitals are public community or university hospitals, owned by voluntary corporations, religious organizations, or local governments. Basic hospital fees are paid by the public system, although private insurance can be used to pay for a private room during a hospital stay. Hospitals develop separate budgets to cover operating and capital expenditures. The operating budget establishes the overall limit on resources available to the hospital but does not dictate the internal allocation of resources. The hospital administration and medical staff do that. Capital budgets are the mechanisms by which the provinces control the capacity of the hospital system and the implementation of new technologies. The result is that the diffusion of expensive technologies is not nearly as widespread as in the United States. For example, in 1989, Toronto had one radiation treatment center compared to 13 in Boston. Similarly the United States had eight times as many magnetic resonance imaging units per million as Canada. The net result of the limitations on resources in Canada is that there is considerable queuing for services, yet the Canadian people appear to be much happier with their system than Americans are with theirs (Graig 1993).

In Germany, health services are financed through a network of approximately 1150 sickness funds. Everyone who earns less than a specified amount, approximately $41,000 in 1993 in former West Germany and $30,000 in former East Germany, must belong to one of these funds. Only about 1 percent of the population, all above the income limits, opt out of the system. The system provides benefits that are among the most comprehensive in the world, covering medical, dental, inpatient hospital care, and prescription drugs, with no deductibles or minimum copayment amounts. Physicians provide ambulatory care either through a regular office setting or through a hospital in which they work. Office-based physicians do not provide services once a patient enters a hospital, and those physicians who work in a hospital do not provide outpatient services. Doctors are paid by regional physician associations but must operate their practices on a fixed budget. Physician associations monitor the volume of services provided by each doctor as a cost-control device. If the volume of services exceeds the budgeted volume, then fee levels are adjusted downward to bring actual expenditures back in line with the budget. Physicians must accept the amount paid as payment in full for the services rendered. At the hospital level, regulated hospital planning coupled with per-diem rates and physician fees control overall budgets. The payers and providers of services deal with each other as large organizations that engage in collective bargaining to set rates. Germany had one of the most impressive records among major developed countries on controlling health cost growth during the 1980s, yet their system exhibits scant evidence of rationing or widespread queuing, and their system garners almost universal support from the general public that it covers (Graig 1993).

In Japan, large companies can set up their own independent plans for employees. Small- and mid-sized firms are covered by plans managed by the government. Mutual aid associations provide coverage for government workers and school workers, as well as for ship crews and day workers. The National Health Insurance program covers everyone else, including the self-employed, unemployed, and retirees. None of the plans has a deductible, but all have copayments that were introduced in 1984 to stem the rate of growth in national health expenditures that had been relatively high during the 1960s and 1970s. Employees insured under employer plans pay 10 percent of covered costs, whereas their dependents pay 20 percent of inpatient services and 20 percent of outpatient services. Those covered under the National Health Insurance plan pay 30 percent of all costs. These copayments are limited to $400 per month for most of those covered, or $200 per month for low-income individuals.

The government sets targets for health spending growth based on the growth in GDP. To control costs, it sets a uniform, nationwide fee schedule for inpatient and outpatient services. Billing beyond the government set prices is not allowed. The fee schedules are set by negotiation that includes representation from health care providers, payers, and consumers. Because no overall global budget exists or no limits have been set on health care expenditures, some providers tend to increase the volume of services as they game the system. Still, after fairly strong inflationary increases in health costs during the 1960s and 1970s, Japan was able to stabilize the growth in their health care outlays as a percent of GDP during the 1980s, maintaining more widespread support from their population than the United States has been able to maintain from its citizenry (Graig 1993).

Facing the Moral-Economic Conflict

Daniel Callahan noted that health research investment and health care costs correlate extremely closely. For example, he notes that between 1979 and 1987 costs in health research and development increased by 180 percent and national health costs rose by the same number (Callahan 1992). He concluded that evolving health technology is the culprit behind much of the increasing health cost burden in the United States. He is especially concerned about the prevalence of life-extending technologies that get more expensive because they keep health care consumers around longer in an increasingly debilitated state of existence. He argues that much of the extension-of-life-at-all-costs philosophy ignores the quality of life that is being extended.

The trade-off between the reasonable extension of life and the residual quality of life most certainly is not a one-to-one relationship in many cases. The person with end-stage renal kidney failure who undergoes hemodialysis certainly does not enjoy the same quality of life after the onset of illness and initiation of treatment as before. Yet, the relatively normal functioning of patients who receive dialysis suggests that coexistence between life and treatment regimen can be achieved to a tolerable state that allows them to enjoy much that life has to offer and to contribute to their families and society in many ways. Egregious cases can occur at the margin, however, especially when vast sums of resources are devoted to treatments and all parties already have conceded that those expenditures will not overcome the hopelessness of the medical situation. In some cases, the providers make the Herculean commitment; in others, the patient's family refuses to let go of a dying loved one; finally, the state often plays a role in committing resources to extending lives by forcing continued treatment in cases where the medical professionals involved and the families involved already have agreed that nontechnological treatment is the only humane way to proceed.

Burton Weisbrod has written an essay that examines the interrelationship between the growth in health insurance in the United States and evolving technology (Weisbrod 1991). He argues that the expansion of health insurance, which, for many years, paid doctors and hospitals on the basis of submitted charges, has encouraged the development of cost increasing technologies, which, in turn, have increased the demand for insurance.

Weisbrod observes that some technologies increase expected costs of treatment for a given disease, whereas others may decrease it. Similarly, some technologies increase the variance in the cost of treating a disease, whereas others may decrease it. If a technology increases not only the expected cost but also the variance in the cost of treating a disease, then such a technology will increase the demand for insurance. If the technology reduces both, it will tend to reduce the demand for insurance. He views the spectacular growth in private and public health insurance since the end of World War II as evidence that technologies have increased both the cost *and* variance of treating diseases.

Weisbrod uses Lewis Thomas's three levels of technology in medicine to develop this analysis (Thomas 1975). The first level is "nontechnology," which helps patients cope with diseases that are poorly understood or that have no known cures. Nontechnology medicine is essentially the equivalent of the "caring medicine" that Callahan advocates in hopeless cases where no cure is available. Next is "halfway technology," which encompasses treatments that are not curative but that sustain life, although they often produce some reduction in quality of life. These technologies include transplants, treatment of cancers, and the like. The third level is "high technology," which includes truly preventive and curative procedures that can be used because of the disease mechanism and ways to treat it are well known. Nontechnologies and high technologies tend to be relatively inexpensive to deliver; halfway technologies, however, can be expensive.

Weisbrod reasons that the type of insurance available to consumers affects the kinds of technologies developed in the health sector. He notes that the historical pattern of providing coverage for new products and procedures once they move beyond the "experimental" stage is particularly important. If developers of technology believe that the potential costs of delivering a future product or service will be paid by insurance upon delivery, even though it might not be covered currently, it still is in their best interests to invest in the technology. An insurance system that tends to pay for almost any service once it is no longer experimental and one that tends to pay for the costs incurred in the delivery of health ser-

vices on a retrospective basis encourages the development of halfway technologies that extend life with no regard for cost. Weisbrod also contends
that the retrospective payment structure characteristic to health insurance in the United States since the end of World War II has tended to
encourage the development of halfway technologies because no incentive is given to providers to avoid expensive technologies, even if only
marginally effective.

In contrast, a prospective payment system encourages health care providers to seek out technologies that reduce costs, because prospective
payment gives providers a flat rate without regard to the actual costs incurred in delivery. Throwing expensive, unproven, or marginally beneficial technology at a health problem significantly increases the likelihood
that the prospective payment will not cover the costs of treatment. Prospective payment encourages the development of high technologies, but,
in its absence, more nontechnology care would be given than occurs under a retrospective payment system.

If the United States were to move to a universal prospective payment
health delivery system, it would cast many health care providers into a
much different role than they are in today. To adopt such a system would
inevitably raise questions about the general availability of services and
whether or not providers were not reducing overall quantity and quality
of services to meet budget constraints.   Alan Hillman has pointed out
that many HMOs already present doctors with a potential conflict of interest because the level of care provided to a patient can directly affect
remuneration (Hillman A 1987). The same is true, however, when a doctor bills an insurance company retrospectively on a fee-for-service basis.
In that case, the conflict of interest operates in the opposite direction. In
trying one more treatment, prescribing one more x-ray, or requesting
one more laboratory test, the doctor influences compensation directly. It
would seem that only doctors compensated on a direct-salary basis, with
no incentives for the economic performance of their employer, are truly
free of the conflict-of-interest situations discussed at length earlier. In
such cases, though, the employer undoubtedly would oversee the doctor's
use of resources in treating patients.

Some doctors have made it clear that they are troubled by having to
take an active role in the explicit allocation of health services among the
service population. Doctors of earlier generations, however, faced the
same dilemma of allocating scarce resources. Under the modern widespread practice of reimbursement for "reasonable and customary" charges
for whatever services provided, many doctors no longer faced the earlier,
traditional need to limit services to individual patients. Even as Medicare
and Medicaid began to curtail reimbursement rates, it often was possible
to shift expenses that were not being reimbursed from patients who had

public insurance or no insurance to patients covered by private insurance. As employers have become increasingly aware of the extra burdens that their plans have had to shoulder, they have moved to limit the extent to which they become a dumping ground for costs that others refuse to cover. Although some doctors may not want to participate in allocation

TABLE 8.11   Area Variations in Selected Medicare Procedures: Utilization Rates Per Thousand Beneficiaries[a]

	Number of Areas	5th	25th	50th	75th	95th	Coefficient of Variation
Office visits (per enrollee)	344	2.58	3.01	3.36	3.79	4.59	0.18
Hospital visits (per enrollee)	344	1.57	2.15	2.59	3.16	3.95	0.27
Consultations	340	162.07	221.70	276.72	349.19	548.15	0.42
CT scans (head)	344	34.29	46.01	53.42	64.41	77.84	0.26
CT scans (other)	344	25.45	36.26	44.59	54.55	76.55	0.33
Arthrocentesis	344	7.42	18.81	28.15	41.53	72.83	0.64
Upper GI endoscopy	344	9.84	16.66	20.73	25.36	36.83	0.36
Colonoscopy	344	9.42	15.63	20.30	27.46	422.25	0.44
Electrocardiogram	344	448.96	603.69	708.37	841.34	1130.30	0.27
Coronary angiography	303	2.04	5.08	7.38	9.78	14.05	0.52
Cystoscopy	344	5.80	13.49	19.68	24.16	37.63	0.47
Transurethral resection of the prostrate	312	11.19	15.96	19.62	22.94	31.40	0.30
Destruction of benign lesions, facial	339	14.63	29.09	43.02	69.15	112.75	0.63
Destruction of benign lesions, nonfacial	339	16.93	30.69	49.93	72.12	160.60	0.98
Carotid endarterectomy	144	0.77	1.41	2.03	2.93	4.66	0.57
Cataract removal/ lens implant	316	6.36	15.76	22.23	29.33	41.02	0.46
Cholecystectomy	233	2.63	3.88	4.81	5.85	8.71	0.38
Modified radical mastectomy	148	1.87	3.01	3.93	4.77	6.22	0.33
Breast biopsy with excision	201	2.65	4.66	6.03	7.90	11.20	0.44
Total hip procedures	171	1.19	1.92	2.53	3.54	4.89	0.42

[a]*Source:* 1985 Part B Medicare Annual Data Beneficiary File as reported in Holahan J, Berenson RA, Kachavos PG. Area Variations in Selected Medicare Procedures. *Health Affairs.* Winter 1990; 169.

decisions, the practical reality is that they no longer can avoid it. In many cases they already are making explicit allocation decisions to limit the services that they provide to some patients. And the general public may be more comfortable with a physician in the role of judge than a politician.

A highly variable allocation of health services already exists for some elderly people. John Holahan, Robert Berenson, and Peter Kachavos have analyzed area variations in the provision of 20 different medical procedures to Medicare beneficiaries who received fee-for-service benefits in 1985 (Holahan et al. 1990). In developing their analysis, they used a five percent sample of beneficiaries and aggregated them into groups by metropolitan statistical area (MSA) for each MSA in the United States and for non-MSA parts of each state except for Rhode Island and New Jersey. This gave them 344 potential areas to compare procedures that were fairly common. Some procedures were not provided frequently enough in some areas with smaller populations to give statistically reliable estimates of the actual treatment patterns for that whole population. In these cases, the analysis focused only on treatment patterns in areas that produced enough observations to support the analysis.

The gross results of their analysis are presented in Table 8.11, which reveals wide variation in the utilization rates for most procedures included in the study. The authors found several factors to be statistically significant in explaining these variations. For example, they found that the prevalence of specialists in a geographical area increased utilization rates. Their major conclusion, however, was that much of the variation in treatment patterns could not be accounted for by the individual characteristics of the area populations, the service providers, or other criteria that had been measured. It is possible that the practice of medicine tends to take on a local pattern as doctors in any given locale adopt treatment regimens similar to those used around them or with which they are already familiar. The common practice in one area might differ significantly from those in other areas. The overall variations in the provision of health services under Medicare may be attributed largely to common practice variations of physicians across localities. This suggests that more widespread dissemination of information regarding effective treatment regimens might result in more consistent and appropriate treatment patterns across the country.

One specific finding in this study that relates to the elderly does not follow from the data in Table 8.11. In their analysis, the authors found that "The seventy-five and over population is less likely to have CT scans, both of the head and the rest of the body, and less likely to have upper GI endoscopies, coronary angiographies, transurethral resections of the prostate, and cataract removal with lens implants. It appears that some procedures are simply not done on very old persons" (Holahan et al. 1990). It is possible that the de-facto, decision-making process on selective limitation of health services in this country is similar already to the processes that exist in Canada, Great Britain, or Germany, for instance, where doctors clearly face allocation decisions because of the national budget constraints imposed on their health delivery systems.

Any further constraint of resources to the health sector in the United States will create some moral dilemmas, but lack of constraint is creating the same moral dilemmas. At the federal government level, the size and persistence of federal deficits gives rise to long-term equity questions among generations. Although some individuals have argued that national priorities should be rearranged to divert certain existing government expenditures to the delivery of yet more health care services, no absolute moral standard can certify that the current priorities are inferior to some other politically acceptable priorities. At the state government level, the relative burden of medical costs has infringed recently on other public obligations. Although the trade-off between providing a liver transplant for a small child and building a road or staffing a school room is not something anyone relishes, the orderly evolution of society depends on governments meeting the latter obligations. Although employers in this country have accepted an unusually large role in providing health insurance protection to workers and their dependents, these same employers have not been freed from their obligations to provide safe jobs and fair compensation to their workers, or from their responsibility to provide a reasonable return to the members of society that make ongoing operations possible.

One area that must be addressed under the possibility of an allocation system is the general availability of good information on what works, what is cost effective, and the probabilities of favorable outcomes. It is ironic that our "high technology" medical system has placed so little emphasis on outcomes research. Prescription drugs and some medical devices are the only major categories of services or products that must be proven effective before new technologies can be adopted and paid for under the current reimbursement system. Elaborate clinical outcomes studies will not be developed quickly. In the short term, more emphasis should be placed on expert panels to develop treatment protocols derived from a consensus on what works and what does not. This information, combined with a move to capitated payment systems, could eliminate much of the unnecessary and ineffective care provided today. If medical practitioners begin to use this information to determine their own practice patterns, then potential elimination of inefficient and ineffective care will ameliorate the breadth and depth of allocation decisions that otherwise must be faced.

If medical providers cannot help establish and implement the mechanisms for making health service delivery affordable and equitable in America, then, ultimately, more programs like the one that Oregon has proposed for its Medicaid program will be needed. It is not clear whether the Oregon approach is any less fraught with moral dilemmas than one in which medical providers work out treatment regimens and protocols among themselves to provide a finite level of services to those who need them. The hope that Americans are willing to pay for every possible health service or product that the current system might devise and make that service or product available to anyone who might want it is not viable in the current economy and is unlikely to be so any time in the foreseeable future.

References

Aaron H, Schwartz WB. Rationing Health Care. *Across the Board.* July/August, 1990; 34-39.

Blank RH. *Rationing Medicine.* New York: Columbia University Press. 1988; 85.

Blendon RJ, Leitman R, Morrison I, Donelan K. Satisfaction with Health Systems in 10 Nations. *Health Affairs.* 1990; 9(2); 188.

Burner ST, Waldo DR, McKusick DR. National Health Expenditures Projections Through 2030. *Health Care Financing Review.* 1992; 14(1): 19.

Califano Jr. JA. The Last Time We Reinvented Health Care. *Washington Post.* April 1, 1993; A23.

Callahan D. *What Kind of Life: A Challenging Exploration of the Goals of Medicine.* New York: Simon & Schuster Inc., 1990.

Caplan AL. *If I Were a Rich Man Could I Buy a Pancreas?* Bloomington: Indiana University Press. 1992; 289.

Churchill LR. *Rationing Health Care in America: Perceptions and Principles of Justice.* Notre Dame, Indiana: University of Notre Dame Press, 1987.

Congressional Budget Office. *The Economic and Budget Outlook.* Washington, DC: Congress of the United States, August, 1992.

Congressional Budget Office. *Universal Health Insurance Coverage Using Medicare's Payment Rates.* Washington, DC: Congress of the United States. 1991; 22-33.

Etzioni A. Health Care Rationing: A Critical Evaluation. *Health Affairs.* 1991; 10(2): 89-95.

Evans RW. Health Care Technology and the Inevitability of Resource Allocation and Rationing Decisions. *Journal of the American Medical Association.* 1983; 249(15): 2048.

Gallant MH. Limits on Medicaid Program Fund Transfers. *Healthcare Financial Management.* October 1992; 34.

Gallup Organization. *Public Attitudes on Setting Health Care Limits, 1992.* Washington, DC: Employee Benefit Research Institute. October 1992; 24.

Gleicher N. Cesarean Section Rates in the United States: The Short-Term Failure of the National Consensus Development Conference in 1980. *Journal of the American Medical Association.* 1984; 252(23): 3273.

Graig LA. *Health of Nations.* 1st ed. Washington, DC: Wyatt Company, 1991.

Greenfield S, Nelson EC, Zubkoff M, Manning W, Rogers W, Kravitz RL, Tarlov

AR, Ware JE. Variations in Resource Utilization Among Medical Specialties and Systems of Care. *Journal of the American Medical Association.* 1992; 267(12): 1624-1630.

Grogan CM. Deciding on Access and Levels of Care: Comparison of Canada, Britain, Germany, and the United States. *Journal of Health Politics, Policy and Law.* 1992; 17(2): 213-232.

Hemenway D, Killen A, Cashman SB, Parks, CL, Bicknell WJ. Physicians' Responses to Financial Incentives, Evidence from a For-Profit Ambulatory Care Center. *New England Journal of Medicine.* 1990; 322(15): 1059-1063.

Hillman AL. Financial Incentives for Physicians in HMOs, Is There a Conflict of Interest? *New England Journal of Medicine.* 1987; 317; 1743-1748.

Hillman AL. Health Maintenance Organizations, Financial Incentives, and Physicians' Judgments. *Annals of Internal Medicine.* 1990; 112(12): 892.

Hillman AL, Pauly MV, Kerstein J. How Do Financial Incentives Affect Physicians' Clinical Decisions and the Financial Performance of Health Maintenance Organizations?. *New England Journal of Medicine.* 1989; 321(2): 86-92.

Hillman BJ, Joseph CA, Mabry MR, Sunshine JH, Kennedy, SD, Noether M. Frequency and Costs of Diagnostic Imaging in Office Practice—A Comparison of Self-Referring and Radiologist-Referring Physicians. *New England Journal of Medicine.* 1990; 323(23): 1604-1608.

Hillman BJ, Olson GT, Griffith PE, Sunshine JH, Joseph CA, Kennedy SD, Nelson WR, Bernhardt LB. Physicians' Utilization and Charges for Outpatient Diagnostic Imaging in a Medicare Population. *Journal of the American Medical Association* 1992; 268 (15): 2050.

Holahan J, Berenson RA, Kachavos PG. Area Variations in Selected Medicare Procedures. *Health Affairs.* 1990; 166-175.

Iglehart JK. Health Policy Report, The American Health Care System, Medicaid. *New England Journal of Medicine.* 1993; 328(12): 898.

Insurance Information Institute. Medical Malpractice Insurance, 1982-1991. *The I.I.I. 1993 Fact Book.* 1993; 29.

Kusserow RP. *Financial Arrangements Between Physicians and Health Care Businesses.* Washington, DC: Office of the Inspector General. U.S. Department of Health and Human Services. May 1989.

Levit KR, Lazenby HC, Cowan CA, Letsch SW. National Health Expenditures, 1990. *Health Care Financing Review.* 1991; 13(1): 36.

Localio AR, Lawthers A, Bengtson J, Hebert L, Weaver S, Brennan T, Landis R. Relationship Between Malpractice Claims and Cesarean Delivery. *Journal of the American Medical Association.* 1993; 269(3): 366.

Menzel PT. *Medical Costs, Moral Choices: A Philosophy of Health Care Economics in America.* New Haven: Yale University Press. 1983; 184-212.

Mitchell JM, Scott E. New Evidence of the Prevalence and Scope of Physician Joint Ventures. *Journal of the American Medical Association.* 1992; 268(1); 80-84.

Mitchell JM, Scott E. Physician Ownership of Physical Therapy Services, Effects on Charges, Utilization, and Service Characteristics. *Journal of the American Medical Association.* 1992; 268(15): 2055-2059.

Mitchell JM, Scott E. Physician Self-Referral: Empirical Evidence and Policy Implications. *Advances in Health Economics and Health Services Research.* 1992; 13; 27-42.

Mitchell JM, Sunshine JH. Consequences of Physicians' Ownership of Health Care Facilities—Joint Ventures in Radiation Therapy. *New England Journal of Medicine.* 1992; 327(21): 1497-1501.

Morgan D. Loopholes Closing for Strapped States. *Washington Post.* February 7, 1993; A23.

Morgan D. Tennessee Medicaid Crunch Mirrors a National Ill. *Washington Post.* March 29, 1933;Al, A6.

Myers SA, Gleicher N. A Successful Program to Lower Cesarean-Section Rates. *New England Journal of Medicine.* 1988; 319(23): 1511-1516.

Newhouse JP. An Iconoclastic View of Health Cost Containment. *Health Affairs.* 1993; 12(Supplement): 152-171.

Pallarito K. Budget Deficits Threaten to Shut Out Medicaid Benefits. *Modern Healthcare.* April 22, 1991; 26.

Reinhardt UE. Health Care Spending and American Competitiveness. *Health Affairs.* 1989; 8(4): 5-21.

Riley K. Task Force Mulls Law on Medical Liability. *Washington Times.* March 19, 1993; Cl.

Reischauer RD. CBO Testimony before the Subcommittee on Health, Committee on Ways and Means. U.S. House of Representatives. Washington, DC: March 2, 1993; 17.

Rosenblatt RA. Medicaid Bills for Poor Up 25% in U.S., 36% in California. *Los Angeles Times.* March 18, 1993; Home Edition, Part A; 25.

Schieber GJ, Poullier JP, Greenwald LM. Health Care Systems in Twenty-Four Countries. *Health Affairs.* 1991. 10(3):22-38.

Schieber GJ, Poullier JP, Greenwald LM. U.S. Health Expenditure Performance: An International Comparison and Data Update. *Health Care Financing Review.* 1992. 13(4):3.

Sloan FA, Bovbjerg RR, Githens PB. *Insuring Medical Malpractice.* New York: Oxford University Press. 1991; 206-218.

Social Security Amendments. Section 1801, Title SVII. Health Insurance for the Aged and Disabled. 42 USCS 1395:6811.

Social Security Administration. *Social Security Bulletin, Annual Statistical Supplement, 1991.* Washington, DC: Social Security Administration. 1991; 271.

Thomas L. *The Lives of a Cell.* New York: Bantam Books. 1975; 37-40.

Thorne JI. The Oregon Plan Approach to Comprehensive and Rational Health Care. *In:* Strosberg MA, et al., eds. *Rationing America's Medical Care: The Oregon Plan and Beyond.* Washington, DC: The Brookings Institution. 1992; 25-26.

U.S. Department of Commerce. Bureau of the Census. *Statistical Abstract of the United States: 1992.* 112th ed. Washington, DC: U.S. Government Printing Office. 1992; Table no. 86; 67.

U.S. General Accounting Office. *Canadian Health Insurance, Lessons for the United States.* Washington, DC: United States General Accounting Office. 1991; 60-66.

Weiler PC, et al. *A Measure of Malpractice, Medical Injury, Malpractice Litigation, and Patient Compensation.* Cambridge, Mass: Harvard University Press. 1993; 2.

Weisbrod BA. The Health Care Quadrilemma: An Essay on Technological Change, Insurance, Quality of Care, and Cost Containment. *Journal of Economic Literature.* 1991; 29; 523-552.

Wyatt Company. Employer-Sponsored Health Benefits Programs: A Chronic Affliction or a Growing Malignancy? *Management USA: Leading a Changing Work Force.* Washington, DC: Wyatt Company. 1990; 2.

Wyatt Company. Unpublished data from its 1987 *Group Benefits Survey* and *1992 Wyatt COMPARE Survey.*

Commentary: David A. Asch

Sylvester Schieber entitles the last section of Chapter Eight, "Facing the Moral-Economic Conflict." This commentary focuses on the last section of his chapter and begins, in a sense, where Dr. Schieber ends. He concludes with the statement that, "The hope that Americans will be willing to pay for every possible health service or product that the current system might devise and then make that service or product available to anyone who might want it is not viable in the current economy."

Dr. Schieber should be commended for his comprehensive analysis in support of this last statement. He brings together a tremendous amount of thought and information about the resources that presently support health care in this country, comparisons across developed nations, and potential trends for the future. Dr. Schieber's figures tell much about the United States' capacity to deliver health services. Ultimately, however, the important question to answer is how much of that capacity should be supported?

This question assumes a perspective slightly different from the view of many health economists. The common view, as Dr. Schieber suggests, is that "no absolute moral standard exists that would certify the current priorities as inferior to other politically acceptable priorities." Indeed, there is no obvious reason why 20% or even 50% of the United States gross domestic product (GDP) should not be devoted to health care if that is what Americans want. Although the current ruckus over health care reform suggests there may be some absolute political standards for setting priorities, there are no absolute moral standards that dictate how much health care capacity to support.

The position expressed in this commentary is that there is an absolute moral requirement for a society to make some sort of *decision* about how much health care spending to support, regardless of what that level is. The current political interest in health care reform is as convenient a reason as any to begin that process now, but, in the abstract, it makes

Support from the John A. Hartford Foundation is gratefully acknowledged sense for societies to develop a formal mechanism with which to set priorities, something that in this case, perhaps, should have begun long ago.

The argument presented here is that we must make active decisions to set priorities and that setting priorities has more to do with supporting health than anything else. In the end, the title of Dr. Schieber's paper is misleading, because it suggests that we can resolve the conflict between cultural values and limited resources in some absolute sense. The position of this commentary is that there is no satisfactory resolution to this problem. Instead, in the area of health care benefits for the elderly or, indeed, in any area that addresses health care justice, there simply is no way to avoid conflict. The search for some sort of acceptable solution is destructive because it wastes time and prevents us from making the hard choices that we cannot avoid.

The remainder of this discussion will touch upon three related issues. Each of these represents a basic concept that underlies the conflict that Dr. Schieber addresses. These underlying concepts explain why the conflict between values and resources is irreconcilable and why we should stop seeking resolution.

The first issue is that the health care system is like a commons upon which we all graze, and unless a commons is actively managed and regulated, everyone loses. The message is that if we are to share common resources, we must cooperate as a group; to do this, we must learn to restructure personal incentives. The second issue is that the whole point about limited resources is that we sometimes have to say no to some truly beneficial services. The message here is that despite the reduction in costs we might achieve by reducing administrative hassles or defensive medicine, trimming the fat is never enough. We must learn to set reasonable limits, and *reasonable* limits will always exclude some truly beneficial services. The third issue is that even if we establish health as our most important priority, we must stop thinking of health as something only medicine can provide. The message here is that there are alternative paths toward health, and we must focus on the goals rather than on the process.

The goal of this paper is to demonstrate that these three concepts are connected; that they are indeed the basic concepts that underlie this problem; and that, although each of us already understands and accepts these three concepts, at the same time we seem unable to accept their logical implications.

The Tragedy of the Commons

Each of us has had the experience of going to a restaurant with a group of friends and deciding what to eat. When ordering from the menu, we may choose differently if we are getting separate checks or if, instead, we will later split the bill. A single diner ordering within a group will order more than otherwise, because increases in the cost of one meal will increase the total bill relatively little. Since each diner faces the same choice, however, all may overorder. The end result is that the entire bill becomes progressively larger, and each person's share of this bill turns out to be perceptibly higher than it might have been had each planned to pay separately.

This general phenomenon has been called the tragedy of the commons (Lloyd 1833). Imagine a pasture open to a group of shepherds. As each shepherd allows his animals to graze the land, he may conclude that the cost to him of adding one more sheep to the herd is more than offset by the gains. He gets all the benefit of the additional animal but only a share of the cost. As a result, the rational shepherd adds one more animal to his herd, and then another, and yet another. But since all rational shepherds reason the same way, in time the commons becomes so overcrowded with sheep that there is insufficient grass for grazing. As Garrett Hardin observed, there is no technical solution to this common problem: "Ruin is the destination toward which all men rush, each pursuing his own best interest in a society that believes in the freedom of the commons. Freedom in a commons brings ruin to all" (Hardin 1968).

The resources available for health care have been likened to a medical commons (Somers 1971; Hiatt 1975). Health insurance sustains that similarity because health insurance insulates individuals from the costs of their choices and, thereby, attenuates the financial implications of individual decisions on individual decisionmakers. The issue really is no different from the problem of moral hazard (Pauly 1968). As in the restaurant, where the diners are prompted to order the more expensive entree or the second dessert, the tragedy of the health care commons is that individuals will demand more health care than they would if they faced the full cost themselves.

There is no reason to blame health insurance alone for creating a medical commons. Physicians and other health care providers have been coconspirators, for they have long supported the view that whatever can be done for the patient should be done. Professional norms like these induce demand (Eisenberg 1986).

Still, the central issue is that health insurance sustains the medical commons. Deductibles and copayments help patients sense on a personal level the costs of their individual decisions, but deductibles and copayments in the end merely turn full insurance into partial insurance. The same issues remain—patients are still at least partially numb to the potentially painful financial implications of their decisions, and so they will tolerate more than if they were not insured.

This is a fundamental problem that has no solution. As long as we allow individuals to purchase health insurance—and there are many compelling reasons why health insurance is, all told, probably a good thing—our aggregate demand for health services remains artificially high.

Most people intuitively understand and accept this idea. What is surprising is that, despite the simplicity of this concept, so many seem unwilling to accept its implications. As Daniel Callahan has observed:

> There is a widespread belief that we can find some managerial fix, some wonderful incentive scheme to get doctors to use only proven treatments based on parsimonious diagnostic procedures, for instance. That belief is matched in fervor only by the hope that we can find some entitlement fix, some scheme that reduces government expenditures while leaving patients satisfied with their nicely calibrated out-of-pocket expenses. (Callahan 1990)

The commons represents a marketplace where the invisible hand does not support equilibrium. The tragedy of the commons is that the invisible hand leads to destruction. The only way to avoid that destruction is to establish an active process that sets limits.

Beyond Trimming the Fat

This notion leads to the second point. Dr. Schieber outlines several ways to reduce health care costs without changing the amount of services provided. These mechanisms include streamlining the health care system to reduce its administrative costs; altering the malpractice tort liability system so that awards are reduced, awards are directed more toward patients than attorneys, and the practice of defensive medicine is undermined; and restructuring the financial incentives that lead to the oversupply of and induced demand for unnecessary medical services. Each of these mechanisms represents one form of trimming the fat. Individually, each may produce various amounts of savings, but the actual amount of savings is less important than the obvious point—we ought to eliminate wasteful practices in health care no matter how small the gains.

It is one thing to suggest that we ought to trim the fat, but it is entirely another thing to suggest that trimming the fat somehow might address or even solve the cost problem we face in health care. Trimming the fat is not a *solution* to anything. Even if United States health care expenditures amounted to only 1% of the GDP, we ought to try to eliminate waste. Waste is inherently bad.

The problem with focusing on waste is not that it gets us nowhere. The problem is that the exercise is an excuse not to address the real issue.

The real issue is the problem of diminishing marginal returns. This is a basic principle from elementary microeconomics: Firms ought to stop producing when the marginal costs of production exceed their marginal gains. At this point, there is still unmet demand for goods and services, but the demand cannot support the cost of producing those goods and services.

The implications of this very basic idea ought to be clear in the case of health care, whether it is for the elderly or any other segment of the population. If we are unwilling to put a price on health benefits, then we immediately commit an unlimited amount of resources to health and go bankrupt. As soon as we put a finite value on health benefits, there is some point at which the cost of the next health service is not worth its benefit. If we stop providing services at that point, as we should, we will have failed to provide services that convey some benefits.

What this means is that trimming the fat is never sufficient. There is no way we can avoid the situation in which we fail to provide services that convey true benefits. You have to cut lean. This is the price of Lewis Thomas' "halfway technologies" that Dr. Schieber discusses (Thomas 1974). As Howard Hiatt has argued, "[a]s we develop more and more practices that may be beneficial to the individual but not to the interests of society, we risk reaching a point where marginal gains to individuals threaten the welfare of the whole" (Hiatt 1975).

As in the case of the tragedy of the commons, this is a simple point that flows inescapably from a basic concept that we all understand. Nevertheless it is surprising how many believe that by trimming the fat, or by identifying some other managerial fix, we can somehow avoid the situation in which we say no to truly beneficial services. The message is that we must learn to set reasonable limits, and *reasonable* limits will always exclude some medical care that really does make a difference.

Alternative Paths to Health

The degree to which we cut into the lean will be determined by the priority we place on health. This notion introduces the third point. No matter where health sits on our list of priorities, the goal is health, not the provision of medical care. So much of the current thinking about health seems to confuse the goal with the process. The distinction is a simple concept, like the tragedy of the commons or the law of diminishing marginal returns, and yet, once again, the implications of this simple concept continue to be ignored.

In fact, medical care is probably much less relevant to aggregate health than many other social institutions. Historically, the really important advances in health have come from significantly more fundamental changes, like public sewers and fresh water, or overall improvements in the economy.

Dr. Schieber notes how some believe that "any expenditure is justified in preserving an individual life" (Blank 1988). That statement needs to be qualified. Americans have been able to establish budgets for highway or product safety, building codes, and a host of nonmedical interventions whose explicit goals are to promote health and preserve life. The uproar over the prospect of global health care budgeting is a recent example of the distinction made between medical and nonmedical paths to health and welfare. The glib explanation for the current interest in health care cost containment is that for years the medical enterprise has been given an unlimited budget, and they have "exceeded" it. No other path toward health and welfare has been similarly endowed.

A variety of political and psychological reasons explain how the distinction between medical and nonmedical paths to health can be maintained in the minds of otherwise thoughtful people who clearly understand—on some level—that there is no distinction at all. One political reason may be the power of the medical lobby. One psychological reason may be the urgency and compelling plight of the identifiable patient versus the unknown statistical highway fatality (Churchill 1987).

Whatever the reasons, the distinction leads to waste and inefficiency. As Howard Hiatt notes, the "widely accepted but narrow interpretation of health as an exclusively medical concern . . . contributes to continuing raids on the commons by expensive practices" (Hiatt 1975). The ultimate tragedy of maintaining this artificial distinction is that we forego opportunities for real improvements in health. Each dollar we contribute to some expensive medical practice of limited value might instead have been used to widen highway lanes or strengthen bicycle helmets.

This discussion began with Dr. Schieber's claim that there may be no absolute moral standard by which to judge any system of priorities. This claim may be legitimate; nevertheless, there is an absolute moral requirement that we set some priorities. If we are able to set priorities in some areas that affect health, like highway safety, we ought to be able to do the same for medical care. And unless we are willing to tolerate inefficiencies in the ways we allocate resources across alternative paths toward the same goal, those priorities need to be consistent—which is to say that they must be based on those goals, not on any one specific process.

Conclusion

Recognizing medical care as only one of many means to an end highlights the alternative uses for our resources and, in itself, provides a compelling argument for allocating those resources on the basis of the marginal gains that they can achieve. These are the micro issues in health care resource allocation. The macro issues are all the same, although they take various names: setting priorities, determining the size of the medical commons, or, more currently, establishing global budgets.

The argument presented in this commentary is that there is no resolving the conflict between individual needs and social goals. The reason this conflict is irreconcilable can be found in very simple notions that we all learned to accept before we finished high school. Yet the inescapable conclusion of these three notions—the tragedy of the commons, the law of diminishing marginal returns, and the distinction between process and goals—seems to be continually lost on those who search for the perfect copayment or deductible, the perfect reimbursement system for physicians, or the perfect way to trim the fat. These are all good things, but, in the end, they are no substitute for actually saying no to some truly beneficial medical services that will help real patients.

Garrett Hardin notes that "Every new enclosure of the commons involves the infringement of somebody's personal liberty" (Hardin 1968). The practical implications of this comment may not be perfectly clear in the case of health care, but it would seem that the elderly are at great risk, and that arguments such as these could redefine how their health care benefits are determined. Most of the popular and useful measures of health benefits rely in some way on counting up the years of life saved by alternative health interventions. Because older people, by and large, have fewer years left to live no matter what, interventions targeted to the elderly have a lower ceiling of potential gain than those targeted to the young. Without getting more specific, it seems logical that if we are able to accept the commons as a finite resource, to allocate that resource according to the benefits we receive, and to recognize alternative paths to the same goal, then many medical interventions for the elderly are going to seem very frivolous indeed. We need to say no more often in the provision of medical care. We need to say it to our physicians, and our physicians need to say it to their patients. If we learn, finally, how to say no, then the elderly are going to hear that word a lot more than other segments of the population.

References

Blank RH. *Rationing Medicine.* New York: Columbia University Press. 1988; 85.

Callahan D. *What Kind of Life: The Limits of Medical Progress.* New York: Simon and Schuster. 1990; 27.

Churchill LR. *Rationing Health Care in America: Perceptions and Principles.* Notre Dame, IN: University of Notra Dame Press. 1987.

Eisenberg JM. *Doctors' Decisions and the Cost of Medical Care.* Ann Arbor: Health Administration Press. 1986; Chapters 2-4.

Hardin G. The Tragedy of the Commons. *Science.* 1968; 162:1243-1248.

Hiatt HH. Protecting the Medical Commons. *New England Journal of Medicine.* 1975; 293:235-241.

Lloyd WF. *Two Lectures on the Checks to Population.* Oxford: Oxford University Press. 1833.

Pauly MV. The Economics of Moral Hazard. *American Economic Review.* 1968; 533-539.

Somers AR. *Health Care in Transition.* Chicago: Hospital Research and Educational Trust. 1971; 153-157.

Thomas L. *The Lives of a Cell.* New York: Viking. 1974; 31-36.

Commentary: John M. Burns

In Chapter Eight, Sylvester Schieber discusses extensively the fundamental conflicts that have led to the current state of affairs in the American "nonsystem" of health care. The prominent issues examined by Schieber include runaway costs, excessive care, and growing numbers of underinsured or uninsured. This commentary evaluates the success of Schieber's presentation.

In 1944, Tinsley Harrison noted, "the present day tendency is toward the fine minute history followed by a five day barrage of special tests in the hope that the diagnostic rabbit may suddenly emerge from the laboratory hat" (Harrison 1944). Medical benefit plans that provide entitlement to services lead to the indiscriminant use of diagnostic testing, one factor that contributes to the high cost of health in the United States, as compared to Canada and Europe for instance. Additional causes are (1) administrative cost excesses; (2) unbridled technology and specialization without concern for yield; (3) insatiable demand for services; (4) unrealistic expectations and poor medical judgment; (5) medical legal concerns; and (6) greed (Hadler 1990). The major reasons for the conflict described by Schieber are the secondary costs of excessive and unnecessary care. For example, Milliman and Robertson, the Seattle-based actuaries and consultants, recently projected that "nearly 60% of the time patients spend in hospital is medically unnecessary" (Axene and Doyle 1993).

The entitlement to health care benefits, especially that provided to the elderly and encouraged by the vested interests of the stakeholders, contributes significantly to the excessive demands of the patient consumer. Certainly, Americans must learn to cope with an aging society that now consumes almost 40% of all health care in the country. The entitlement orientation of consumers and the failure of the health care nonsystem to minimize unnecessary care has created a situation in which " the amount of health care that the elderly can consume is limited only by the imagination and ingenuity of scientists, physicians, drug companies, and other producers of other health care goods and services" (Fuchs 1993).

If excessive costs were the only consequence of the situation, it would be bad enough; but, keep in mind a 1981 finding that 36% of patients admitted on a general medical service at a university hospital acquired an iatrogenic illness. Indeed, in 9% of all persons admitted, the incidence was considered major in that it threatened life or produced considerable disability, and that 2% of iatrogenic illness was believed to contribute to the death of the patient (Steel et al. 1981).

Schieber's views are debatable, particularly when he states that chronic ailments are problematic because their treatment often means that yet some additional chronic ailments will result from treatment and will require further treatment. As Dr. Alexander Leaf (Harvard Medical School) stated in a recent article, "the objection is invariably raised that preventing illness early will only increase the burden of chronic diseases at a later age. This, it is argued, would increase the sum total of human suffering and adversely affect health costs. But evidence for such gloomy outcome from optimizing health as the major goal of the health care system is what is lacking. . . . Disease prevented is not necessarily disease postponed" (Leaf 1993). The perverse incentives of the system undoubtedly contribute to the lack of emphasis on preventive care. After all, it is the doers, not the preventers, who reap rewards. Prevention is too invisible and even boring. Watching a fire is more exciting than a smoke detector (Dans 1993).

Schieber also contends that "state and local governments are large *purchasers* of health services through a variety of programs." (author emphasis) This statement also is debatable. Undoubtedly, government is a *payer* of benefits, but whether or not the government purchaser has the sophistication to specify a particular product so that an informed purchase can be made is highly doubtful.

The issue of rationing is raised by Schieber as the inevitable consequence of cost control. The definitions proposed by Hadorn and Brook would help resolve this apparent dilemma (Hadorn and Brook 1991). They suggest the following:

- Rationing is the societal toleration of inequitable access to health services acknowledged to be necessary by reference to necessary care guidelines;
- Health care needs are desires for services that have been reasonably well demonstrated to provide significant net benefit for patients with specified clinical conditions;
- Basic benefit plans or insurance packages should provide for all and only acknowledge health care needs, again by reference to appropriate clinical guidelines.

The definition of care on the basis of standards of necessity and appropriateness should help resolve the conflict between cultural values and limited resources, a conflict that is one of perception more than of reality. According to a recent editorial, "Restriction of care to that which is known to be appropriate or to that which an informed patient consents and redesign of the processes of care or the provision systems are approaches that do not require rationing of care" (Schoenbaum 1993).

An excellent review is available from the Washington Business Group on Health that addresses malpractice reform. It might be advisable for both Schieber and interested readers to examine this work, especially in light of the presentation on malpractice in Chapter Eight.

With regard to excessive care, Schieber offers the Chicago Mt. Sinai caesarean section study as an example. A better reference for the appropriate number of necessary caesarean births might be the massive work done by Chalmer, Enkin, and Keirse (1990). In this analysis, which reviewed studies of 60 key journals from 1950 onward and which included surveys from over 40,000 obstetricians and pediatricians in 18 countries, the authors were able to document that little improvement occurs in outcome of pregnancy when caesarean rates rise above 7 percent! Finally, the moral and economic conflict in providing care for the elderly, as discussed in Chapter Eight, appears to be based on the false assumption that whatever is done should be done, and, as a result, "values" come into conflict.

The fundamental issue involved in addressing health care, the cost of health care, and the apparent real conflicts with societal cultural values and norms is the failure to address the issues of necessity and appropriateness. The provision of excessive or futile care should not produce conflict in values and affordability. Instead it should lead to the requirement that the payer or purchaser document that any health care for which reimbursement is sought should be necessary and appropriate. For many older persons, hospitalization results in functional decline despite cure or repair of the condition for which they were admitted. This is called a "cascade to dependency," a phenomenon common to the treatment of the elderly that only creates a need for further care and costs. Unless the appropriateness of care and the consequences of incomplete care are addressed, the cascade will continue to be a self-fulfilling promise. Studies have been completed on the effectiveness of specially designed units for treatment of the elderly (Creditor 1993).

Equally disturbing in the discussion of health care delivery is the notion of compulsory payment for unwanted treatment or court-ordered reimbursement for unproven medical technology (Annas 1992; Ferguson et al. 1986). Undoubtedly, the cascade effect of medical care—referring to a process once started that proceeds step-wise to its full and seemingly inevitable conclusion—is a major cost factor in medicine (Mold and Stein 1986). As so frequently stated, the first mistake is often the biggest. In addition, the subject of medical futility is being raised more frequently in medical journals.

All in all, Schieber's chapter provides a significant amount of information on comparative costs and utilization patterns. Most of the relevant issues that contribute to the dilemma are raised. Until the health care product is defined on the basis of medical necessity and appropriateness, however, the conflict between cultural values and limited resources remains a perception, not a reality.

References

Annas GJ. Adding Injustice to Injury. *New England Journal of Medicine.* 1992;327:1885-1887.

Axene DV, Doyle RL. *Analysis of Medically Unnecessary Inpatient Services.* Seattle: Milliman and Robertson, Inc., 1993.

Chalmer I, Enkin M, Keirse MJNC. *Effective Care in Pregnancy and Childbirth.* Oxford: University Press at Oxford; 1989.

Creditor MC. Hazards of Hospitalization of the Elderly. *Annals of Internal Medicine.* 1993;118:219-223.

Dans PE. Perverse Incentives, Statesmanship, and the Ghosts of Reforms Past. *Annals of Internal Medicine.* 1993;118:227-229.

Ferguson JH, Dubinsky M, Kirsch PJ. Court-Ordered Reimbursement for Unproven Medical Technology. *Journel of the American Medical Association* 1993;269:116-2121.

Fuchs VR. Dear President Clinton. *Journal of the American Medical Association.* 1993;269:1678-1679.

Hadorn VC, Brook RH. Toward Fewer Procedures and Better Outcomes. *Journal of the American Medical Association.* 1991;266:3328-3331.

Hadler S. The Internal Destruction of the American System of Medical Practice. *Bulletin of Hennepin County Medical Association.* 1990;March/April:6-9.

Harrison TR. The Value and Limitation of Laboratory Tests in Clinical Medicine. *Journal of the Medical Association of Alabama.* 1944;13:381-384.

Leaf A. Preventive Medicine for our Ailing Health Care System. *Journal of the American Medical Association.* 1993;269:616-618.

Mold JW, Stein HF. The Cascade Effect in the Clinical Care of Patients. *New England Journal of Medicine.* 1986;314:512-514.

Schoenbaum SC. *Journal of the American Medical Association.* 1993;269:794-796.

Steel K, Gertman PM, Crescenzi C, Anderson J. Iatrogenic Illness on a General Medical Service at a University Hospital. *New England Journal of Medicine.* 1981;34:638-642.

Contributors

JOSEPH R. ANTOS is Director of the Office of Research and Demonstrations in the Health Care Financing Administration (HCFA) and served as Chairman of the HCFA wide task force that implemented Medicare physician payment reform. Previous positions held by Dr. Antos include Deputy Assistant Secretary for Management and Budget and Deputy Chief of Staff, both for the U.S. Department of Health and Human Services. He also has held senior positions on the President's Council of Economic Advisers, the Office of Management and Budget, and the U.S. Department of Labor. Dr. Antos received his B.A. in mathematics from Cornell University and Ph.D. in economics from the University of Rochester.

DAVID A. ASCH is an Assistant Professor of Medicine in the Division of General Internal Medicine of the University of Pennsylvania School of Medicine. Dr. Asch has clinical appointments at the Hospital of the University of Pennsylvania and the Veterans Affairs Medical Center in Philadelphia, where he is Director of Health Services Research. He is a senior fellow at the Leonard Davis Institute of Health Economics and the Associate Director of the Robert Wood Johnson Foundation Clinical Scholars Program at the University of Pennsylvania. Dr. Asch received an A.B. in philosophy from Harvard College and an M.D. from Cornell University Medical College. Following his residency in internal medicine at the Hospital of the University of Pennsylvania, Dr. Asch became a Robert Wood Johnson Clinical Scholar at the University of Pennsylvania and a fellow in the Division of General Medicine at the Hospital of the University of Pennsylvania. He also received an M.B.A. in decision sciences and health care from the Wharton School of the University of Pennsylvania.

G. LAWRENCE ATKINS is the Director of Health Legislative Affairs in the Washington office of the New York law firm of Winthrop, Stimson, Putnam & Roberts. Before his current job, Dr. Atkins served for eight years as a staff member of the U.S. Senate Special Committee on Aging, most recently as Minority Staff Director. Before joining the Special Committee on Aging, Dr. Atkins was Director of Planning of the Human Services Coordination Alliance and Senior Planner of the Office of Policy and Budget, Kentucky Department for Human Resources. He is a founding member of the National Academy of Social Insurance and was a member of the 1991 Advisory Council on Social Security. Dr. Atkins graduated from Kenyon College. He holds an

M.S. from the University of Louisville and an M.A. from the University of Kentucky. He earned his Ph.D. in Social Welfare Policy from the Heller School at Brandeis University.

JOHN M. BURNS is the Vice President for Health Management at Honeywell Inc. Dr. Burns is a member of the American College of Physicians and the American College of Occupational and Environmental Medicine. He has served on the boards of the Midwest Business Group on Health and of the American College of Physician Executives. He is a member of the board of the Washington Business Group on Health and has served as its chairman. Before beginning a full-time career in corporate health care management, Dr. Burns maintained a private practice in internal medicine and acted as Medical Advisor and Assistant Medical Director for Northwestern Bell Telephone Company. He earned a B.S. in chemistry and an M.D. from St. Louis University and an M.B.A. from the University of St. Thomas (St. Paul, Minnesota). Dr. Burns completed a residency in internal medicine through the University of Minnesota and served two years as Director of Nephrology at Ancker Hospital in St. Paul.

DEBORAH J. CHOLLET is an Associate Director at the Alpha Center in Washington, DC. Previously she was an Associate Professor of Risk Management and Insurance and the Director of the Center for Risk Management and Insurance Research at Georgia State University. Dr. Chollet is a member of the National Academy of Social Insurance, the American Risk and Insurance Association, the American Public Health Association, the American Economic Association, and the Association for Health Services Research. She serves on the advisory boards of the Robert Wood Johnson Foundation, the March of Dimes, and the Office of Technology Assessment of the U.S. Congress, and on the editorial board of *Benefits Quarterly*. Previously, Dr. Chollet an expert advisor to the Governor of Georgia's Commission on Health Care was and the Senior Research Associate at the Employee Benefit Research Institute. She has been the Executive Director of the quadrennial Advisory Council on Social Security, a senior researcher at the National Center for Health Services Research, and a member of the economics faculty at Temple University. Dr. Chollet earned a B.S. in economics at the University of Missouri at St. Louis and an M.A. and Ph.D. in economics at Syracuse University.

PEGGY M. CONNERTON works for the Service Employees International Union, AFL-CIO as Chief Economist and as Director of Public Policy. Dr. Connerton participates in the National Leadership Coalition on Health Care Reform, the Health Policy Agenda Task Force on Medicaid, and the Dunlop Group of Six. Dr. Connerton has held positions in the House Energy and Commerce Committee, the Joint Economic Committee, and the Office of Policy at the U.S. Department of Labor, where she was the liaison to the Office of Management and Budget on the economic impact of Department of Labor regulations. Dr. Connerton received her Ph.D. in economics from Harvard University.

WILLIAM S. CUSTER is the Director of Research at the Employee Benefit Research Institute (EBRI). Before joining EBRI, Dr. Custer was an economist in the Center for Health Policy Research at the American Medical Association and served as an Assistant Professor of Economics at Northern Illinois University. Dr. Custer earned a B.S. in economics at the University of Minnesota and received his Ph.D. in economics from the University of Illinois at Urbana.

PAUL B. GRANT is an Associate Professor of Human Resources and Industrial Relations in the graduate Institute of Human Resources of Loyola University Chicago. Professor Grant is secretary of the University's pension committee, which is responsible for a TIAA-CREF program for faculty and a defined benefit program that covers 6000 other employees. He received a B.S. in history and an M.S. in labor relations from Loyola University Chicago and an M.A. in economics from Northwestern University.

WILLIAM R. GREER is a Clinical Scholar with the Four Schools Physician Scientist Program, funded by the Lucille P. Markey Charitable Trust. He graduated from Yale University with a major in English and worked for six years as a staff reporter for *The New York Times* before attending the University of Pennsylvania Medical School. He is a Senior Fellow with the Leonard Davis Institute of Health Economics and Health Policy. Currently he is a house officer in Internal Medicine at the Hospital of the University of Pennsylvania.

ALAN L. HILLMAN is an Assistant Professor of Medicine at the School of Medicine, Assistant Professor of Health Care Management at The Wharton School, and Director of the Center for Health Policy at the Leonard Davis Institute of Health Economics, all of the University of Pennsylvania. Dr. Hillman also is a senior scholar in Penn's Clinical Epidemiology Unit and a member of its Comprehensive Cancer Research Program, a member of the editorial boards of *PharmacoEconomics* and *Business and Health*, and a fellow of the American College of Physicians. Dr. Hillman graduated with honors from Cornell University with an interdisciplinary degree in science, technology, and society and received awards as the outstanding member of his graduating class at Cornell University Medical Center. Following a residency in internal medicine at New York Hospital-Cornell Medical Center, he pursued a fellowship in Penn's Robert Wood Johnson Foundation Clinical Scholars Program, during which time he received an M.B.A. with distinction from The Wharton School.

CAROL H. MALONE is a member of the Washington Resource Group of
William M. Mercer, Inc. Ms. Malone is in regular contact with federal
and state government staff to provide Mercer's consultants and clients
with up-to-date information and analyses of health and welfare legislative and regulatory actions. She also consults on a national level with
Mercer's clients to maximize coordination and responsiveness of the
firm's advice and communications on health care issues. Before to
joining Mercer's Washington Resource Group, Ms. Malone was a consultant with the Segal Company, where she designed and analyzed
health benefit plans for employees and retirees. Ms. Malone received
her undergraduate degree from Columbia University and holds a
Master's degree in Health Services Administration from George Washington University.

JUDITH F. MAZO is Senior Vice President and Director of Research for The
Segal Company. Ms. Mazo is a member of the Pension Research Council
and the Editorial Advisory Boards of the BNA Pension Reporter and
the Benefits Law Journal. She is active in the American Bar Association, serving as chair of the Welfare Reform Subcommittee of the
Employee Benefits Committee of the Tax Section and chair of the Plan
Termination Committee of the Real Property, Probate, and Trust Sec-
tion. Before joining The Segal Company, Ms. Mazo was engaged in
private law practice in Washington, DC, specializing in ERISA and serving as special counsel to the Pension Benefit Guaranty Corporation
(PBGC) and as consultant to the Pension Task Force of the House
Committee on Education and Labor. She was senior attorney for the
PBGC and executive assistant to its general counsel from 1975 to 1979.
Ms. Mazo graduated with honors from Yale Law School and Wellesley
College and has been admitted to the bar in the District of Columbia
and the State of Louisiana.

OLIVIA S. MITCHELL is the International Foundation of Employee Benefit
Plans Professor of Insurance and Risk Management and Executive Di-
rector of the Pension Research Council at The Wharton School of the
University of Pennsylvania. Dr. Mitchell is a Research Associate at the
National Bureau of Economic Research. She previously was a Professor of Labor Economics at Cornell University's Industrial and Labor
Relations School, represented the public on the ERISA Advisory Council for the Secretary of Labor, and has been a visiting scholar at Harvard
University's Department of Economics. Dr. Mitchell received a B.S. in
economics from Harvard University and an M.A. and Ph.D. in economics from the University of Wisconsin, Madison.

DIANA L. MURRAY is the Senior Manager of Group Insurance Plans for the
Sara Lee Corporation, where she is responsible for the analysis, development, and communication of all group program benefits. Before

to assuming her position at Sara Lee Corporation, Ms. Murray was Manager of Retiree Benefits for FMC Corporation and Assistant Director of Benefits for the University of Chicago. Previous to that, she taught German to high school students. During her teaching career, Ms. Murray was awarded fellowships for summer study by the Goethe Institute and the Midwest National Endowment for the Humanities. She received a B.A. in German with a French minor from Kalamazoo College and studied theology at McCormick Theological Seminary. Ms. Murray is a Certified Compensation Professional and is working toward certification as an Employee Benefit Specialist (CEBS).

J. PETER NIXON is a Policy Analyst with the Services Employees International Union. Mr. Nixon has a Master's degree in Public Policy (M.P.P.) from Georgetown University and a B.A. from McGill University. He is the author of many monographs and articles on health care reform, the most recently being, "Health Care Reform: A Labor Perspective," which was published in the July 1993 issue of the *American Behavioral Scientist.*

MARK V. PAULY is the Bendheim Professor, and Chairman of the Health Care Systems Department, and Professor of Insurance and Public Policy and Management in the Wharton School of the University of Pennsylvania. Dr. Pauly also is Professor of Economics in the School of Arts and Sciences and Director of Research at the Leonard Davis Institute of Health Economics (LDI) of the University of Pennsylvania. He is a member of the Institute of Medicine, an adjunct scholar of the American Enterprise Institute, and a member of the advisory board of the Washington-based Capital Economics group. Before joining the faculty at the University of Pennsylvania, Dr. Pauly was a visiting research fellow at the International Institute of Management in Berlin, (West) Germany, and professor of economics at Northwestern University. His other appointments have included visiting scientist to the International Institute for Applied Systems Analysis in Laxenburg, Austria, and faculty research fellow at the National Bureau of Economic Research. Dr. Pauly is a graduate of Xavier University. He received an M.A. from the University of Delaware and a Ph.D. in economics from the University of Virginia.

ANNA M. RAPPAPORT is a Managing Director of William M. Mercer, Inc. and a benefits strategy consultant to major clients of the firm. Ms. Rappaport is a member of the Pension Research Council and coedited and contributed a chapter to its 1991 symposium volume, *Demography and Retirement: The Twenty-First Century.* Ms. Rappaport has taught graduate and undergraduate courses at the College of Insurance in New York. Before joining William M. Mercer, Inc., she served as a Vice President of the Equitable Life Insurance Society of the United

States and as Senior Vice President and Chief Actuary of the Standard Security Life Insurance Company of New York. Ms. Rappaport holds an M.B.A. from the University of Chicago. She also is a Fellow of the Society of Actuaries, a member of the American Academy of Actuaries, and an enrolled actuary. She previously served as Chairman of the Midwest Business Council and as Vice President, Treasurer, and elected Board Member of the Society of Actuaries.

JOHN ROTHER is Director of the Legislation and Public Policy Division for the American Association of Retired Persons (AARP). Before coming to the AARP, Mr. Rother served as Special Counsel for Labor and Health to Senator Jacob Javits and as Staff Director and Chief Counsel for the Special Committee on Aging under its Chairman, Senator John Heinz. He has served as a member of the ERISA Advisory Council for the Secretary of Labor, the Blue-Ribbon Advisory Commission on the FDA for the Secretary of Health and Human Service (Edwards Commission), and the Commonwealth Fund's Commission on Elderly People Living Alone. He cofounded the National Long-Term Care Campaign and serves as Public Policy Cochair of Generations United. Mr. Rother is a graduate of Oberlin College and the University of Pennsylvania Law School, where he was editor of the Law Review.

SYLVESTER J. SCHIEBER is a Vice President of The Wyatt Company, the Director of its Research and Information Center, and a member of its Board of Directors. Dr. Schieber is a member of the Pension Research Council and a coeditor of and a contributor to its 1991 symposium volume, *Demography and Retirement: The Twenty-First Century*. Before joining The Wyatt Company, Dr. Schieber was the first Research Director of the Employee Benefit Research Institute (EBRI), and he currently serves on EBRI's Board of Directors. Previously, he was the Deputy Director, Office of Policy Analysis, Social Security Administration, and Deputy Research Director, Universal Social Security Coverage Study, Department of Health and Human Services. Dr. Schieber received a Ph.D. in economics from the University of Notre Dame.

DONALD C. SNYDER is the Assistant Director of the Human Resources Division in the U.S. General Accounting Office. Dr. Snyder has been a professor of economics at Goucher College and Howard University and a consultant to several government agencies, including the Bureau of Labor Statistics, Department of Labor, Social Security Administration, Senate Special Committee on Aging, and the Joint Economic Committee. He has published numerous articles for academic and professional journals. Dr. Snyder received a Ph.D. in economics from the University of Maryland.

Index

Pension Research Council Publications

Concepts of Actuarial Soundness in Pension Plans. Dorrance C. Bronson. 1957.

Continuing Care Retirement Communities: An Empirical, Financial, and Legal Analysis. Howard E. Winklevoss and Alwyn V. Powell with David L. Cohen, Esq. and Ann Trueblood-Raper. 1983.

Corporate Book Reserving for Postretirement Healthcare Benefits. Edited by Dwight K. Bartlett. 1990.

Demography and Retirement: The Twenty-First Century. Edited by Anna M. Rappaport and Sylvester J. Schieber. 1993.

An Economic Appraisal of Pension Tax Policy in the United States. Richard A. Ippolito. 1990.

The Economics of Pension Insurance. Richard A. Ippolito. 1989.

Employer Accounting for Pensions: Analysis of the Financial Accounting Standards Board's Preliminary Views and Exposure Draft. E.L. Hicks and C.L. Trowbridge. 1985.

Fundamentals of Private Pensions (Sixth Edition). Dan M. McGill and Donald S. Grubbs, Jr. 1988.

The Future of Pensions in the United States. Edited by Raymond Schmitt. 1993.

Inflation and Pensions. Susan M. Wachter. 1987.

It's My Retirement Money, Take Good Care of It; The TIAA-CREF Story. William C. Greenough. 1990.

Joint Trust Pension Plans: Understanding and Administering Collectively Bargained Multiemployer Plans under ERISA. Daniel F. McGinn. 1977.

Pension Asset Management: An International Perspective. Edited by Leslie Hannah. 1988.

Pension Mathematics with Numerical Illustrations (Second Edition). Howard E. Winklevoss. 1993.

Pensions and the Economy: Sources, Uses, and Limitations of Data. Edited by Zvi Bodie and Alicia H. Munnell. 1992.

Pensions, Economics and Public Policy. Richard A. Ippolito. 1985.

Providing Health Care Benefits in Retirement. Edited by Judith F. Mazo, Anna M. Rappaport, and Sylvester J. Schieber. 1994

Proxy Voting of Pension Plan Equity Securities. Edited by Dan M. McGill. 1989.

Retirement Systems for Public Employees. Thomas P. Bleakney. 1972.

Retirement Systems in Japan. Robert L. Clark. 1990.

Search for a National Retirement Income Policy. Edited by Jack L. VanDerhei. 1987.

Social Investing. Edited by Dan M. McGill. 1984.

Social Security (Fourth Edition). Robert J. Myers. 1993.